# EURO-MEDITERRANEAN
## AFTER THE ARAB

# Euro-Mediterranean Relations after the Arab Spring
## Persistence in Times of Change

*Edited by*

JAKOB HORST
ANNETTE JÜNEMANN
DELF ROTHE

*Helmut-Schmidt-University Hamburg, Germany*

Routledge
Taylor & Francis Group

LONDON AND NEW YORK

First published 2013 by Ashgate Publishing

2 Park Square, Milton Park, Abingdon, Oxfordshire OX14 4RN
711 Third Avenue, New York, NY 10017

*Routledge is an imprint of the Taylor & Francis Group, an informa business*

First issued in paperback 2017

**British Library Cataloguing in Publication Data**
A catalogue record for this book is available from the British Library

**The Library of Congress has cataloged the printed edition as follows:**
Euro-Mediterranean relations after the Arab Spring : persistence in times of change /
edited by Jakob Horst, Annette Jünemann and Delf Rothe.
    pages. cm
  Includes bibliographical references and index.
  ISBN 978-1-4094-5552-3 (hardback) 1. European Union countries—Foreign relations—
Arab countries. 2. Arab countries—Foreign relations—European Union countries.
3. European Union countries—Foreign relations—Mediterranean Region.
4. Mediterranean Region—Foreign relations—European Union countries. 5. Arab Spring,
2010- 6. Arab countries—Politics and government—21st century. 7. Mediterranean
Region—Politics and government—21st century. I. Horst, Jakob. II. Jünemann, Annette,
1959- author, editor of compilation. III. Rothe, Delf, author, editor of compilation.

  JZ1570.E898 2013
  327.4017'4927—dc23

                                                                                2013015215

  ISBN 978-1-4094-5552-3 (hbk)
  ISBN 978-1-138-57257-7 (pbk)

# Contents

# List of Tables and Figures

**Tables**

**Figures**

# List of Contributors

*Ingrid El Masry* is scientific assistant to the head of the department of Political Science at Philipps University Marburg and researcher at the departments of politics and economics at the Center for Near and Middle East Studies (CNMS) in Marburg, Germany. Her main fields of research are comparative, interdisciplinary and theory-orientated development and transformation studies on the Near and Middle East.

*Kerstin Fritzsche* is a PhD candidate at the Center for Near and Middle East Studies (CNMS) in Marburg, Germany. She studied political science, Middle East Studies and journalism in Leipzig and Stockholm. Her research is dedicated to new political actors in the MENA-region as well as economic, environmental and energy-related questions and their implications for the development and stability of Arab countries.

*Cilja Harders* is a professor of political science and the director of the 'Center for North African and Middle Eastern Politics' (CMP, http://www.polwiss.fu-berlin.de/vorderer-orient) at the Otto-Suhr Institute for Political Sciences at Freie Universität Berlin since 2007. She has extensive research experience in the Middle East, including in Egypt, Jordan, Syria, Lebanon, VAE and Morocco. Her research focuses on politics 'from below' and the current transformations in the Arab world, Euro-Med relations as well as gender and violence.

*Jakob Horst* is a research assistant at the Institute of International Politics of the Helmut Schmidt University/University of Federal Armed Forces in Hamburg, Germany. He is preparing a PhD thesis dealing with the political implications of free trade implementation in the context of the Euro-Algerian association agreement.

*Annette Jünemann* is professor of International Relations at the Helmut-Schmidt-University, University of the Federal Armed Forces in Hamburg. She qualified as a professor (Habilitation) in 2000 at the University of Kassel and did her PhD in 1993 at the University of Hamburg. Her main fields of research are International Relations, EU-Foreign Relations, Mediterranean Studies and Democratisation.

**Florian Kühn** is Senior Researcher and Lecturer at Helmut Schmidt University, Hamburg. Currently, he is a Visiting Professor for International Politics at Humboldt University in Berlin. His research on security and development, on risk and resilience as well as on aspects of ambiguity has been widely published, among others in *International Peacekeeping, International Relations* and *Canadian Foreign Policy Journal*. His book *Security and Development in World Society. Liberal Paradigm and Statebuilding in Afghanistan* (VS Verlag, 2010) won the German Association for Middle East Studies dissertation award. He is co-editor of the *Journal of Intervention and Statebuilding* since 2013.

**Ivesa Lübben** works as a research assistant at the Center for Near and Middle East Studies (CNMS) in Marburg, Germany and has been engaged in research on Islamist parties and Islamic-political discourse since the mid-90s. From 1990 to 2004, she lived in Cairo, working as a freelance journalist and academic editor for German media (TAZ, GEO, INAMO, West German Broadcasting Corporation WDR) and Al-Jazeera, as well as for several foundations and research institutes.

**Eva-Maria Maggi** is PhD candidate in Political Science at the Institute for International Studies, at the Helmut Schmidt University in Hamburg/Germany and Research Assistant at the EU Center of Excellence at the Henry M. Jackson School for International Studies of the University of Washington, Seattle, USA. Her dissertation examines policy change in Morocco and the role of the European Union (EU) as an external actor in these processes.

**Rachid Ouaissa** is professor of political science and head of the Center for Near- and Middle Eastern Studies at the Phillips-University Marburg. His main fields of research are political, economic and societal developments in the Near- and Middle East since the nineteenth century, the rise of Islamist movements in the region, the EU's Mediterranean policy, the foreign policy of Arab countries and questions of energy policy.

**Delf Rothe** is working as a research fellow to Prof. Annette Jünemann at the Helmut Schmidt University Hamburg. His main research interests are securitisation theory, international climate governance and energy governance as well as interpretive methods in International Relations. He has recently finished his PhD thesis on the securitisation of climate change and its policy implications at international, regional and national level.

**Peter Seeberg** is Associate Professor and Director of Studies at Centre for Contemporary Middle East Studies, University of Southern Denmark. He is also Director of the DJUCO-project, an academic cooperation project in Amman, Jordan. Peter Seeberg has published on EU and the Middle East, Arab nationalism, migration and security issues in a Mediterranean perspective and ethnic minorities in Europe and Denmark.

**Tina Zintl** is a PhD candidate at the University of St. Andrews/Scotland, where she also works as research assistant at the Centre for Syrian Studies. Her research interests focus on economic and political transformation, higher education, and state-society relations in Arab countries, as well as on international migration and development cooperation.

# Chapter 1

# Logics of Action in the Euro-Mediterranean Political Space: An Introduction to the Analytical Framework[1]

Jakob Horst, Annette Jünemann, Florian Kühn,
Eva-Maria Maggi and Delf Rothe

## Preface

Although it is not conceivable yet whether the 'Arab Spring' will trigger a new 'wave of democratization' (Huntington 1991), one can already call it a historical event that some commentators compared with the East European revolutions in 1989 (see for example Coates Ulrichsen, Held and Brahimi 2011). It all started in December 2010 when the Tunisian greengrocer Mohamed Bouazizi set himself on fire after having suffered harassment and humiliation by municipal officials. Arbitrarily they had denied him permission for his fruit and veg stall and had repeatedly confiscated his wares, thereby depriving him of his basic means of existence. His suicide became a catalyst for nationwide revolts under the slogan 'we all are Mohamed Bouazizi'. They signified the overwhelming discontent with the social and political shortfalls of authoritarian Tunisia and resulted in the fall of President Zine el-Abidine Ben Ali after 23 years in power. The demise of Ben Ali soon encouraged protesters in other Arab countries to follow suit, although the context and impact is different in each specific country. While Egypt's president Husni Mubarak had to give up in February 2011 after weeks of impressive mass-demonstrations on Kairo's Tahrir Square, Muammar al-Gaddafi was killed on October 20 by rebels after he had lost the war which he had fought against the Libyan people and their Western supporters. Syria's President Baschar al-Assad reacted likewise repressing the revolts in his country and thereby triggering a civil war. In contrast to that, the Monarchies in Jordan and Morocco try to survive with a mix of moderate repression, economic incentives and half-hearted reforms. Saudi Arabia has sufficient resources to appease not only its own people but to

---

1   For helpful comments and suggestions we would like to thank Kerstin Fritzsche, Ivesa Lübben, Rachid Ouaissa, Peter Seeberg and Tina Zintl who acted as discussants and critical interlocutors at two workshops in Hamburg and Odense and thus contributed much to the final result presented here.

interfere also in its neighbourhood, supporting *inter alia* the military clamp down in Bahrain.

It is too early to predict whether or when the 'Arab Spring' will put an end to 'Arab autocracy'. Some of the regimes may survive for quite some time and those that started a process of transformation like Egypt or Tunisia may need years to complete it. Nevertheless, henceforward all of them will have to take the needs and requirements of their people into consideration, since the Arab people have 'lost their fears' (Asseburg 2011). It is the courage to revolt against autocratic regimes that had been in power for decades that has enforced this change and justifies calling the 'Arab Spring' already a historical event.

However, what is called the 'Arab Spring' did not and will not change 'everything'. We believe that there is a tendency to exaggerate the impact of historical events; in our understanding there is no such thing as a 'zero hour'. The aim of this volume is to find out *to what extent* the 'Arab Spring' has triggered political change. In some countries we might witness a revolution, in others incremental reforms and yet in others restauration or the dissolution of the state. Democracy can be an outcome, but also any other form of government. Governments might be more or less resilient with regard to the challenges of the 'Arab Spring', so that authoritarianism might persist in one form or the other. The same counts for economic structures, which are decisive in the context of change. Although the call for economic equity was one of the core requests of the protestors in all Arab countries and should therefore be in the focus of change agents coming to power, rentier economies or other economic structures might survive the political upheavals, due to other logics that superpose the demands of the protestors.

On a societal level the 'Arab Spring' has an important impact within and beyond national borders that might change traditional power relations. Obvious are intergenerational tensions transcending the established political rifts. Less obvious is the impact of the 'Arab Spring' on gender relations. In general, it is not yet clear to what extent discourses on tradition and modernity are affected. All these manifold dynamics do not emerge independently from one another, but are highly interrelated developments, be it on personal, local or transnational level within what we call the Euro-Mediterranean political space.

The notion of a Euro-Mediterranean political space, which will be explained in detail below, implies that Europe is part of this space, due to dense interactions with its southern neighbourhood. Not only the EU and its member states react in some way or another to cope with the changes outlined above. Also non-governmental interactions, be it in the private, the cultural or the economic sphere, are affected. To what extent will the 'Arab Spring' change European perspectives, interests and policies? Are legally binding treaties like the Euro-Mediterranean association agreements or the agreements on repatriation to be re-negotiated? Italian attempts to convince Libya's provisional government to abide by bilateral agreements on migration control, once negotiated with Gaddafi, are an example for continuity rather than change. In this context, discourses matter too, since migration is an extremely securitised issue especially in southern Europe. The new image of Arab freedom fighters might mollify current discourses on a securitised Islam but that is not for sure. The blurry political situation after the 'Arab Spring' might just as well confirm and aggravate the scary image of instability and chaos in what is perceived as the Islamic world. These examples might suffice to explain why we do not believe that political change triggered by a historical event like the 'Arab Spring' is total or all embracing.

On the contrary we presume that there are manifold *logics of action*[2] that are characterised by persistence. Instead of assuming an indiscriminate 'overall change' triggered by the 'Arab Spring', the contributions in this book look at the *quality of change* and identify fields where logics of action show a considerable degree of stability. To grasp these logics, we seek to identify patterns of interaction – and their inner logics – between governmental institutions, economic entrepreneurs, religious groups and other diverse groupings that we presume to have remained at least in parts rather static in times of change.

This introduction is structured in three sections. Following this preface in section two we introduce the Logics of Action (LoA) approach. Here we explicate the theoretical background of our analytical framework and discuss literature that inspired LoA. Based on this preliminary work we argue that to identify logics of action *context matters*. In our understanding, logics of action are shaped in particular in the context of time, space, identity and power, four notions that will be discussed in detail. Finally, section three gives an overview of the contributions to this volume that investigate Euro-Mediterranean interactions from different angles to paint a comprehensive picture of change and persistence after the 'Arab Spring'. Based on the LoA approach, all of them seek to detect logics of persistence in times of change, triggered by the 'Arab Spring'.

## Logics of Action

This volume is more than a loose collection of case studies on the 'Arab Spring'. To be able to paint a more elaborate and comprehensive picture of the 'Arabellions' the contributions in this volume draw on a common analytical perspective – the LoA framework. This perspective provides coherence between the chapters and comparability – as a prerequisite for the identification of broader patterns or logics of change and persistence. Moreover, LoA, as developed in this volume, is an

---

2    In the following, we write Logics of Action in capitals when we refer to the analytical concept of our approach focused on continuity and change in what we understand to be processes taking place in the Euro-Mediterranean political space. In contrast, logics of action in lower case is used to describe the empirically observable practices which take place within a given repertoire of potential political options, which are related to a given political environment, convictions etc.

analytical framework that focuses on change and particularly the quality of change within political processes.[3] Herein it follows two basic assumptions:

- Political processes are shaped through the co-determination of agents and structures
- Causal laws that claim universal validity are too static and general to explain political processes in the Euro-Mediterranean political space

These two general assumptions shall be explicated and specified in the following:

*Political Processes are Shaped Through the Co-Determination of Agents and Structures*

Change or stagnation in political interactions are neither solely the result of actor's interests and dispositions nor are they merely determined by structural conditions. It has been the merit of social constructivist approaches in the discipline of International Relations (IR) to explicate that agents and structures co-determine each other (see Wendt 1987).[4] This is to say that collective or individual actors follow certain logics of action that are made up of interests, beliefs and internalised norms. Likewise structures, such as culture or political discourses, display certain logics that provide templates for (individual) political action. Yet, none of these two levels of logics is independent from the other. While norms and beliefs of individuals are influenced by their social environment, these structures themselves are nothing more than the cumulated result of individual actions – and thus prone to change and contestation.

To give an example: the EU's weakness as an international actor is a consequence of the EU's legal structures as laid down in the EU-Treaty. However, the EU member states themselves have produced them: In fear of losing too much of their national sovereignty they preserved intergovernmentalism as a key concept within the legal structure of Common Security and Defence Policy (CSDP) that now limits the EU's room for manoeuvre in international politics. Thus, the often lamented weak 'actorness' of the EU is produced and reproduced by its actors as well as its structures. LoA, then, is the analytical concept introduced to grasp

---

3    Political processes in our understanding are not reduced to institutionalised (inter-) actions that follow from intended political rationales or aims. Based on the assumption that societal interactions which are not directed towards a certain political aim – think for example of migratory practices – can have political impacts, we include institutionalised as well non-institutionalised political (inter-) actions in our analyses.

4    The LoA approach thus explicitly situates itself within the the constructivist branch of IR-theory.

exactly this 'in-between' site of interplay between the two levels.[5] The perspective of the approach works in two ways: It can take actors or certain structures as a starting point, analysing their impact on specific logics of action. Conversely, taking changing or persistent logics of action as a starting point allows analysing their impact on actors and/or structures. In the given example the logic of relevance would be intergovernmentalism as a core concept in the discourse on EU-integration that has come under pressure due to the growing necessity to overcome the EU's weakness as an international actor and is thus prone to change.

*Causal Laws that Claim Universal Validity are Too Static and General to Explain Political Processes in the Euro-Mediterranean Political Space*

To analyse politics according to logics allows identifying plausible reasons for and driving forces of political developments instead of establishing fixed causalities or causal laws. The argument here is that specific political processes in the cases under investigation cannot be sufficiently explained by causal laws which claim to be spatially and temporarily universal. Logics of action instead can change over time and they might be 'regional'[6] peculiarities. They can give plausible reasons for political interactions in a given context but might not be generalisable for all similar phenomena in the world.

With the help of LoA, in sum, we want to disentangle the vast complexity of the political processes and analyse the relevant factors shaping their evolution. This rather demanding objective, however, requires substantiation. Where does LoA derive from and what is its added value? So far, the observations and ideas of logics of action have been rarely specified but often used in various academic disciplines, including the social sciences. Generally speaking, most disciplines use *logics* as mechanisms shaping social action, but so far no analytical framework has consistently incorporated those logics themselves. Inspirational for the development of our approach was New Institutionalism (see March and Olsen 1989: 160pp) as it helps explain the complex interdependencies between actors' behaviour and their social environment. Actors, March and Olsen argued, do not always act rationally according to their individual interests, i.e. according to a 'logic of consequence'. Their behaviour is often influenced by considerations of what is 'proper' and correct in a given situation – March and Olsen call this a 'logic of appropriateness'. What appears rational or appropriate for actors heavily depends on the context of the respective situation. March and Olsen themselves, yet, did not provide us with a sufficient concept to grasp exactly these contextual factors, which need to be considered to explain a certain logic of action at stake.

---

5   Another example would be the economic dependence on energy exports in some MENA countries. The rentier character of their economies produces rent-seeking behaviour of individual actors within those countries, but at the same time, the rentier-structure is fostered and reproduced by the same individual practices.

6   For a discussion of the problematic concept of regions see below.

To fill out this gap, we therefore build upon Robert E. Goodin's and Charles Tilly's findings that can be summarised as 'context matters' (Goodin and Tilly 2006). One important element of getting the context right consists of identifying, describing, and explaining the *operation* of explanatory stories (Goodin and Tilly 2006: 446). How does the situation look from the actor's perspective? What are the options and constraints on action? According to Goodin and Tilly, psychology matters, ideas matter, culture matters, history matters, place matters, population matters, technology matters. This long list of parameters can easily be prolonged and adapted with regard to specific situations. The goal of their approach is to extract rules of the game and analyse the effect of different contexts: 'So context matters, and context often varies. But these contextual effects are not random. There are patterns to be picked out, and understood from within each distinct historical, cultural and technological setting' (Goodin and Tilly 2006: 25).

While we share the basic assumptions of Goodin and Tilly, this broad range of parameters is also a weak spot in their approach: By adding a potentially indefinite number of different factors without providing a comprehensive notion of how they are actually interlinked, their approach is at risk of ending up with extensive descriptions but little analytical precision. Instead, we develop categories of contextual parameters (which are outlined below) and, most importantly, weigh them and relate them to each other. In addition, we develop a set of guiding key assumptions, which are in themselves interrelated. They include notions of space, identity, power and time: Space helps to connect our research agenda with regionalist approaches without the restricting geographical concept of the 'region'; identity is closely related to the space within which interaction takes place, and describes the construction of collectives and their delimitation; power refers to the observation that, across ideational and material structures, hierarchies shape political interaction in productive and/or coercive ways; finally, to include time means to be sensitive to change and unfolding processes rather than identifying static explanations. By providing such elements of a research design LoA allows to analyse very precisely the evolution of political processes and thereby to grasp the *quality of change* within them.

## Space

As mentioned above, the 'Arab Spring' has a spatial dimension that goes far beyond single Middle Eastern and North African (MENA) countries – it affects the Euro-Mediterranean 'region' as a whole. But what exactly is what is commonly referred to as the 'Euro-Mediterranean Region'? Looking at the map and considering the arbitrariness of the EU's changing definitions of the Euro-Mediterranean 'region' illustrates that there is nothing essential or natural about it. It is a social construction (Bicchi 2004; Pace 2006) which is currently being re-defined through the upheavals in the Arab world. The most noteworthy characteristic of this construction is that many theoretical perspectives understand the region as composed of two distinct, if not conflictive sub-regions. Realist perspectives tend to conceptualise an antagonism between threatened Europe and a threatening 'arch of crisis' in the southern Mediterranean. But not only realism, also liberal approaches back the perception of a dichotomy between 'the North' interacting with 'the South'. This is for example mirrored in the liberal concept of democratic peace that draws upon a binary opposition between democratic and authoritarian regimes. Another example is the Regional Security Complex theory by Barry Buzan and Ole Wæver (Buzan and Wæver 2003). Applied in our context it could come to the result that the Euro-Mediterranean region is not one regional security complex, but two (Bremberg-Heijl 2007). A regionalism perspective that builds on economic integration would – again – contrast a highly integrated Europe against a poorly integrated southern neighbourhood.

We believe that intraregional interaction is much more complex than suggested by all these binary narratives that are all connected to the notion of the 'region'. In this sense the term fails to capture aspects like the changing and changeable nature of discourses that take place in specific historical, political and social contexts and is, thus, too static. As Jeandesboz puts it: 'Looking at the logics of action [...] directs us towards an analysis of the neighbourhood in terms of the social practices that give shape to it' (Jeandesboz 2007: 390). To distance the LoA approach from any territorially defined concept of a Euro-Mediterranean 'region', we introduce the concept of a Euro-Mediterranean political space. This cannot be defined through recourse to geographical and cultural communalities or borders. Nor can it be reduced to those political institutions that were built to systemise Euro-Mediterranean relations like the Euro-Mediterranean Partnership (EMP), the Neighbourhood Policy (ENP) or the Union for the Mediterranean (UfM). Rather, it is constituted and constantly renegotiated through the practices and interactions of political and social actors that are consciously or unconsciously referring to the 'Euro-Mediterranean region' (or subparts of it).[7]

The Euro-Mediterranean political space and all political interactions within it are composed of various policy fields. As an example for a specific policy field one could point to the Euro-Mediterranean migration regime. It is shaped by a multitude of actors (political institutions, non-state organisations, individual migrants etc) but also by specific structures. Material structures shaping the Euro-Mediterranean migration regime are amongst others economic or political push and pull factors,

---

[7]    At the same time, the studies in this volume show that the construction of a political space (like 'the Euro-Mediterranean') also means the exclusion of other political communities or spaces that function as a negative point of reference. In the construction of a common 'Euro-Mediterranean region' such negative reference points are for example groups like radical Muslims or illegal immigrants from Sub-Saharan Africa that are presented as a security threat for both the EU and the MENA countries (see for example Seeberg in this volume). Rothe (in this volume) moreover shows that also discursive entities – such as the notion of dangerous climate change as a common threat for all Mediterranean countries – can take up this role of an 'other' constituting a novel political space.

but also legal settings of the EU treaty and repatriation agreements between the EU and MENA countries. Ideational structures of relevance are discourses that frame migration either as a security threat or as a solution to the aging of the European society. Global dynamics may just as well have an impact, for example 9/11 as a trigger for the securitisation of migration. The *interplay* of actors and structures means that structures shape but at the same time are shaped by the logics of action in this specific policy field. Every contribution in this volume deals with interactions within specific policy fields, which together constitute the Euro-Mediterranean political space.

The added value of this conception of space is that it first enables us to overcome the conventional binary perceptions of Euro-Mediterranean relations and hence to better detect their complexity. The analytical focus shifts away from the construction of dichotomies that are usually static towards the identification of logics of action that shape and thereby change political processes transcending the Euro-Mediterranean political space. Second, the construction of a Euro-Mediterranean 'region' can itself be studied as political practice. Lastly, and most important, the perspective enables us to study change (and persistence) in a more nuanced and elaborate manner as it shows how political communities and policies are subject to change.

## Identity

The discourses on the Euro-Mediterranean 'region' are also shaped by mechanisms of inclusion and exclusion that interact with identity and strategy. To give an example, the EU's definition of the Euro-Mediterranean 'region' can be interpreted as a strategic instrument of a hegemonic European policy to achieve European interests or, on the contrary, as a visionary attempt of region-building, based on the idea that shared institutions, norms and values are not the premise of socialisation and integration, but their outcome. In either case, the construction of identity needs the dissociation from something or someone 'other' (Pace 2006). Emphasising the difference between 'us' and 'them' strengthens the coherence and thus the identity of the we-group. 'Othering', that is the construction of identity through the construction of a different, if not adversary or threatening 'other' is usually based on incompatible binary categories that are perceived as essential and static, like modern/traditional, civilised/uncivilised, good/bad (see Said 1978).

The construction of identity through processes of 'othering' implies that identities are themselves influenced and shaped through political interaction. Therefore, on the one hand, identity is an important factor to explore and explain logics of action in the Euro-Mediterranean political space. Change or persistence of specific logics of action cannot be explained without taking into account the particular identities – and their potential transformation – of the individual actors, groups, organisations or institutions involved in a political process. On the other hand, processes of identity construction through 'othering' can be shaped by specific logics of action. The logics that stand behind the framing of Islam as an essential and threatening part of Arab identity can be taken as an example for the latter.

Identity is not least related to the factor space. As mentioned above, the factor space often plays an important role as a point of reference for identity construction through processes of 'othering'. The differentiation between 'the north' and the 'the south', including certain essential features attributed to the respective geographical entities, played an important role for processes of 'othering' in the Euro-Mediterranean political space.

By taking into account the complexity of identity construction processes and their relevance for any form of political interaction, LoA calls into question simplistic dichotomised notions of the Mediterranean 'region'. The existence of transnational actors that are neither 'north' nor 'south', to give only one example, illustrates the artificiality of the allegedly natural and incompatible attributions of the 'we' and the 'other' (see for example Zintl in this volume). Although identities are subject to processes of social construction they certainly have a concrete and sizable political impact. To identify this political impact is one aim of the LoA approach.

**Power**

Perceptions of Euro-Mediterranean relations are often based on the notion of power – the dominance of 'the north' over 'the south'. From our perspective, drawing on a 'classical' conception of power (Dahl 1957: 202, Weber 1976: 28) is not elaborate enough to grasp the complexity of power relations in the Euro-Mediterranean political space. We hold that power is structural and nothing that can be owned by individual actors. Power is inscribed into the relations between societal and political actors. It thus takes the form of a network or grid – made up of the material and ideational structures that characterise the Euro-Mediterranean political space. On the one hand, power is inscribed in material structures as economic asymmetries and trade relations. On the other hand, power is inscribed in ideational structures that are manifest in specific systems of knowledge, norms and institutions.

Rather than working solely coercive or repressive the effect of power is often a productive one (Foucault 1978: 35). An example for productive power is delivered by Seeberg in this volume, who shows how immigration from MENA countries is framed as a (non-traditional) security issue by various actors. This securitisation opens up the possibility for EU actors to take up a variety of (exceptional) measures that otherwise would appear inappropriate, i.e. too drastic. This productivity of power not lastly shows how closely the latter is related to the concept of identity. Securitisation does not only enable certain political measures but also shapes the (collective) identities of the individuals it addresses – in this case the collective identity as (illegal) immigrants, which undoubtedly affects or changes the logics of action of these actors.

As this example shows power can have different 'faces', which can be analytically distinguished (Lukes 2005). It can be repressive and coercive as it was in the era of colonialism, when military and economic power of states indeed had a major impact. This is quite different from the persuasive character of 'soft power' (Nye 2004) that can be deployed with economic and political incentives and is therefore often associated with the EU. The execution of repressive power can also be covert or hidden, if one takes the ability of actors to silence politically sensitive issues (see Bachrach and Baratz 1962). Finally, the concept of heteronomous power relations describes a situation where actors are formally equal. Nevertheless, the actors commit themselves, or feel constrained to commit themselves, to rules and obligations that produce and reproduce inequality. The LoA approach does not come up with one definition of power but sheds light on the diversity of 'faces' power can have according to the specific context of each case study. To detect the subtle and often unnoticed power relations in the Euro-Mediterranean political space it is crucial to explain the resilience of political practices, institutions and systems during and in the aftermath of the 'Arab Spring'.

**Time**

All three context factors mentioned above are not static imperturbable elements, just as little as political processes and their logics of action. Constructions of space, identities and power relations are all subject to change over time. To grasp this evolutionary dimension of political processes, we consider time to be of special relevance. For this sake all contributions to this volume take up a diachronic perspective at the events before during and after the 'Arab Spring'. To account for the quality or depth of change the LoA approach furthermore borrows from the concept of *political learning* (Levy 1994; Sabatier and Jenkins 1993), which provides different categories to grasp change. Following this argument, logics of action are informed by different types of beliefs – no matter if situated at the level of actors (as individual convictions) or social structures (as cultural discourses). Following Sabatier (1999), beliefs can be distinguished on three levels: *deep core, policy core* and *secondary beliefs*. In short, *deep core beliefs* such as fundamental ontological beliefs are almost resistant to change. *Deep core beliefs* constrain and influence all subsequent levels of the belief system. An example for a collective *deep core belief* could be the social-cultural identity of the EU as a community based on the values of liberalism, democracy and human rights. Another example for a *deep core belief* on the individual level might be the perception of mankind as being either peaceful or hostile. Compared to the rather static level of *deep core beliefs*, *policy core beliefs* are less rigid. They comprise basic perceptions concerning the general seriousness of a political problem and convictions concerning its causes. The EU's conviction that the MENA region's problems have their roots in a lack of democracy and market economy is a good example for a *policy core belief*. *Policy core beliefs* often have a strategic dimension since they also comprise strategies to realise *deep core beliefs*, in the given example the strategy of external democracy promotion.

*Secondary beliefs* are of minor importance since they only comprise the manifold instruments that need to be adjusted when new political goals are defined due to changes on a higher belief level. Frequent change on this third level of the belief system is quite common but without consequences for *policy core* or *deep core beliefs*. We only talk about substantial political change when the higher levels of *policy core beliefs* or – although not very likely to happen – *deep core beliefs* are affected. If however change is merely restricted to the level of *secondary beliefs*, it will not lead to substantial political changes but rather foster persistence. This mechanism, to give an example, is well known from the literature on 'authoritarian upgrading' (Heydemann 2007). It equates to the famous aphorism in Giuseppe Tomasi di Lampedusa's novel *Il Gattopardo* 'For things to remain the same, everything must change.'[8] Drawing on the concept of the belief system, the LoA approach enables us to differentiate between substantial political change that leads to new policy goals on the one hand and instrumental changes that rather produce stalemate on the other, including the various shades between those two poles.

## Contributions

The aim that unites the contributions of this volume is to find out *to what extent* the 'Arab Spring' has triggered political change. Although it's a historical event in the sense that it marks the starting point of paradigmatic change, we do not believe that this change is all-encompassing. On the contrary, we presume that there are manifold logics of action that bring forward persistence. Thus, all contributions seek to detect these logics of persistence in times of change. To do so, we have conducted a sample of interrelating case studies on various political processes within the Euro-Mediterranean political space. Although the case studies stem from different academic backgrounds and focus on different policy fields of intra-regional relations, they are comparable since all of them are based on the LoA approach. This means that all contributions share the theoretical assumptions described in section two. Since all studies focus on the Euro-Mediterranean political space the explanatory value of our results is purposely confined.

Together, the single case studies allow us to identify different patterns or logics of action that explain the transformation as well as persistence of political processes in the Euro-Mediterranean political space. The first part of this volume focuses on the EU and/or European actors and their relevance in the Euro-Mediterranean political space before and after the 'Arab Spring'. The contributions of the second

---

8    See Tomasi di Lampedusa 1958 (Translation A.J.). An actual example of this phenomenon is what Haydemann (2007) calls 'authoritarian upgrading'.

part investigate logics of action in specific MENA-countries and new actors within the Euro-Mediterranean political space that gained political leverage as a result of the 'Arab Spring'. Eventually the third part of this volume explores genuinely 'transnational' actors and logics of action within the Euro-Mediterranean political space, analysing whether and how the 'Arab Spring' impacted on this sphere of 'transnationality'.

The contribution of Eva Maggi focuses on institutionalised Euro-Mediterranean relations and analyses their impact in one specific partner country, Morocco. In her chapter Maggi conceptualises European integration and European Union policy standards as an ideational context factor for the logics of action of political reform processes in Morocco. In a first part, by focusing on economic and environmental reforms between 1995 and 2010, this qualitative case study opens up the black box of policy change and sheds light on the quality of change that can be caused by the EU. Maggi argues that, although economic reform is more prominent, it seems as though EU standards on environmental policies show the desired long-term policy change. The outcome is explained by the logics of action of domestic actors to use external norms such as EU integration to benefit their domestic system. In a second part her contribution analyses whether and to what extent the 'Arab Spring' has shaped the ideational context factors regarding policy reform in Morocco. In doing so, she specifically focuses on the question of whether the position of the EU as a provider of specific norms and standards changed or persisted during and after the 'Arab Spring'.

Annette Jünemann analyses the difficulties and contradictions in EU attempts to promote gender equality in the newly evolving political orders of its southern partner countries. Although women made an important contribution to the 'Arab Spring' in the year 2011, they are no longer playing a comparable role in the reorganisation of political life in the Arab transition countries. Before the 'Arab Spring', the EU had been supporting the agenda of secular women's right groups, paradoxically in tacit agreement with the authoritarian regimes in the region that pursued a kind of secular state feminism as an instrument in the fight against political Islam. Since the 'Arab Spring', this promotional practice of the EU appears anachronistic. To adapt the external promotion of gender democracy to the new political realities is perceived in Europe as a dilemma: How to cope with Islamists if women's rights are at stake? Jünemann argues that the lack of gender equality should not be taken as a problem of especially Muslim societies. It is rather the European perception of Islam, informed by stereotypical narratives and binary identity constructions that created the so-called Muslim exceptionalism. EU perceptions are shaped by a logic of culturalism that reduces the patriarchal character of MENA-societies to the seemingly backward ideology of political Islam. As a result other impact factors for gender injustice are blurred and potential partners for cooperation are overlooked.

Peter Seeberg's contribution studies the European immigration policies towards the southern Mediterranean. While it is often suggested that such policies would form a more or less homogenous common European migration policy approach, Seeberg argues that this perception has been contested in 2011 by the events related to the 'Arab Spring'. The increasing inflow of migration from Tunisia and other MENA-countries has provoked several unilateral actions by different EU member states. Indeed, resulting from their specific material and ideational context, Seeberg shows that single EU-members have very different concepts of the Euro-Mediterranean space – which in turn result in very different positions towards a European migration policy. Seeberg points out how the 'Arab Spring' has affected this setting of rather fragmented national immigration policies in the EU. Of particular importance in this respect, Seeberg argues, is the security dimension of immigration. This relates to the question if a further securitisation of migration in the aftermath of the 'Arab Spring' fuels unilateral approaches to the problem – or if it fosters a common threat perception and thus the development of supranational immigration policy narratives and approaches.

Jakob Horst also focuses on the question of whether the 'Arab Spring' altered the EU's policy approach towards the southern Mediterranean, but his contribution is concentrated on Euro-Mediterranean economic relations. Even though political upheavals in Tunisia, Egypt and other countries in the Arab World have led to new discussions about 'adapting' the EU's foreign policy Horst argues that the EU's general economic approach was until now not inflicted by the developments in the southern partner countries. Focusing on asymmetric material (economic) power relations as an important context factor of the EU's logics of action towards the southern Mediterranean he assumes that these context factors are going to stay the same and therefore change in the economic logic of action of the EU's Mediterranean policy is highly unlikely. Horst takes the example of the EMP-association agreement between the European Union and Algeria, signed in 2002, and includes the development of the Algerian political economy and its failed economic 'transition'-process in his analysis. Thereby his contribution also investigates the potential political impacts of free trade implementation within a rentier economy context, such as the Algerian.

In contrast to the contributions in the first part of this volume the contributions in the second part focus on changing or persistent logics of action in specific MENA-countries and the Arab world as a whole. Cilja Harders investigates the impact of the Egyptian revolution on the logics of action of the authoritarian social contract in Egypt. In the first part of her contribution she analyses five different logics of action that constituted the authoritarian social contract under the Mubarak regime: limited political liberalisation, repression, limited economic liberalisation, Islamisation and informalisation. Harders then explores how under these repressive circumstances a revolutionary mass mobilisation was possible and identifies dominant new and old actors and their logics of action in the Egyptian political field. All in all, Harders concludes that even though persistent logics of repression can be identified the ongoing politicisation and mobilisation of a previously demobilised population should be seen as a major reshuffling of the old authoritarian social contract.

In his analysis of the role of the 'blocked' middle classes as an engine of change in the Arab world Rachid Ouaissa draws a more pessimistic picture. Within the middle classes he identifies upper opportunistic segments, which tend to form alliances with the bourgeoisie. Their political ambitions differ quite a lot from the logics of 'anxious' lower segments that fear nothing more than social decline. The lack of collective identity is reflected in the lack of a common strategy, a lack of fighting spirit and in consequence a lack of common political goals. Their remote ability to draw alliances is one explanation for the low 'potential' of the middle classes as carriers of democratic transition in Arab countries. Another explanation is their embeddedness in the persistent structures of rentier economies. In a rentier system labour cannot be mobilised as an element of protest, so that the middle classes tend to resort to discourses on primordial identity for mobilisation. These however will not form a structural democratic counterweight to the ruling class. Despite their calls for dignity, freedom and justice, Ouaissa argues, the Arab middle classes have no mechanisms for structural leverage. The consumer behaviour of today's Arab middle classes might serve to liberate their individual ways of life but will not compel the establishment of lasting and stable democracies.

Ivesa Lübben and Kerstin Fritzsche concentrate on one specific actor group that gained relevance through the 'Arab Spring', raising scepticism and fears within the EU. They shed light on moderate Islamist parties during the dawn of the 'Arab Spring' and its direct aftermath. Their contribution raises the question, if the revolts have triggered changes in the logics of action of these organisations and explores the depth of these changes: do we see substantial redirections or rather strategic adaptations to a new situation? Lübben and Fritzsche address these questions with regard to the Jordanian Islamic Action Front Party (IAFP) and the Moroccan Development and Justice Party (in French PJD). While Morocco's and Jordan's political systems show several similarities (both are monarchies), significant differences exists with regard to how these countries have been influenced by the 'Arab Spring' and the role that moderate Islamists played in these developments. In Morocco, the PJD acted in favour of the top-down reform process which was launched by the king as a reaction to the country-wide protests. In Jordan, to the contrary, the IAFP criticised the new constitutional amendments that were proposed by a Royal Commission in August 2011 and boycotted the elections in January 2013. Lübben and Fritzsche explain these different outcomes with distinct logics of action of the two parties and draw on their singular structural and historical backgrounds.

Ingrid El Masry explores in her contribution the Egyptian Revolution of 25 January as a civil revolution with social impacts. She proves that the Egyptian revolution is not adequately described by labels like a 'Facebook' or a spontaneous 'youth revolution'. Rather, it has to be understood as a subversive movement which began long before the overthrow of the Mubarak Regime. El Masry traces back the historical roots of the upheavals and asks for the actual outcomes of the popular struggle. El Masry shows how a changing ideational and structural logic of the postcolonial Egyptian development model produced the context of an agent-action frame of changing individual and collective interests. She analyses different power structures and respective logics of action such as labour-capital relations, civil-religious relations, civil-military relations, and gender relations that are decisive for a societal and political transformation. After all, El Masry argues, many of these structures display a high degree of continuity and persistence under the Morsi presidency as compared to the pre-revolutionary system. Yet, this does not mean that the Egyptian revolution will not be able to alter these structures substantially, as the events of the 'Arab Spring' in Egypt do not mark the end of a revolutionary process but rather its beginning.

The third section of this volume has a focus on transnational logics of action, analysing whether and how the 'Arab Spring' impacted on this sphere of 'transnationality'. Delf Rothe explores the puzzling, growing attention given to the Desertec project, which aims to set up an EU-MENA renewable energy cooperation, since the late 2000s. Rothe shows that the success of the project – in terms of public and political resonance – was based on the establishment of a transnational discourse coalition around the label 'Desertec'. He traces back the evolution of this discourse coalition and studies how it became influential. In a second section, then, Rothe's contribution analyses how ideational and material structures are challenged and changed through the 'Arab Spring'. He shows that the recent upheavals reveal a second face of Desertec: it ultimately reproduces existing structures in the Euro-Mediterranean like rentier economic political economies in MENA countries or a discourse of economic modernisation. Lastly, his chapter explores the Desertec project's reaction to this substantial challenge and asks whether this has changed the logics of action behind the project.

Finally, Tina Zintl focuses in her contribution on one specific 'transnational' actor group within the Euro-Mediterranean political space. Her chapter investigates the dialectics of 'transnationality' as a distinctive attribute of foreign-educated Arab return migrants. Zintl argues that they are both indispensable interlocutors and unpredictable roamers in the Euro-Mediterranean political space; they challenge the monopoly of states' authorities while being subject to states' coercive power; they are both praised and feared as 'agents of change'. 'Transnationality' – here understood as the internationalised elements of economic, cultural, social, and symbolic capital – is used by different agents: the returnees themselves; authoritarian Arab states seeking legitimacy and international reputation, and European states looking for reliable partners. Focusing on Syria, Zintl asks whether and how these actors' logics of action have changed during the 'Arab Spring'. She argues that returnees, who developed a *modus vivendi* towards the regime, have not decisively acted as agents of change. The regime, which had coopted highly-skilled returnees and showcased them as a reformist 'young guard', largely sidelined them when accusing foreign conspirators of instigating unrest. Finally, although the EU might diversify its cooperation partners and over-hastily discard former 'friends' now perceived as old regimes' footmen, her contribution maintains that its logics of action compel it to search for new 'untainted' transnationalised elites.

## Bibliography

Asseburg, M. 2011. Der Arabische Frühling. Herausfordrungen und Cancen für die deutsche und europäische Politik, Studie der Stiftung Wissenschaft und Politik, Berlin, July 2011.

Bachrach, P. and M.S. Baratz. 1962. The Two Faces of Power, *American Political Science Review*, 56, 941-952.

Bicchi, F. 2004. *The European Origins of Euro-Mediterranean Practices.* Berkeley: Institute of European Studies Working Paper.

Bremberg-Heijl, N. 2007. Between a Rock and a Hard Place: Euro-Mediterranean Security Revisited, *Mediterranean Politics*, 12(1), 11-16.

Buzan, B. and O. Wæver. 2003. *Regions and Powers: The Structure of International Security.* Cambridge: Cambridge University Press.

Calhoun, C. 2002. *Dictionary of the Social Sciences.* Oxford/New York: Oxford University Press.

Coates Ulrichsen, K., D. Held. 2011 and A. Brahimi. The Arab 1989? Open Democracy [Online, 11 February 2011] Available at: http://www.open democracy.net/kristian-coates-ulrichsen-david-held-alia-brahimi/arab-1989 [accessed: 13 March 2011].

Dahl, R. 1957. The Concept of Power, *Behavioural Science*, 2, 201-215.

Foucault, M. 1978. *Dispositive der Macht: Über Sexualität, Wissen und Wahrheit.* Berlin: Merve.

Goodin, R.E. and C. Tilly. 2006. *The Oxford Handbook of Contextual Political Analysis.* Oxford/New York: Oxford University Press.

Heydemann, S. 2007. Upgrading Authoritarianism in the Arab World, Saban Center Analysis Paper No. 13, Washington D.C, October 2007.

Huntington, S.P. 1991. Democracy's Third Wave, *Journal of Democracy*, 2(2), 12-34.

Jeandesboz, J. 2007. Labeling the 'Neighbourhood': Towards a Genesis of the European Neighbourhood Policy, *Journal of International Relations and Development*, 10(4), 387-416.

Levy, J.S. 1994. Learning and Foreign Policy: Sweeping a Conceptual Minefield, *International Organization*, 48(2), 279-312.

Lukes, S. 2005. *Power. A Radical View.* 2nd Edition. New York: Palgrave MacMillan.

March, J.G. and J.P. Olson. 1989. *Rediscovering Institutions: The Organizational Basis of Politics.* New York: The Free Press.

Nye, J.S. 2004. *Soft Power. The Means to Succes in World Affairs.* New York: Public Affairs.

Pace, M. 2006. *The Politics of Regional Identity: Meddling with the Mediterranean.* London: Routledge.

Sabatier, P.A. 1999. *Theories of the policy process.* Boulder, CO: Westview Press.

Sabatier, P.A. and H. Jenkins-Smith. 1993. *Policy change and learning: An advocacy coalition approach.* Boulder, CO: Westview Press.

Said, E. 1979. *Orientalism*. New York: Vintage Books.

Tomasi di Lampedusa, G. 1958. *Il Gattopardo*. Milan: Feltrinelli.

Weber, M. 1976. *Wirtschaft und Gesellschaft. Grundrisse der verstehenden Soziologie*. 5th Edition. Tübingen: Mohr.

Wendt, A. 1987. The agent-structure problem in international relations theory, *International Organization*, 54(3), 335-370.

# PART I
# The EU's Mediterranean Policy after the 'Arab Spring'

Chapter 2

# Change to Stay the Same: The European Union and the Logics of Institutional Reform in Morocco[1]

Eva-Maria Maggi

## Introduction

'Those who make peaceful revolution impossible,' John F. Kennedy once said, 'make violent revolution inevitable.' Fifty years after Kennedy passed this famous line on to his diplomatic corps in the White House in 1962, the democratic movement in the Middle East and North Africa (MENA) countries seemed to have proven Kennedy right. The most oppressive leaders in North Africa were the first to fall in the aftermath of spring 2011 while mainly the monarchies such as Jordan[2] and Morocco seem to have successfully accommodated public demands and stayed in power. This analysis takes a closer look at the Moroccan case where the so-called 'Arab Spring' did not lead to a revolution but a reform process guided by the Royal circle of power.

If there is one pattern of institutional reforms in Morocco it is called guided change, induced from the top-down and lead from above. But different to most processes of change in Morocco in the past, the 'Arab Spring' vitalised the population to demand reform through widespread public protest. The King responded swiftly with a draft of a new constitution that was approved shortly after its publication by 98 per cent of the votes in a referendum in July 2011. The election followed in November with moderate Islamist Party of Justice and Development (PJD) winning the plurality of the vote for the first time and appointing the new Prime Minister Abdelilah Benkirane. The guided constitutional change by the Palace paired with elections calmed the protests.

The European Union (EU) as most international organisations and countries in Morocco's international environment was taken by surprise when the democratic wave hit the MENA countries. After decades of blurry and inconsistent democracy promotion efforts in the region, domestic demand for change seemed to be unstoppable. For the first time the EU responded swiftly reiterating the Union's commitment to democracy in North Africa and the Middle East (European

---

1    I thank the editors for their valuable comments and the interviewees for their time.
2    At the time of the article protests in Jordan are ongoing (Kirkpatrick 2012).

Commission 2011c, High Representative of the Union for Foreign Affairs and Security Policy and European Commission 2011). The EU chose a double strategy to respond to the 'Arab Spring'. Democratic movements were welcomed if the country faced an overhaul of the system such as Egypt, Tunisia or Libya and the regimes supported if the country remained relatively stable like Morocco or Jordan.

So to what extent did the 'Arab Spring' trigger political change and persistence in North Africa? And what are the consistent patterns of reform in Morocco? Connected to the general questions of persistence and change in this volume, this chapter compares the logics of action of domestic change processes in Morocco before and after the 'Arab Spring'. It explores the extent ideational context factors such as cooperation with the European Union (EU) as well as internal factors such as the interest of the domestic elite on the impact of institutional change. The EU has not only an important financial stake in Morocco but also an elaborated and institutionalised form of cooperation. Not only is the EU and its member states Morocco's most important trade partner, the Kingdom also has close relations with the EU in various areas including the economic and environmental policy analysed here.

Field research for this chapter was conducted in the immediate aftermath of the 'Arab Spring' and was able to collect important insights about patterns of reform processes in Morocco and the EU's change of policy towards the MENA region. The single country research design allows looking more deeply at selected processes of domestic change in economic and environmental policy. The in-case comparison of two policy reform processes ensures a differentiated outcome of the analysis without overemphasizing domestic or external explanatory factors over the other (see also Radaelli and Exadaktylos 2010). Empirical data was collected through semi-structured qualitative expert interviews conducted in Rabat, Morocco in autumn 2011 and spring 2012, email and phone interviews, document and secondary literature analysis.

Following this introduction, the chapter continues with laying out the Logics of Action framework and placing it within the broader context of recent studies looking at the possible impact of EU policy on domestic reform processes. Next, the logics of action of domestic reform focusing on two parameters – space and time – are examined. The space as well as the time parameter is central to analyse what and if any level of learning and diffusion took place in the circle of Morocco's ruling elite during the 'Arab Spring'. The chapter ends by laying out the specific patterns of interaction between Morocco and the EU as well as patterns of change detected throughout the analysis.

## Logics of Action: Space, Identity, Power and Time

The Logics of Action framework is an analytical tool to systemise variables which can influence the process of change. Instead of solely focusing on causal explanations, Logics of Action breaks down the complex interaction between domestic actors into basic components. In the case of domestic change in Morocco, four different categories not only allow analysing the evolution of political processes but also the quality of change within them. Space, identity, power and time are parameters to explore specific logics of action which seek to explain *why* international as well as domestic actors act in a certain way and to systemise variables that affect the logic of domestic interaction and change in Morocco before and after the 'Arab Spring'. For detecting the patterns and depth of domestic reforms in Morocco as well as exploring the role of external context factors such as the cooperation with the EU, space and time are the most promising parameters.

At the same time, the Logic of Action parameters *power* and *identity* are underlying processes of domestic change. The construction of the 'other side', as captured by the *identity* parameter is apparent in reform processes as well as the *power* relations influencing the process. In Morocco different blueprints for reform are discussed by domestic actors following a sense of competition with the goal to perform better in policies compared to neighbouring countries or the international cooperation partner. Reasons for this identity construction of 'us' versus 'them' can also be seen in the cooperation between the EU and Morocco. *Power* relations expressed through asymmetries of resources, know-how and trade leverage influence all aspects of international cooperation. These asymmetries can sometimes hinder reform progress when the EU is involved. But power asymmetries between domestic actors may also block or lessen reforms. While *identity* as well as *power* are important underlying parameters in processes of domestic change, this study looks in more detail at the role of space and time to explore the depth of reform as well as the role of EU factors in this process.

The Moroccan policy reforms compared here are embedded in a complex network of international cooperation within the Euro-Mediterranean Political *Space* which connects the northern and southern shore of the Mediterranean Sea in various forms. As can be seen in the economic as well as environmental policy reform in Morocco, the cooperation of Morocco with the European Union played into the course of reforms, supported, and sometimes even hindered the domestic agenda of change. Especially interesting in the Moroccan case is the quality of domestic change that the Logics of Action framework catches with its *time* parameter. While the policy reform record in the country is quite remarkable, implementation rarely takes place. The further exploration of learning in policy reform processes sheds light on this phenomenon. Change, so it seems, is complex and even a historical unique event like the 'Arab Spring' does not necessarily trigger comprehensive, long-lasting reforms, at least not in the short run.

*Quality of Domestic Change and EU Impact*

With its focus in different parameters instead of the detection of causal laws, the Logics of Action framework fits perfectly into the broader picture of European

Union studies. Not only does the Logics of Action framework direct the attention to crucial parameters of political interaction, it also touches upon one of the key puzzles of recent EU studies research: to what extent can processes of institutional change be triggered externally by the EU? Similar to the Logics of Action applied here, domestic change is in all studies on Europeanisation the decisive dependent variable while the collection of independent variables varies between EU rules and norms, power as well as domestic actors' interest and constellation. The less the EU formulates and demands reform, one of the main conclusions of Europeanisation research, the less likely change is going to be triggered in EU member and candidate states (Börzel and Risse 2000, Cowles, Caporaso and Risse 2001, Grabbe 2003). Studies on the effect of European policy on its neighbouring states confirm that the quality and clarity of EU norms influence the scope of impact, but even more important is the interest and preference of domestic actors (Freyburg et al. 2009, Héritier and Knill 2001).

The concept of learning sets out to explore the quality of impact of European Union policy on processes of domestic change within and outside Europe (Farrell 2009, Radaelli 2008, 2009). Learning allows looking into the black box of institutional change and the role of domestic actors and see how 'deep' the reform taken goes (Dolowitz and Marsh 2000, Stone 1999). Logics of Action can expand the perspective of Europeanisation studies with placing domestic change in the quad of space, identity, power and time and unfolds the complexity of processes of domestic change rather than focusing on single explanatory variables and causal laws.

The Logics of Action time parameter extends upon former studies done in institutional analysis that learning can alter actor beliefs on different levels and in different time frames (Levy 1994, Sabatier and Jenkins-Smith 1993, Bennett and Howlett 1992). Sabatier and Jenkins (1993) identified three forms of belief change: deep core, policy core and secondary beliefs. Deep core beliefs are mostly resistant to change. The EU's social-cultural identity based on values of liberalism, democracy and human rights is such a deep core belief unlikely to change because it constitutes the base of the community and its actions. In Morocco, a deep core belief could be the supremacy of the King as 'the commander of the faithful'. Policy core beliefs are still quite resilient to change. The belief that for example economic liberalism will lead to democratic structures, is a policy core belief that the EU is applying in its neighbourhood and development policy (see Horst in this volume). In Morocco, a policy core belief is that economic liberalism leads to economic growth or that policies should be generally guided from a central institution rather than a decentralised decision-making structure. Policy core beliefs often have a strategic nature because they are based on deep core beliefs. The lowest belief on the totem pole of institutional change and learning are secondary beliefs. They are responsive to change and entail mostly policy instruments that need to be adjusted after new policy goals are defined. One example is the revision of the European Neighbourhood Policy (ENP) after the 'Arab Spring' which now also encompasses a European Civil Society instrument whose goal is to support NGOs and civil society groups in MENA (European Commission 2011b, High Representative of the Union for Foreign Affairs and Security Policy and European Commission 2011, 2011a). Secondary beliefs, such as policy instruments, are quickly adjusted and do not necessarily need a change in deep or policy core beliefs. This quicker adjustment can lead, as observed in the ENP revision at the moment, to a more superficial change that is not supported by core beliefs and that can hinder its implementation (Youngs 2012).

In the following, this notion of learning processes and the depth of institutional change is used to analyse reform processes in Morocco before and after the 'Arab Spring' and further explore the Logics of Action parameters of time and space. While examining institutional change in time and space, domestic as well as external factors that triggered the institutional change are examined. Special attention is given to the effect of European policy on economic and environmental policy reform and on patterns of domestic change in Morocco.

## Policy Reforms in Morocco Before and After the 'Arab Spring'

Moroccan domestic reforms follow patterns that are closely related to the belief system of the domestic actors. Before further exploring this connection between belief system and reform pattern with the Logics of Action framework, the following section lays out the effect of the 'Arab Spring' protests on day-to-day reform processes in economic and environmental policy. While economic policy reform is at the core of political as well as international interest, environmental policy has a lower political priority. Both policy reform agendas were halted by the events of the Moroccan 'Arab Spring'.

Inspired by the protests in Tunisia and Egypt in spring 2011, smaller and decentralised protests also rose across Morocco (see also Fritzsche and Lübben in this volume). Following the examples of their neighbours the 20 February movement – named after the start of the protests in Morocco – hoped for overall political change while the ruling elite around the palace were alarmed and acted more quickly than their neighbouring regimes. After a series of reforms induced by the palace, including the formulation of a new constitution and the call for new elections for November 2011, the public support of the protests dwindled. What looked from the outside like a forward-looking government acknowledging the changes demanded by its population was seen by some observers as a 'pyrrhic victory for the King' (Ottaway and Muasher 2011). However, the win of the moderate Islamist PJD in the November 2011 elections can be seen as a real novum in Moroccan politics that would have been unlikely without the wave of the Arab Spring (Benchemsi 2012: 57) (see for more details Fritzsche and Lübben in this volume). The 2011 election was the start of Morocco's claim to have found a third path between violent suppression of protests from above and revolutionary change (Ottaway 2012).

But the genuine partnership between the King and PJD after the election did not change the overall reform pattern since Morocco's independence in 1956 that is dominated by the interest in political stability of the palace (Pennell 2000, Perthes 2004). For example, five hundred of the country's most senior positions are appointed by the new prime minister, Abdeliah Benkriane. King Mohammed VI instead chooses 37 of the most pivotal posts including all ambassadors. Further article 41 of the new constitution enables the King to overrule any laws decided in the legislature with the royal *dahir* or decree. Similar to Jordan, the old Moroccan elite found its way to maintain its hold on the reins of power in a more subtle way than before the protests (Benchemsi 2012, McManus 2012, Colombo 2011).

The Moroccan 'third way' through the 'Arab Spring' and the new constitution and election cemented the official discourse about Moroccan exceptionalism and the country's role model for North Africa in the wake of the 'Arab Spring' and beyond. In practice the induced reforms – at least in the core areas of government – remain mainly unchanged and heavily guided from the Royal circle of power. The Logics of Action framework helps to unfold these general patterns of persistence in times of change. The general tendency of guided change from above and preservation of the King's power in Morocco trickles down to all levels of policy reform and becomes especially apparent in the reform process of the two policies discussed below.

## Economic Policy

'The King is [...] the first banker, insurer, exporter and farmer in his country' (Graciet and Laurent 2012: 11, *author's translation*). The prominent role of the monarchy in all realms of the Moroccan economy has not changed with the 'Arab Spring'. On the contrary, the more public enterprises were privatised through economic policy reform and liberalisation efforts the more royal wealth was accumulated (Graciet and Laurent 2012: 9, Benchemsi 2012, Catusse 2008). While most other Monarchs around the world lost parts of their fortune in the early financial crisis in 2008, King Mohammed VI was able to double his to 2.4 billion US dollars which makes him the seventh richest monarch in the world (Pendleton 2009). This was mainly because of the lucrative phosphate trade which is controlled by the Royal Office of Phosphates (OCP) and the so-called '500 families' or *makhzen* who are also in charge of other large, multi-sectoral holdings and have close relations with the Palace. The OCP has the monopoly over phosphate production, employs 19,000 workers and contributes 2 to 3 per cent to GDP (Arieff 2011). Although no statistics are publicly available, observers report that the National Investment Company (SNI) of which the royal family holds the majority, controls significant domestic financial, insurance, construction, and commodity interests (Karam 2011). Only a few investment projects in Morocco are done without the King's involvement (Benchemsi 2012: 57).

The major economic reforms in the past fifteen years included a wave of privatisation in the telecommunication, banking and insurance sectors among others. A 206 million US dollar state-guaranteed public-private sector fund was introduced in 2010 to increase competiveness of automobiles, aeronautics, services and telecommunication (Arieff 2011). Further privatisation and support for key industrial sectors were especially supported by the World Bank, the International Monetary Fund, as well as the European Union – Morocco's major trading partner – to mobilise the private sector, generate jobs and make the Moroccan economy less dependent on the agricultural sector (European Commission 2010, 2011d, 2011e). As of today, 17.1 per cent of the GDP is generated on farms which give jobs to more than 44.6 per cent of the population. Several efforts to change this economic focus towards macroeconomic management and sustained growth in non-agricultural sectors were unsuccessful to trigger a major shift in labour distribution: the government remained the biggest employer outside agriculture (Arieff 2011).

This triad of Morocco's labour economy – phosphate, agriculture and government jobs – was not affected by the 'Arab Spring'. On the contrary, the regime relies even more heavily on these traditional areas to generate state income and jobs. In the height of the protest in spring 2011, the government started to hire young university graduates (numbers vary from 200-1000). Interviews indicated that new employment in these areas was not planned before the protests.[3] Additionally the Monarchy reiterated the strength of Plan Maroc Vert, which describes how to effectively expand the agricultural sector and boost its productivity by 2020 (La Vie éco 2009) and is supported by the loan programmes of the World Bank as well as the European Investment Bank (European Investment Bank 2012, World Bank 2012). Especially in times of change the Moroccan economy continues to build on its traditional strengths.[4]

Another important stepping stone on the way to economic modernisation in Morocco in the last 10 years was the cutting back of extensive government subsidies, especially on oil and propane. As discussed in more detail in the next section, the water prices were also envisaged to be adjusted to their real price in summer 2011. Both reforms would have generated a rise in prices which affects the majority of the population directly. None of the above changes were implemented.[5] In 2011, subsidies skyrocketed to a record level of 5.93 billion US dollars, 76.5 per cent higher than in 2012 and now represents a serious contingent liability on public finances (World Bank October 2012). Combined with one of the most severe cold winters and droughts in Moroccan history in spring 2012, agricultural productivity dropped and resulted in higher unemployment (Schemm 2012). Morocco's economy is expected to grow in 2012 by only 2.2 per cent instead of the previously predicted 7 per cent. The economic crisis in Europe contributed to this downslide – tourism which generates around 10 per cent of

---

3    Interviews with Moroccan officials in Rabat, autumn 2011.
4    Interviews with Moroccan bureaucrats in Rabat, autumn 2011 and spring 2012.
5    As of December 2012.

GDP is down 9 per cent especially because of fewer tourists from crisis stricken Spain, Portugal and France.

In summary, economic policy before the 'Arab Spring' was at the core of the domestic reform process with the goal of redirecting job creating and productivity to non-agricultural sectors. While most of these reforms were adapted into laws, their implementation in some areas was hindered by the 'Arab Spring' because of the fear for more mass protests. Instead, old reform patterns of economic policy were revitalised with special emphasis on the creation of more governmental jobs and the suspension of price reforms. The central role of the *makzhen* interest and the stake of the King himself in economic policy reform in Morocco did not seem to be affected by the changes proposed with the new constitution and with the election of a new government. The overall wind of change through the 'Arab Spring' so it seems, did not only come to a halt in Morocco but also hindered the ongoing economic reform agenda.

*Environmental Reform*[6]

While economic reforms facilitating free trade lay unchanged at the core of interest of domestic actors as well as any international cooperation with Morocco, environmental policy always had a lower priority on the political agenda. Nevertheless, reforms such as in the water or energy sector especially affect the population directly and are therefore delicate domestic changes in times of popular protests and rising criticism of the ruling elite's wealth. At the same time, environmental policy reforms allow taking a closer look at the effect of the 'Arab Spring' in day-to-day reforms and diverging actors' interests.

Before the developments of the mass protests, environmental reform in Morocco was pushed forward. Numerous reform strategies for the environment were adopted but only a few were implemented. The Environmental Protection Plan of 2003 as well as the 2010 National Environment and Sustainable Development Charta established fundamental principles of government action to organise environmental protection in waste or water management for example (European Commission 2009, 2010). Water management is a pressing issue for Morocco because the strong agricultural sector depends on reliable (and cheap) water supply. But water is also a scarce resource: With over 17 per cent of arable land being irrigated, the 29 cubic metres of available renewable fresh water per year is not sufficient if shared with a population of about 33 million (in 2000) (Central Intelligence Agency 2009).

Both the 2003 Environmental Protection Plan as well as the 2010 Environmental Charta mention the need for more effective water management including the improvement of water supply to rural areas, the building of more dams for agricultural irrigation as well as an increase in water fees. While water supply measures as well as dams were successfully implemented, water prices remained

---

6    This paragraph is based in parts on Maggi 2012.

unchanged. The role of the 'Arab Spring' should not be overemphasised to explain lagging policy reform implementation. Structural problems such as insufficient administrative capacity and concurring interests of the domestic actors are equally crucial to explain this lack of implementation. While one group of actors – mainly situated in the Agricultural ministry – push for extensive water use and the building of more dams, the Environmental ministry, backed by some international donors such as Germany is more interested in an intensifying water use strategy. This controversy does not only result in difficult cooperation between the ministries but also in an incoherent water strategy. Compromises like law no. 10 of 2010 did indeed establish a decentralised water management administration, but the water authorities not only lack sufficient personnel, but also financial means to finance, for example, the gas to drive water well inspections.

Renewable energy instead has experienced an unprecedented pace of reform and support in the last ten years. By establishing independent agencies, the Moroccan government and more importantly the Royal Palace circumvented the potential rivalries of interest between ministries. In 2009 the National Agency for the Development of Renewable Energy (Agence Nationale pour le Développement des Energies Renouvelables et de l'Efficacité Energétique, ADEREE) and the Moroccan Agency for Solar Energy (MASEN) were established with the goal to support renewable but especially solar energy. While ADEREE is staffed by former ministry employees, MASEN is completely 'outsourced' from public administration. Supported by the King, MASEN gained international and national attention quickly. What for his father Hassan II were dams and irrigation, the reform of Morocco's energy supply seems to be the life project for Mohammed VI (Graciet and Laurent 2012: 192ff). In 2009 alone five laws passed parliament with the goal of promoting renewable energy in Morocco. In the same year, the King inaugurated the Moroccan Solar Plan with the aim of producing 42 per cent of the national energy consumption with renewable energy to which solar energy is supposed to contribute 3500 MW. To minimise Morocco's dependency on foreign energy imports, various solar plants are planned. Ouarzazate on the slopes of the Atlas Mountains will be the biggest solar power plant with a planned production of 2000 MW. But to realise the Moroccan Solar Plan, major international investment such as the European investment consortium Desertec are needed (see also Rothe in this volume).

Economic and environmental policy reforms are showing a different logic of action and patterns of institutional change. Environmental policy reform gives interesting insight in the day-to-day change of a policy that has not extended political stake. If multiple actors' interest is diverging, policy reform and especially its implementation is more unlikely such as in water policy reform. If policy preferences merge and are backed by the palace, policy reform can show an impressive speed as seen in the renewable energy sector. The logics of action of environmental and economic policy reform differ depending on the interest of the involved domestic actors.

*Patterns of Domestic Reform*

Whether it be public protests resulting in a new constitution, a new majority in parliament, and a new prime minister through elections, or daily reforms in economic and environmental policy – all processes of domestic change in Morocco seem to have one pattern in common: the development, speed and depth of reforms is dependent on the consent of the palace or are heavily influenced by the interest of the King and the *makzhen*. While the events of the 'Arab Spring', especially the new PJD majority in parliament might have the potential to trigger an incremental process of change in the long run, the events do not influence the course of day-to-day reforms. Quite to the contrary, the 'Arab Spring' did not lead towards overarching change in every limb of the state but did hinder sensitive reform such as the suspended price increase for gasoline and water. In the case of economic policy it even reversed the seeds of change planted by the election and brought the focus back on the traditional strength of the Moroccan economy with the generation of more government jobs and a refocus on agriculture. Reform in the daily administration of environmental policy continued to be blocked by diverging interest between ministries, which lead to a chronic lack of reform implementation. As argued below, lasting political change depends on the interest of a majority of ruling domestic actors and on the space and time frame in which the political interaction takes place.

## Logics of Action and Domestic Policy Change

The Logics of Action framework explains the patterns of domestic change by placing it in the quad of space, identity, power and time. While all four parameters help to unfold the complexity of reform processes, this section focuses on time and space. Space leads the attention to the environment surrounding political interaction in which domestic change in Morocco is embedded while the time parameter looks at the depth of change and possible processes of learning underlying them. In the following, the role of the 'Arab Spring' as well as the effect of EU-Morocco cooperation on processes of domestic change, its pattern and depth of reform are analysed in the broader context of Logics of Action. Change, so it seems, is complex and even a historical unique event like the 'Arab Spring' does not necessarily trigger comprehensive, long-lasting reforms on all levels of domestic politics.

*Domestic Change and the Euro-Mediterranean Political Space(s)*

For every process of domestic change the environment in which it takes place is crucial. This includes the domestic as well as the international environment surrounding it. Being situated in the Euro-Mediterranean Political Space influenced the course of reform processes during the 'Arab Spring' as well as economic and environmental policy change. The EU mainly welcomed Morocco's handling of the 'Arab Spring' protests and followed the preference of the King and the palace for political stability. Similar behaviour hindered further economic and environmental reform processes in some cases.

The changing character of EU engagement in its neighbourhood – reflected in numerous cooperation approaches to the region – also changed the EU's role in the Moroccan domestic change agenda. The EU sought cooperation with traditional key actors rather than the inclusion of new, eventually change promoting actors (Kausch 2008, Pace 2005). The Advanced Status granted due to Morocco's long term relationship with the EU in 2008 as well as the European Neighbourhood Policy (ENP) illustrate this pattern well. Different to the precise participation conditions of the EU enlargement policy, the ENP is characterised by a loose carrot and stick policy (Böttger 2010, Kelley 2006, Youngs 2001). ENP Action Plan and Progress Reports point out courses of reform and areas in which more change is needed without a legal obligation for an ENP partner country like Morocco to meet them. The main legal basis of the relationship is the Association Agreement between Morocco and the EU which follows its own time schedule. The ENP instead is connected to the wider EU foreign policy and budget cycle – a procedural discrepancy that was already creating complications within the Euro-Mediterranean Partnership (Johansson-Nogués 2004). The Advanced Status of 2008 simply adds a layer of cooperation to the existence framework of Association Agreement and Action Plan to reiterate the political and economic integration between the EU and Morocco rhetorically (Kausch 2010, Martín 2009). Especially during the events of the 'Arab Spring' the Advanced Status fulfilled an important symbolic effect, used by EU as well as Moroccan officials to underline the robust and persistent relationship.[7] The EU's preference seems to have shifted away from reform support towards favouring the persistence of relations.

The popularity of budget support as the major financial EU assistance illustrates this shift well. Budget support promotes the domestic reform agenda along relatively generous conditions of funding such as national or sectoral development or reform strategies, existence of a stable macroeconomic framework and ongoing improvement of public financial management (European Commission 2010, 2011a, 2011b, 2011e). Hence, the deliberately-limited capacity of the EU to intervene in domestic reform processes leads to a focused support of key actors instead of the promotion of innovative policy change (see further Maggi 2012). Whether this focus on traditional actors shifts with the implementation of the review of the ENP after the 'Arab Spring' is seen as sceptical by non-governmental actors on the ground as well as by some commentators (Youngs 2012).[8]

The EU's preference for persistence of relations is also true for economic as well as environmental policy reform in Morocco. The EU and its member states remain the biggest and most important trading partner sharing 51.3 per cent of

---

7   Interviews with Moroccan and EU officials in Rabat, autumn 2012.
8   Interview with civil society actors in Rabat, spring 2012.

Morocco's total trade and have undeniable leverage within negotiations (Dawson 2009).[9] The trade imbalance with Morocco importing goods worth 14.1 billion Euros and exporting 8.1 billion Euros to the EU, contributes to this asymmetric power relationship that gives the EU some leverage for domestic reforms. While the privatisation of public companies was demanded by the EU as well as other international donors, its practical implications were of secondary importance.[10] The monopolistic role of the Royal family and the ruling circle surrounding it in Morocco's private sector was therefore silently welcomed over the last two decades (see also Graciet and Laurent 2012: 185ff). The cementation of economic influence of the old elite through privatisation and the EU budget support hindered any form of economic innovation outside the ruling elite.

The reform agenda of environmental policy specifically of renewable energy illustrates well that domestic reform heavily depends of the orientation and preferences of the domestic ruling elite. Strongly promoted by the Royal circle and King Mohammed VI himself, solar energy has not only seen strong domestic reform progress but also the institutionalisation of two new agencies fostering renewable energy – ADEREE and MASEN within one year. The project has also attracted international investment interest, with the EU remaining relatively silent. Even though the 2008 Union for the Mediterranean (UfM), another initiative to foster political interaction around the Mediterranean Sea, envisioned a Mediterranean Solar Plan, little EU involvement is seen in the renewable energy sector. A different picture can be drawn from EU engagement in water policy reform. With water policy being one of the oldest fields of cooperation between Morocco and the EU, it was the first sector to receive budget support in 2002. By 2006, around 120 million Euros were transferred to the Moroccan budget to pursue the domestic reform agenda marked by inter-ministerial rivalries and unclear priorities. Hence the ever more untargeted EU financial assistance contributed rather to a halt of the day-to-day reform process than progress or active solutions to problems of reform implementation.

*Morocco's Third Way: Change and Persistence Over Time*

The 'Arab Spring' set out to change everything that was held true for the MENA countries: stable authoritarian regimes, passive civil society and the never-ending path to democracy. What has changed for Tunisia, Egypt and maybe Libya was not the case for Morocco. Instead Morocco proclaims to have chosen the third way between a revolution and authoritarian suppression of uprisings as seen in Libya or

---

9    In 2012 53.1 per cent of Morocco's total trade was with the EU. Goods worth 23.6 billion Euros were traded in 2011. While Morocco's main export products are clothing (25.5 per cent), agricultural products (23.5. per cent), machinery and transport equipment (23.3 per cent), the EU ships mainly machinery and transport equipment (36.5 per cent) and manufactured goods (22.8. per cent) (European Commission DG Trade 2012).

10    Interview with EU officials, Rabat, spring 2012.

Syria (Ottaway 2012). King Mohammed VI initiated reforms; a new constitution was followed by elections and the rise of the moderate Islamic PJD which seems to have a genuine partnership with the Royal palace. To put it in the vocabulary of learning research: Even though it seemed like and was communicated that deep core beliefs at the roots of the belief system have changed, only secondary beliefs were adjusted to a change in strategy of the ruling elite to preserve their power. This followed a common logic of action of reforming domestic policy in the country: While comprehensive changes are announced, adjustments are only put into practice if they coincide with the preferences of the ruling elite who are eager to preserve and build upon the *status quo* (Benchemsi 2012, Boukhars 2011, Willis 2009).

While the 'Arab Spring' overhauled many basic principles in other MENA countries, the overarching deep core belief in Moroccan politics that the central role of the King as 'commander of the faithful' remains untouched. Neither the majority protesters and to a lesser extent the leading circle of the country were supporting the idea of a constitutional monarchy after the British or Spanish example (Benchemsi 2012, Pelham 2012). The King kept most of his core functions throughout the 'Arab Spring' but allowed for the first time a moderate Islamist party to win the election and build a government (Benchemsi 2012, Ottaway and Muasher 2011, Pelham 2012). This has two important consequences: First, the general policy core belief that only the King can have a public religious and political affiliation at the same time is now also granted to the PJD. Secondly, the rise of the PJD in Moroccan politics will probably alter the strategic action and secondary beliefs of key actors within future processes of domestic change in Morocco.

While changing policy core beliefs are a very rare occasion, secondary beliefs in the form of policy instruments seem to constantly change in Morocco. The 'Arab Spring' affected their pace and also brought some such as the scheduled rise in water prices to a halt. Other reform efforts like the reduction of jobs in public administration were reversed out of the fear of more protests and upheavals. Changing few policy core beliefs while leaving deep core beliefs mainly untouched and adjusting secondary beliefs instead, is a common pattern of learning processes to avoid public resistance and conserve the *status quo* (Sabatier and Jenkins-Smith 1993). While the change of policy core beliefs through the public rise of the PJD can be seen as a substantial domestic change with long term effect due to the 'Arab Spring', none of the state fundamentals or deep core beliefs have been altered. This reform path of least resistance is a common feature to be seen also in economic and environmental policy reform in Morocco. While policy instruments were adjusted quickly, the lack of change at deeper levels of the belief system leads to inconsistent or non-implemented reforms. Therefore one can also conclude that secondary beliefs can only be expected to change if policy core beliefs are changed as well.

## Conclusion

Former US president Kennedy seemed to have rightly foreseen the revolutions in Tunisia, Egypt and Libya. But the MENA monarchies are the big exception to Kennedy's rule of thumb. So far Morocco's potential revolution was tempered by the guided reform initiated by the palace and the inclusion of an Islamic party in politics. The analysis has shown that this strategy has lead for the most part to rather cosmetic changes. It is also questionable if the dispensing of public subsidies can sustain this strategy in the long run.

The parameters *time* and *space* of the Logics of Action framework helped to decode the domestic changes during the 'Arab Spring' in Morocco and identify reform patterns before and after the protests. The parameter *space* unfolded the complex layers of political interaction in which reform processes can take place. It helped not only to focus on political instruments surrounding political interaction, such as the European Neighbourhood Policy but to highlight domestic interaction as well. Switching towards less targeted financial assistance through budget support, the EU has limited leverage to promote policy change beyond adaptation of reforms that are already on the agenda of domestic actors. Further, existent power structure of the political elite and the prominent role of the king in the economic sector were enhanced with the promotion of privatisation policies without considering the building of monopolies through them. Throughout the process of domestic change in economic as well as environmental policy, EU involvement was conditional to the interest and goals of the ruling elite. Hence the EU cannot be seen as a reform innovator in Morocco but rather a facilitator for the domestic reform agenda.

The *time* parameter grasped the complexity of processes of domestic change and underlined how these can be transformed by an extraordinary event such as the 'Arab Spring'. At the same time, looking closer at the time dimension of domestic change allowed us to open the black box of reform processes and classify the different levels of change. Working with a belief system enabled not only the analysis of how domestic and international actors reacted to big political events but also permitted statements on how durable the induced change might be. While the 'Arab Spring' was unable to trigger the big revolution that would change everything, policy core beliefs seem to have altered the domestic logic of action with impact on future reforms. The PJD will gain more political experience which could ultimately contribute to further independence of the government from the palace. The reaction to the 'Arab Spring' as well as the detected patterns in ongoing reform processes in economic and environmental policy, show a change of secondary beliefs that hindered the implementation of policy reform and helped to calm the protests, probably avoiding more comprehensive changes. The alteration of a few policy core beliefs while leaving deep core beliefs mainly untouched and adjusting secondary beliefs instead, is a common pattern of learning processes to avoid public resistance and conserve the *status quo*. The political developments in Morocco after the 'Arab Spring' have delivered more evidence for this finding, but have also shown that comprehensive change in times of revolutions have a rather incremental character. How deep policy diffusion can go and if this is due to a learning process at a deeper level of the belief system depends not only on the design of the policy being adapted. Domestic actor constellation and interest seem to play a large role because of their position within the reform processes.

## Bibliography

Arieff, A. 2011. *Morocco: Current Issues.* Washington D.C.: Congressional Research Service.

Benchemsi, A. 2012. Morocco: Outfoxing the Opposition. *Journal of Democracy*, 23, 57-69.

Bennett, C.J. and M. Howlett. 1992. The Lessons of Learning: Reconciling Theories of Policy Learning and Policy Change. *Policy Sciences*, 25(3), 275-294.

Boerzel, T.A. and T. Risse. 2000. When Europe Hits Home: Europeanization and Domestic Change. *European Integration online Papers* 15. Available at: Http://papers.ssrn.com/sol3/-papers.cfm?abstract_id=302768 [accessed 19 November 2012]

Boettger, K. 2010. *Die Entstehung und Entwicklung der Europäischen Nachbarschaftspolitik: Akteure und Koalitionen.* Baden-Baden: Nomos.

Boukhars, A. 2011. *Politics in Morocco: Executive Monarchy and Enlightened Authoritarianism.* London/New York: Routledge.

Catusse, M. 2008. *Le Temps Des Entrepreneurs? Politique Et Transformations Du Capitalisme Au Maroc.* Paris: Institut de recherche sur le Maghreb contemporain.

Central Intelligence Agency (CIA). 2009. *The World Factbook 2009: Morocco.* Washington D.C.: Central Intelligence Agency.

Colombo, S. 2011. Morocco at the Crossroads: Seizing the Window of Opportunity for Sustainable Development. *MEDPRO Technical Report*, 1-17.

Cowles, M.G., J.A. Caporaso and T. Risse. 2001. *Transforming Europe: Europeanization and Domestic Change.* Ithaca, N.Y.: Cornell University Press.

Dawson, C. 2009. *EU Integration with North Africa – Trade Negotiations and Democracy Deficit in Morocco.* London: Tauris Academic Studies.

Dolowitz, D.P. and D. Marsh. 2000. Learning from Abroad: The Role of Policy Transfer in Contemporary Policy-Making. *Governance*, 13(1), 5-24.

European Commission DG Trade 2012. Morocco: Main economic indicators, based on Eurostat (New Cronos). March 21, 2012.

European Commission. 2011a. *Document De Travail Conjoint Des Services, Mise En Oeuvre De La Politique Européenne De Voisinage En 2010, Rapport Pays: Maroc.*

———. 2011b. *The Future Approach to the EU Budget Support to Third Countries.*

————. 2011c. *Increasing the Impact of EU Development Policy: An Agenda for Change.* 637 final.

————. 2011d. *National Indicative Programme Morocco 2007-2010.*

————. 2011e. *National Indicative Programme Morocco 2011-2013.*

————. 2010. *Mise En Œuvre De La Politique Européenne De Voisinage En 2009 Rapport De Suivi Maro.*

————. 2009. *Mise En Œuvre De La Politique Européenne De Voisinage En 2008 Rapport De Suivi Maroc.*

European Investment Bank. 2012. *Plan Maroc Vert – Programme National De L'économie De L'eau En L'irrigation (PNEE).* Luxembourg: The European Investment Bank.

Farrell, M. 2009. EU Policy Towards Other Regions: Policy Learning in the External Promotion of Regional Integration. *Journal of European Public Policy,* 16 (8), 1165-1184.

Freyburg, T., S. Lavenex, F. Schimmelfennig, T. Skripka and A. Wetzel. 2009. EU Promotion of Democratic Governance in the Neighbourhood. *Journal of European Public Policy,* 16(6), 916-934.

Grabbe, H. 2003. Europeanisation Goes East: Power and Uncertainty in the EU Accession Process, in *The Politics of Europeanization,* edited by K. Featherstone and C. M. Radaelli. Oxford: Oxford University Press, 303-330.

Graciet, C. and É. Laurent. 2012. *Le Roi Prédateur: Main Basse Sur Le Maroc.* Paris: Seuil.

Héritier, A. and C. Knill. 2001. Differential Responses to European Policies: A Comparison, in *Differential Europe: The European Union Impact on National Policymaking,* edited by A. Héritier, D. Kerwer, D. Lehmkuhl, C. Knill, M. Teutsch and A. Douillet. Boulder: Rowman & Littlefield, 257-294.

High Representative of the Union for Foreign Affairs and Security Policy and European Commission. 2011a. *A New Response to a Changing Neighbourhood.* COM(2011)303.

————. 2011. *A Partnership for Democracy and Shared Prosperity with the Southern Mediterranean.* COM(2011)200 final.

Johansson-Nogués, E. 2004. A 'Ring of Friends'? The Implications of the European Neighbourhood Policy for the Mediterranean. *Mediterranean Politics,* 9(2), 240-247.

Karam, S. 2011. Morocco Regulator in Pledge on Monarchy-Owned Firms. *Reuters* [Online, 30 September]. Available at: http://www.reuters.com/article/2011/09/30/idUSL5E7KU2VA20110930 [accessed: 19 November 2012]

Kausch, K. 2010. Morocco's 'Advanced Status': Model Or Muddle? *FRIDE Policy Brief, 43.*

————. 2008. Morocco: Negotiating Change with the Makhzen – Project on Freedom of Association in the Middle East and North Africa. *FRIDE Working paper, 54.*

Kelley, J. 2006. New Wine in Old Wineskins: Promoting Political Reforms through the New European Neighbourhood Policy. *Journal of Common Market Studies*, 44(1), 29-55.

Kennedy, J.F. 1962: Address on the First Anniversary of the Alliance for Progress, White House reception for diplomatic corps of the Latin American republics, March 13, 1962. Public Papers of the Presidents – John F. Kennedy.

Kirkpatrick, D.D. 2012. Protests in Jordan Continue, with Calls for Ending the King's Rule, *The New York Times* [Online, 15 November] Available at: http://www.nytimes.com/2012/11/16/world/-middleeast/protesters-in-jordan-call-for-ending-king-abdullah-iis-rule.html?_r=0 [accessed: 19 December 2012]

La Vie éco. 2009. *La Révolution Agricole Commence.* Special issue to La Vie Eco no.4 507.

Levy, J.S. 1994. Learning and Foreign Policy: Sweeping a Conceptual Minefield. *International Organization*, 48(2), 279-312.

Maggi, E.-M. 2012. A Leopard can (Not) Change its Spots: Promoting Environmental Policy in Morocco, in *Policy Change in the EU's Immediate Neighborhood: A Sectoral Approach*, edited by T.A. Boerzel and K. Boettger. Baden-Baden: Nomos, 145-162.

Martín, I. 2009. EU–Morocco Relations: How Advanced is the 'Advanced Status'? *Mediterranean Politics*, 14(2), 239-45.

McManus, A. J. 2012. 'Arab Spring', Moroccon Winter. *Jadaliyya* [Online, September 9] Available at: http://www.jadaliyya.com/pages/index/7278/arab-spring-moroccan-winter [accessed: 19 November 2012].

Ottaway, M. 2012. Morocco: Can the Third Way Succeed? *Commentary – Carnegie Endowment for International Peace.*

———. 2011. Arab Monarchies: Chance for Reform, Yet Unmet. *Carnegie Papers*.

Pace, M. 2005. The Impact of European Union Involvement in Civil Society Structures in the Southern Mediterranean. *Mediterranean Politics*, 10(2), 239-244.

Pelham, N. 2012. How Morocco Dodged the Arab Spring. *The New York Review of Books – Blog* [Online, 5 July] Available at: http://www.nybooks.com/blogs/nyrblog/2012/jul/05/how-morocco-dodged-arab-spring/ [accessed 19 November 2012].

Pendleton, D. 2009. King of Rock. *Forbes* [Online, 17 June] Available at: http://www.forbes.com/2009/06/17/king-morocco-phosphate-business-billionaires-royal-conflict.html [accessed: 19 November 2012].

Pennell, C.R. 2000. *Morocco since 1830: A History.* New York: New York University Press.

Perthes, V. 2004. *Arab Elites: Negotiating the Politics of Change.* Boulder, Colo.: Lynne Rienner Publishers.

Radaelli, C.M. and T. Exadaktylos. 2010. New Directions in Europeanization Research, in *Research Agendas in EU Studies: Stalking the Elephant*, edited by M.P. Egan, N. Nugent and W.E. Paterson. Basingstoke/New York: Palgrave Macmillan, 189-215.

Radaelli, C.M. 2009. Measuring Policy Learning: Regulatory Impact Assessment in Europe. *Journal of European Public Policy*, 16(8), 1145-1664.

———. 2008. Europeanization, Policy Learning, and New Modes of Governance. *Journal of Comparative Policy Analysis: Research and Practice*, 10(3), 239-254.

Sabatier, P.A. and H.C. Jenkins-Smith. 1993. *Policy Change and Learning: An Advocacy Coalition Approach.* Boulder: Westview Press.

Schemm, P. 2012. Drought, Falling Tourism Threaten Morocco Economy. *The Guardian* [Online, 14 April] Available at: http://www.guardian.co.uk/world/feedarticle/10195107 [accessed: 19 November 2012].

Stone, D. 1999. Learning Lessons and Transferring Policy Across Time, Space and Disciplines. *Politics*, 19(1), 51-59.

Willis, M.J. 2009. Conclusion: The Dynamics of Reform in Morocco. *Mediterranean Politics*, 14(2), 229-237.

World Bank. October 2012. *Morocco Overview.* Washington D.C.: The World Bank.

———. 2012. *Morocco – Second Development Policy Loan in Support of the Plan Maroc Vert Project.* Washington D.C.: The World Bank.

Youngs, R. 2012. *Funding Arab Reform?* Washington. D.C.: The German Marshall Fund of the United States.

———. 2001. *The European Union and the Promotion of Democracy.* Oxford/New York: Oxford University Press.

## Chapter 3

# Facing a Dilemma: The EU's Promotion of Gender-Democracy after the 'Arab Spring'[1]

Annette Jünemann

## Introduction

Although women made an important contribution to the 'Arab Spring' in the year 2011 by being involved in initiating and carrying out the protests, they are no longer playing a comparable role in the reorganisation of political life in the Arab transition countries (Agapiou-Josephides, Benoit-Rohmer 2012). Not all are willing to accept the absence of a gender-specific revolution dividend and therefore demand full participation in the newly emerging political structures. Their involvement comes at the right time because the establishment of gender democracy is not a luxury that can be addressed once all the other problems of the transition have been solved.[2] On the contrary, it is necessary to exploit the window of opportunity in which constitutions and electoral laws are emerging, new political elites are forming and new economic structures are being established. If women do not introduce their own gender-specific demands into the transformation process from the outset, this window can quickly close again, as for example happened after the Algerian War of Liberation in the 1960s (Brac de la Perrière 1997) or the end of apartheid in South Africa in the 1990s (Hassim 2003). Not all female activists from the 'Arab Spring' are aware of the fact that phases of revolutionary upheaval are usually followed by an increased demand for security and order. This is the reason why post-revolutionary transition processes leave little room for a fundamental realignment of gender relations, which nevertheless affect the core of every restructuring process (Harders 2011: 49). Nawal El Saadawi, a well known Egyptian women's rights activist warns that 'women can lose their rights after the success of a revolution, since the patriarchal class laws and values are embedded

1    This contribution has benefited a lot from critical discussions with the co-editors, colleagues and women's rights activists. I owe special thanks to Amal Basha, Zeineb Ben Othmann, Nezah Alaoui, Majdouline Lyazidi, Hoda Salah, Rihab Gamaoun, Ashwaq Bateha and Cilja Harders. I also thank Colin Hawkins for his translation of an earlier German version of this text and Phillip Ständer for helping with editing and formatting.

2    This contribution was written in spring 2013, before the setback in the process of transformation in Egypt as well as – to a lesser extent – in Tunisia. The basic assumptions of my analysis, however, remain the same.

in the society' (El Saadawi 2011). From this perspective, the 'Arab Spring' offers great opportunities but also considerable risks.

Not until women and men, regardless of their differences, can participate with equal entitlement on all levels, namely in politics, economics, culture, science and all other socially relevant areas, will the postulate of gender democracy be fulfilled. Reference to this objective occurs in the *Arab Human Development Report* of the United Nations, which as long ago as 2002 came to the conclusion that the systematic unfair treatment of women in political, economic, social and legal terms was a key obstacle to development in the Arab societies (Arab Human Development Report 2002). However, as demonstrated in the *Gender Index* prepared on behalf of the OECD, most of the Arab states lie at the far bottom end of the scale so that it is reasonable to speak of an Arab exceptionalism (SIGI 2012). Conscious use is made here of the term 'Arab' and not 'Muslim' exceptionalism. Like other religions, Islam too stabilises established structures in society and thus contributes to the persistence of traditional gender relations. It is important to note, though, that it is only one factor amongst others and that European decision makers tend to overestimate the importance of Islam as a primary cause of deficiencies in Arab (gender) politics.

The 'Arab Spring' revealed the hypocrisy of longstanding EU cooperation with authoritarian regimes, which was based on a shared interest in keeping political Islam down.[3] One of the most important lessons the EU has to learn from the 'Arab Spring' is to fully accept democratically legitimised Islamist[4] governments. This contribution examines how the new tolerance to be adopted towards political Islam after the 'Arab Spring' can be brought into harmony with the fostering of women's rights in the MENA region. The latter is a normative policy goal and part of the EU's external promotion of democracy. Prior to the 'Arab Spring', the EU has been supporting the agenda of secular women's right groups, paradoxically in tacit agreement with the authoritarian regimes of the region that pursued a kind of secular state feminism as an instrument in the fight against political Islam. Since the 'Arab Spring', this promotional practice of the EU appears anachronistic. To adapt the external promotion of gender democracy to the new political realities, however, confronts the EU with a dilemma: How to cope with Islamists if women's rights are at stake?

---

3    This does not mean that the toppled Arab regimes had been secular. Apart from Tunisia all regimes in the Middle East and North Africa (MENA) had been striving for religious legitimacy in one way or another (see Harders in this volume). In this overview study the systemic differences between specific Arab countries cannot be dealt with in detail.

4    The terms 'Islamism' and 'political Islam' are used synonymously in this study and denote the very heterogeneous spectrum of political convictions that are guided by religious beliefs. It's a broad concept, covering fundamentalist as well as moderate currents, be they peaceful or not.

# Analytical Framework: Logics of Action and the Concept of 'Othering'

In order to give due consideration to the complexity of the issue, it is decisive to conduct a precise analysis into the logics of action that characterise gender politics in the Euro-Mediterranean political space. Logics of Action, as elaborated in the introduction to this volume, means more than just the rationale behind a political decision and includes all the influential factors that shape actions within a certain political arena. The political arena of gender politics is shaped by norms and values, by interests and strategies, but also by a culturalistic perspective on the issue. From a European viewpoint, most of the problems in the Arab world have their roots in Islam, which is perceived as a delinquent *culture* more than a religion. According to this narrative, Islam is the main reason for the lack of democracy in the Arab world, especially for the lack of gender democracy. To deconstruct this narrative, one first of all needs to know where it derives from. Euro-Mediterranean relations are embedded in age-old discourses, the negative impact of which cannot be captured with a pure rationalist approach. To capture the impact of these discourses on gender politics in the Euro-Mediterranean political space, this study combines Logics of Action with the concept of *othering*;[5] that is the discursive process of constructing the 'other' to focus and stabilise one's own identity.[6] *Othering* is based on cognitive mechanisms of reality reduction that elevate one's own cultural identity against the inferior 'other'. Such binary perceptions have been produced and reproduced over centuries in the Euro-Mediterranean political space and are therefore extremely persistent, even in times of change as caused by the 'Arab Spring'.

This study is based on the assumption that culturalism is *the* dominant logic of action shaping the arena of gender politics. It is supported by two observations: The first one concerns the specific role ascribed to woman as an indication of the difference between supposedly antagonistic cultures. According to Renate Kreile, communities see the relation of the sexes as a key element of respective inner hierarchy that distinguishes the specific identity of one's own culture in the collective consciousness and demarcates it from the 'the other'. The process of collective self-definition always contains a clarification of the status and role-assignment for women, which in many cultures are regarded as the embodiment of collective identity concepts (Kreile 2009: 275). The second observation concerns the fact that the elevated role of the women for the construction of a collective identity seems to be a universal, and not an 'Arab' or 'Muslim' phenomenon. Astonishing parallels between the external fostering of gender democracy in the Arab world, which is the subject of this study, with the implementation of gender

---

5　Edward Said in his standard work 'Orientalism' has traced the genesis and impact of these discourses over several centuries in religious and literary texts and, in doing so, has coined the term 'othering' (Said 1979).

6　The combination of the Logics of Action approach with the concept of *othering* is especially fruitful since identity is a decisive category within Logics of Action. For a detailed description of the Logics of Action approach see the introduction to this volume.

democracy during the course of the EU's eastward expansion, which was the topic of my research a good ten years ago, have contributed to the development of this assumption. The duplicity of the two cases questions all binary identity constructs that ascribe gender-political deficiencies mono-causally to certain 'cultural spaces', in the 1990ies to the 'backward East' and now to the 'Muslim South'.

The study is divided into six sections. The introduction to the analytical framework in this first section is followed by a critical review of the EU's external promotion of gender democracy in section two. As the Logics of Action approach follows the constructivist assumption that agents and structures are mutually constitutive, an examination is conducted, not only into the complex constellations of agents in section three, but also into the closely interconnected discursive constructs of identity and space in section four. In section five alternative explanations for the significant resilience of patriarchy in the Arab world are presented, drawing on the concept of distress. Against the backdrop of this analysis, the final section six presents various options for the EU to overcome its alleged dilemma by adapting persistent patterns in its external promotion of gender democracy to the political changes emerging from the 'Arab Spring'.

## No Democracy Without Gender Democracy

Gender equality is an inherent constituent of what is understood by democracy within the EU.[7] In accordance with this logic, gender equality is also a constituent part of the Unions external promotion of democracy. Following the strategy of gender mainstreaming[8] the EU made gender equality a cross-cutting issue in all fields of policy affecting the external relations. In spite of all the gender mainstreaming rhetoric however, with regard to the MENA region the promotion of gender democracy initially played a minor role, as a report by the transnational *Euro-Mediterranean Study Commission* criticises (EuroMeSCo 2006: 6). This changed at least gradually with the *Euro-Mediterranean Ministerial Meeting on Strengthening the Role of Women in Society*, which took place in Istanbul in November 2006. The so-called Istanbul process is today the most important political framework for the promotion of gender democracy in the context of Euro-Mediterranean relations. Its primary concern is the promotion of women's political rights and the improvement of their opportunities for participation as well as better access for women to education and employment. The EU aroused high expectations with its commitment to promote women's rights, which were,

---

7   Cf. Article 19 TEU (non-discrimination) as well as Articles 21 and 23 of the EU Charter of Fundamental Rights (Non-discrimination and Equality between men and women).

8   Gender mainstreaming is a strategy enshrined in law to achieve *actual* equality. The EU has adopted this strategy in its promotion of gender equality both in internal and external dealings.

however, disappointed with the follow-up to the Istanbul Plan of Action (IPA). The deficiencies mainly lie in the field of implementation, as a shadow report of the transnational *Euro-Mediterranean Human Rights Network* establishes, which was written on the occasion of a follow-up conference in Marrakesh:

> The Shadow Report reveals a wide lack of knowledge about the IPA both among governmental and non-governmental actors in the countries concerned, as well as the absence of policies and laws aimed at enhancing gender equality and women's rights which refer explicitly to the IPA. The 'Progress report', which governments were to submit one year after the adoption of the IPA, failed to raise awareness about IPA; neither encouraged public debate about progress of gender equality. In most cases it was not even published – nor were meetings or consultations held with women's rights organisations. (EMHRN 2009: 16)

The inadequate implementation of the IPA indicates fundamental problems in the promotion of gender democracy as part of the EU's foreign relations. It is interesting to note that precisely the same problems that are described in the shadow report on implementation of the IPA occurred during the accession process of the Central and Eastern European countries (CEE). The accession candidates had to adapt their national legislation to the *acquis communautaire*, including the comprehensive gender-specific legislation in European primary and secondary law, before being accepted as EU-members in 2004. In the CEE as well, the factors responsible for the deficiencies were a mixture of incompetence and disinterest on both sides, namely among both the responsible officials in the accession countries as well as the EU officials in charge of the support and monitoring functions (Pavlik 2005). In this respect, *gender mainstreaming* so far appears to have only reached the documents but is by no means in all minds. A further difficulty was seen to be the insufficient communication with the affected parties. The gender discourse during the accession process was characterised by almost incompatible concepts of 'feminism'. Many women's rights groups in the CEE felt themselves being treated with contempt, not only by EU officials but also by western European women's rights groups who offered their support with the best of intentions yet only paid insufficient attention to the interests and perceptions of those to whom their efforts were directed (Siklova 2005). Incompetence and a lack of interest at state level coupled with insufficient sensitivity (also) at the social level are consequently problems that generally characterise the policy field of externally promoting gender democracy, independently of the location and hence independently of the cultural context as well.

## Actors in Euro-Mediterranean Gender Politics and Their Diverse Logics of Action

Relevant actors in the arena of gender politics within the Euro-Mediterranean political space are first of all the states on both sides of the Mediterranean, but also the EU with its institutions as well as a large number of non-state actors. At the focus of this study, however, are the female change agents themselves.

*Secularism and State Feminism*

'Religious fundamentalisms are a major threat to women's rights and freedoms. As long as religions interfere in the political and public sphere, the word "moderate" to describe them is deprived of meaning' (RDFL/IFE 2011). This statement is typical for all those women's rights groups in the MENA region that follow a logic of action that is marked by secularism and a clear-cut rejection of political Islam. Their gender-political objectives focus above all on the political participation rights of women as well as the civil status law, which puts women at a severe disadvantage in most Arab countries, in issues such as divorce, maintenance law or rights over their own children (Mashhour 2005). In general, the women involved in the secular organisations have a higher level of education, such as lawyers in particular, and have clearly emancipatory intentions. Many of them have studied in Europe, those from the Maghreb region generally in France, and have undergone western socialisation in the process. It would, however, be too easy to draw the conclusion of an unfiltered 'westernisation' from this. The accusation of 'westernisation' is already part of the binary discourse, the problems of which are expounded in this contribution. After all, just as non-existent as the phenomenon of a homogenous 'western' feminism is that of a homogenous 'Arab' feminism. Gender discourses are heterogeneous and fluid everywhere. Political division lines between liberals, conservatives and leftists need to be taken into consideration within the spectrum of secularism as well as Islamism. Nevertheless, a certain influence on the perceptions of how gender relations should be organised to the optimum in a democratic society may be assumed among activists socialised in Europe. All in all, it becomes apparent that the secular women's rights movement is well connected internationally and knows how to use its contacts efficiently, also and especially those to the EU.

The opposition to political Islam provides an explanation for a strategic alliance many secular women's rights groups have entered into with the authoritarian regimes of their respective countries. The interest on both sides in forcing back tendencies towards Islamification in society has caused authoritarian regimes to make concessions towards women's rights campaigners, as long as they did not question state authoritarianism itself. Women's rights groups have in many cases been coopted by the state, derided as Government Organised Non-Governmental Organisations (GONGO).[9] One typical GONGO is the *National Council for Women* (NCW), the chair of which the Egyptian First Lady Suzanne Mubarak took over in 2000. From then on, pro-women laws, which the regime used to legitimise itself to the outside world, were known as *Suzanne Laws* (Sholkamy 2012: 164). Tunisia, where equal rights have also been presented as a personal

---

9    For details concerning the logics of co-optation see Harders in this volume.

project of the (then) president Ben Ali and his wife (Hussein et al. 2012), is a particularly conspicuous example of the strategic interplay between authoritarian regimes and secular women's rights groups. In contrast to all other Arab states, Tunisia has developed a high degree of gender democracy as a result (Kelly 2010) although this has been accompanied by uncompromising repression of all political forces that questioned the regime's claim to power. Testimony to this comes from the fate of the women's rights campaigner Sihem Bensedrine, a figurehead of the resistance to Ben Ali's dictatorship, who was arrested and tortured on numerous occasions during the 1990s. She had to leave the country and did not return to Tunisia until January 2011, on the day when Ben Ali fled. Only few secular women right's activists denounced the first ladies GONGOs and made them responsible for the fragmentation of genuine women's rights movements in the Arab world (El Saadawi 2011). The price that secular women's rights groups had to pay for the gender political concessions extracted from the regime was high. They had been used as a showcase aimed at western financiers and indicating an alleged willingness to conduct reforms, but lost their credibility at home when the regime was brushed away with the 'Arab Spring'.

## *Islamist Feminism – A Contradiction in Terms?*

A more difficult task is to understand the gender political activities of women whose logics of action are shaped by their religious identity. What is meant here are all practices, whether intended or not, that religiously oriented women use to promote the political and social participation of women. Intended and hence clearly emancipatory are approaches to reinterpret the Qur'an from a feminist perspective. Fatima Mernissi (2004), professor of sociology, adviser to UNESCO and a member of the advisory staff to the World Bank for the Near East and North Africa, is perhaps the most well known representative of an 'Islamist feminism', which is organised among other bodies within the *International Congress on Islamic Feminism*. It builds on the conviction that the Qur'an does not justify patriarchy when it is interpreted in a contemporary manner and by incorporating female views. Islamist feminists may be allocated to the liberal groupings of political Islam. They see themselves as part of the global women's rights movement and exhibit openness towards the diversity of even European discourses on gender. Nevertheless, they are the subject of criticism amongst many secular women's rights campaigners, to whom the mere description 'Islamist feminism' appears to be a contradiction in terms. Other religious groupings, however, such as the 'Sisters in Islam', do not want to be associated with the global women's rights movement, since they denounce the term 'feminism' as a 'basically secular paradigm' (Raouf Ezzat 2012).

To be distinguished from feminist Islamism are the practices of self-empowerment of religiously oriented women, who may follow an emancipatory intention but do not necessarily have to do so. One clear example of this is the creation of numerous jobs for women in the charitable institutions of Egypt's

Muslim Brotherhood. In hospitals and schools, even women from extremely traditional social backgrounds obtain the opportunity to leave the private sphere of the home in a legitimate manner, namely as nurses or teachers in a religious establishment. Their role within the family changes due to the reduction in economic dependence on their husband who was formerly the sole earner. If the latter should then also become unemployed, as is not infrequently the case (Kreile 2009: 261), the woman's additional income then becomes the main source of earnings. Such developments are not yet revolutionising gender relations within families but are leading to shifts and upheavals. All of this is able to happen without the need for a politically conscious logic of female empowerment.

Although secular and religiously oriented women are in different, sometimes antagonistic, camps, there are also points at which their logics of action intersect. Commonalities can be found, for example, in the demand for political participation and material improvement in women's status, for example through better access to the educational and health systems. Sometimes there are even joint actions, such as the campaign in Egypt for a new divorce law less prejudicial to women in the year 2000 (Block 2012: 59). Difficult to reconcile, in contrast, are positions on topics such as sexual self-determination or the women's family obligations. Heba Raouf Ezzat (2012) is representative for Islamist positions when she argues 'only few women can practically manage both the responsibilities of family and jurisdiction at a time. Only if they have the compatibility […] they have full choice – even a responsibility – to participate on the political levels in a Muslim society.'

*Additional Division Lines: Rich and Poor, Young and Old*

It is not only religious institutions that create work opportunities outside of the home for the poor and uneducated women from mainly traditional backgrounds. More and more Arab women are finding work in the export-oriented sectors of the textile and electronics industry because the conception of the man in gender ideology as the breadwinner allows women to be employed for low wages. Women are thus cheaper than the men competing for the same job (Kreile 2009: 261). From their at least partial financial independence, they are able to derive aspirations for political and social participation and also receive support in these endeavours from secular women's rights groups, such as the *Association démocratique des femmes du Maroc* (Berriane 2011). However, commendable the activities of individual NGOs may be, the social trend is heading in the opposite direction, namely towards a hierarchisation among women based on social inequality. 'Gender is one factor in these inequities, but class, family, and power are more important' (Sholkany 2012: 165). In Egypt, social inequality and a strong awareness of individual social status have led to the establishment of almost separate lifestyles according to class affiliation (Block 2012: 58). The growing prosperity gap in the Arab societies is not irrelevant in terms of gender politics because it leads to difficulties in creating a large and powerful women's rights movement that encompasses all segments of all societies. Women's politics has hitherto been primarily the topic of a minority of educated women from the upper middle class with a secular agenda, who according to Johanna Block have no contact whatsoever with their clients in their daily lives. They are hardly regarded as role models but tend instead to be perceived as foreign and distant and hence are also not able to take on the function of multipliers with which they are credited by the EU and other western financiers.[10]

Largely uninvestigated to date has been the gender political role of religious women who have made their way into politics at municipal or national level, in ministries or parliaments. Questions as to why and by whom Islamist women politicians are elected and what attitude they have to democracy, how they act as legislators and to what extent they are actually able to develop decision-making power will only be a suitable subject for investigation after some time has passed. Irrespective of their individual political agendas, however, all women in political offices are through their mere existence already a manifestation of the female demand for political participation. While it is primarily young Islamist women who are questioning traditional gender roles, the older Islamist women tend to support the conservative agendas of the religious parties delegating them, with all the restrictions for the development of gender democracy. This refers to the important fact that the 'Arab Spring' was also based on a generational conflict, which manifests itself in all segments of society and transverses all other conflict lines. The uprising against authoritarianism was not only directed at the authoritarian state but also at the rigid structures of a traditional social hierarchy based on seniority that unduly restricted the room for development of the following generations. It may therefore be expected that young women in particular will bring out changes within Islamist parties.

## The EU in Search of the 'Right' Project Partners

In view of the complex constellation of players, it is not surprising that the EU is experiencing difficulty in identifying the 'right' contact points for its gender political projects. Initially, these projects were a thorn in the flesh of the authoritarian regimes in the southern partner countries, since they were perceived as part of a European bottom-up strategy for promoting democracy. The EU however, due to prior interests in security and regional stability, proceeded with exceptional restraint and kept its commitment to supporting the civil society within a framework very narrowly defined by the authoritarian regimes. The target group was therefore only those organisations that did not challenge the power of the ruling regimes and instead acted as mediators in the broadest sense between state and society (Jünemann 2004). Islamist groupings, which the regimes of most southern partner countries regarded as potential opposition to the system,

---

10   In Tunisia's first free elections in October 2012, the female candidates from the secular spectrum were less successful compared to those from the Islamist spectrum, partly due to their campaigns in French. Interview with Zeineb Ben Othmann, expert on women's economic integration, 27 October 2012 in Berlin.

were therefore automatically excluded as cooperation partners for the EU and accordingly all women affiliated to these groupings. In contrast, secular women's rights groups, specifically because of their anti-Islamist agendas, were almost ideal project partners for the EU. Their stance was close to the European ideas of gender democracy and not least because of their French many of their members spoke the 'same language'. This is to be interpreted in the literal sense because the EU generally recruits its project partners through tenders in the official languages of the EU. Those not proficient in French or English and also without the necessary level of education to be able to find such calls for tender at all have barely any chance of participating in an EU project from the outset. Ultimately, it has to be assumed that, due to their anti-western posture, many religious groupings have little interest in establishing contact with the EU of their own accord.[11] Hence a dialogue could only come about if the EU were to actively seek it.

To sum up, a strategic coalition of interest had emerged that had its common ground in an anti-Islamist bias, composed of European and Arab governments as well as secular women's rights groups. However, within this coalition of interest, there was just as little unity on the degree of gender democracy to be strived for as on the general level of political freedom.

### Discursive Constructions of Identity and Space and their Impact on Logics of Action

The following analysis will add a further layer to deepen the analysis of the relevant logics of action. Through an examination of identity constructs established in discourses and their positioning within supposed 'cultural spaces', it becomes clear that the arena of gender politics is not only defined by norms and values nor solely by the interests and strategies of relevant actors as outlined above, but also by a culturalistic perspective to be identified as the dominant logic of action.

*'North versus South', 'West versus Islam', 'Orient versus Occident': Identity Construction through Othering*

*North versus South*, in the broadest sense, labels the discourses in development policy within the context of the so-called North/South conflict. What is meant in this contribution, however, is the narrower context of institutionalised Euro-Mediterranean relations that supply the material framework of reference for this study (Jünemann 2009). From a European perspective, *North versus South* highlights the power relations between the EU considered rich and homogenous and the southern partner countries that depend on it, which are perceived as 'weak'. One example that fits into this category is the theorem of democratic peace,

---

11    Interview with Majdouline Lyazidi, a young feminist and member of Amnesty International Morocco, 27 November 2012 in Berlin.

according to which democratic Europe uses its strength to help the authoritarian Arab world to achieve democracy. For the southern partner countries the relevant discourses tend to be those on neocolonialism and neoimperialism in the context of *North versus South*, in which the European Mediterranean policy is interpreted in a very different manner, namely as an encroachment in power politics following the logics of action of the old imperial and colonial powers.[12] The promotion of gender democracy is part of these binary discourses:

> It seems that the gender question is addressed as a problem of the South, an issue faced by the southern women, and not as a common concern affecting people, both women and men, in the North as well as the South. Therefore the tone seems to be set for the EU to take a paternalistic role vis-à-vis its southern partners: the EU teaches so that the southern partners can learn. (Kynsilehto, Melasuo 2006: 214)

Another discourse on identity with a similarly binary structure in which the construct of supposed cultural spaces becomes even clearer can be labelled with the conceptual pair of *West versus Islam*.[13] After the terrorist attacks of 11 September 2001, this discourse has become more important and primarily refers to the USA yet in the broader sense also to Europe and other 'Western' players. Here the term 'West' denotes both the geographical location and a homogeneously perceived political culture. The term 'Islam' is comparatively imprecise in this discourse in which it remains unclear as to whether the religion or the politicisation of the religion is meant, whether individuals or societies, whether organisations or regimes. Irrespective of this imprecision, however, a homogeneous attitude of mind is established for 'Islam'. Following an essentialistic logic, the religion is declared to be an unalterable core of an 'Islamic culture' that is not only 'different' but also 'threatening'. Narrowly interwoven with this discourse is the older discourse on *Christian Occident versus Muslim Orient*, which can be traced back to the time of the crusades.[14] However, while the *North versus South* discourse, contrasting the 'South' perceived as Muslim with an enlightened secular *North*, leaves space for atheists, in the narrative of *Orient versus Occident*, Christianity functions as a category-generating identity.

Despite the apparent incoherencies, all three discourses blend in a largely unreflected manner within the collective perception and come together to form reciprocal concepts of the enemy. At the centre of these dichotomous culturalistic identity constructs is the role of the woman in each case.

---

12 According to this logic, the *Egyptian Women's Union* is striving for the 'liberation of Egypt from external colonial and internal oppressive exploitative powers' (El Saadawi 2011).

13 For a deepened analysis of this discourse see Kalin 2009.

14 For a deepened analysis of this discourse see Said 1979.

*The Role of the Woman as a Representative of Cultural Identity*

According to the dominant European narrative, a pre-modern and backward Islam faces a modern and enlightened Europe, the progressiveness of which is particularly manifested in the emancipation of women. The latter has seemingly nothing more in common with the 'suppressed Oriental woman'. Freedom of the woman as a distinguishing feature of liberal societies acts like a blind spot on the retina, making potential commonalities with the 'other' invisible. To name but one example, reference is made to the percentages of women in national parliaments as a means of illustrating the difference between Europe and the Arab world, which is allegedly so great. In 2006 Morocco with 10.8%, Italy with 11.5% and France with 12.2% *women* members of parliament were roughly level in contrast to Tunisia with 22.8% women MPs (EuroMeSco 2006: 16). This is not intended to dispute the fact that deficiencies in gender politics are greater in the Arab world than in other regions of the globe. However, the situation is far more complex, not only in an interregional comparison but also in a comparison between countries and within countries. This complexity distances itself from a one-dimensional explanation due to the narrative concerning backward Islam.

If we replace the term 'Islam' with that of 'religion' it becomes clear that the political dividing lines are at right angles to the established dichotomy of allegedly antagonistic cultural spaces, as Louise Chappell (2004) substantiates in a study on the close cooperation of the Vatican with Muslim authorities in the context of internationalising women's rights. Together they had used their political standing to combat the rights agenda proposed by the transnational feminist movement.

Also comparatively one-dimensional, however, is the 'southern' narrative, according to which gender democracy is a purely western concept that was exported aggressively into the rest of the world. According to this narrative, the western woman was robbed of her dignity and degraded to a commodity, while women in the Muslim world enjoy the protection of the community and above all that of men.[15] This identity construction stands also behind the criticism aimed at the UN convention CEDAW,[16] which occurs despite the fact that CEDAW is regarded even by the *Arab Human Development Report* (which is prepared exclusively by Arabs) as a universal reference, and despite the fact that it was transnational women's rights networks that anchored the principle of 'women's rights are human rights' with a legislative force at the level of UN institutions (Kreile 2009: 265). Transnational cooperation agreements and transnational identities have no place in a binary world view because they expose their underlying reduction of reality

---

15    For an extremely rigid perception of sexuality in the West see Qutb ash-Shaheed 1951. He was one of the most influential Islamist theorists within the Egyptian Muslim Brotherhood in the 1950s and '60s.

16    UN-Convention on the Elimination of All Forms of Discrimination against Women, adopted 18 December 1979.

for what it is. They thus resolve the supposed incompatibilities and open up new perspectives for the problems in hand – and their solutions.

## Resilience of Patriarchal Gender Relations Due to National Distress

After it has been shown that Islam alone is incapable of explaining the resilience of patriarchal gender relations in the Arab world, the question still remains as to why political Islam is currently propagating an especially restrictive interpretation of gender relations and why this restrictiveness is apparently met with social approval in large segments of society. One approach at explaining the broad acceptance of patriarchal gender relations, among both men and women, is the feeling of distress. According to this argument, consciousness of one's own cultural roots can be seen as a defence reaction against domination by foreign influences and loss of identity. Just as colonialism was once perceived as an attack on one's own identity, today it is the processes of globalisation and Western dominance. Modernisation on the one hand and the impoverishment of large parts of the populations, on the other, are weakening traditional power relations in which large families and family networks are important, and are therefore also questioning the gender political social contract anchored within them.[17] With its emphasis on the traditional role of the woman in a social order oriented towards community, political Islam offers a religiously legitimised alternative approach to the 'Western' modern age with which a perceived domination by foreign influences is fended off and the individual's own identity which has run into difficulties can be stabilised (Kreile 2009: 259f). Through their connection within the family, namely as mothers and hence socialisers of the next generation, women are accorded a special role for retaining the values and norms of Islamic society. They become bearers of the culture and as the epitome of virtue and morality symbolically embody the foundation of an intact and integral Muslim society (Borkstett 2012).

However, the symbolically charged elevation of the woman as bearer and representative of cultural identity is not a special feature of Islam but can also be observed in other situations where identity comes under pressure. One vivid example of this phenomenon, which continues to have an influence up to the present-day, is the 'Polish Mother' myth, which emerged after the third division of Poland in the eighteenth century, which posed a tremendous threat to the 'Polish' identity at that time. The 'Polish Mother' myth, which Adam Mickiewicz created in his poem 'To the Polish Mother', continues to survive in the national discourse and is impressed upon women in Poland as the ideal of female involvement for the general wellbeing of all Poles (Choluj 2003: 31). The 'Polish Mother' does not fight for gender democracy but for the sovereignty of her nation. And she does not

---

17    This argument is less convincing for the rich Gulf countries where fundamentalist interpretations of Islam follow other logics. This is not to be elaborated in this contribution which has a focus on the South-Mediterranean Arab countries.

do so eye-to-eye with the men but in the background by supporting the men and above all by bringing up the new men in an appropriate manner. In line with that ideology the Polish woman does not make any claims for herself. Bozena Choluj explains the strong dislike amongst Polish women of 'Western' feminism through the sustainability of the patriarchal gender hierarchy that had become manifest in the 'Polish Mother' myth and the fear of Western domination (Choluj 2003: 31). Another analogy to the current development in the Arab world is the seizure of gender politics by religion.[18] While in the Arab world it is the Islamist parties who are conspicuous due to a decidedly patriarchal agenda, Poland saw Catholicism take on a comparable role.[19] Polish Catholicism, which established a political counter identity not only during the divisions of Poland but also during the period of communist oppression, became an important social power after the collapse of the latter regime.[20] However, Catholicism lost political importance to the same extent as Poland consolidated its identity as a sovereign and democratic state. It seems as if modern Poland no longer needs a 'counter identity'.

In the Arab world, however, patriarchal order is now more than ever playing a decisive role in the construction of an identity perceived as authentic. Even if political Islam has primarily taken control of the topic, it must not be overlooked that all members of Arab society are to a greater or lesser extent characterised by patriarchal traditions and practices, regardless of whether they are, like the majority of society, Muslims or belong to a minority of Christians or atheists. The categorisation of the political landscape into 'progressive' and 'reactionary' also says little on how the individual parties and groupings stand in relation to the gender issue. In a thoroughly conservative society, questions on gender are generally allocated to the private and hence unpolitical sphere. The assumption that only political Islam threatens gender democracy is a myth that was recently revealed in a shocking manner through the misogynist practices of the old Mubarak regime. On 9 March 2011, not Islamists but the military police subjected women activists of the 'Arab Spring' to so-called 'virginity tests', a practice tantamount to torture and aimed at degrading and silencing women (Amnesty International 2012). On another occasion, a demonstrator's clothes were pulled over her head revealing her blue bra, which henceforth became a much-cited symbol of the brutality of the expelled regime (Coleman 2012). Not less disturbing is an incidence that happened on Tahrir Square on 8 March 2011, when women

---

18    It is interesting that the communist regime also made use of the 'Polish Mother' myth. Socialist state feminism was based on an equally modest role model for women dedicated to the community.

19    A good basis for this came from the cult of the Holy Mary in Poland, which the Polish King John III Sobieski founded through the coronation of the Holy Mother Mary as the Queen of Poland in the year 1665 (Choluj 2003: 31).

20    In 1993, to give only one example, the church lobbied an extremely restrictive abortion law, which was protected against liberalisation measures during the process of Europeanisation by an additional protocol in the Polish accession treaty in 2004.

in a demonstration commemorating International Women's day were attacked, harassed, and ridiculed by other demonstrators. They obviously accepted women as activists for the revolution but not as activists asking for women's rights (Sholkamy 2012: 168-169). Patriarchy is a universally powerful logic of action that seems to become especially powerful wherever collective identities are under distress. This is currently the case in the Arab world, where patriarchal logics of action crosscut all segments of society.

## Scope for Action in Promoting Gender Democracy after the 'Arab Spring'

The analysis based on the Logics of Action approach provided evidence for the assumption that a core problem of European external promotion of gender democracy is the EU's culturalistic perception of its neighbourhood. Culturalism was identified as a dominant logic of action in the arena of gender politics, based on binary discourses that elevate Europe against the inferior 'other', here 'the Muslim'. These discursive constructions of identity, positioned within supposed 'cultural spaces' are extremely persistent since they evolved over centuries and have become part of the collective logics of action, not only in the European political elites, but also in society. The case study proved that 'othering' resulted in a simplistic view of the problems at stake and thereby provoked inadequate political decisions. The narrow perspective on gender politics as an instrument in the fight against political Islam was misleading and ended in the EU's embarrassing vicinity to Arab autocrats. What are the lessons to be learned, especially with regard to the political changes caused by the Arab Spring?

Many women's rights groups fear that the EU might draw wrong consequences by degrading gender politics to a bargaining counter when dealing with newly evolving Islamist regimes. The EU might be tempted to adopt a forceful approach in negotiations on *high-policy* issues such as terrorism, migration or energy security while in exchange demonstrating willingness to compromise in the *low-policy* area of gender politics. An approach such as this might almost appeal because it could be legitimised as culturally sensitive. In actual fact, however, it would be to the detriment of gender democracy, a declared objective of the EU community of shared values. Not all, but many women's rights activists count on that and expect the EU to support their political struggle.[21] The purpose of this contribution is not to draft specific programmes for the promotion of gender politics. It should, however, enable stimuli on how the EU promotion of gender democracy in its southern partner countries can be placed on a new foundation and adapted to the changed political environment.

In order to overcome its misperception of the Arab world, the EU should henceforth pursue the regional gender discourses more intensively, incorporating

---

21   Interview with Nezah Alaoui, Union de l'Action Féminine in Morocco, 27 November 2012 in Berlin.

Islamist positions. It is above all young women who are questioning traditional stances of society and are therefore important change agents to be focused on. As a reference framework for European demands within the *more-for-more* approach,[22] CEDAW or the *Arab Human Development Reports* are more suitable than the gender political primary and secondary law of the EU. The external demand for gender democracy should not be a project of Europeanisation strategy but should be positioned within the overriding international context in which the transnational women's rights movement plays a key role. Within this context, regional and local approaches to unify the women's rights movement should be promoted. Instead of deepening the rift between secular and religious women's rights activists, the EU could build upon their communalities, such as the demand for political participation, material improvement in women's status and domestic violence. To pave the ground for an open dialogue, language matters. Politically sensitive terms such as 'secularism' or 'feminism' can be avoided in favour of notions that are also compatible with the semantic field of Islamist concepts, such as 'fairness' and 'justice'.[23] To get into an open dialogue with all segments of civil society, the new EU delegations could play a positive role. In order to carry out this role, however, it is necessary to have appropriate personnel and specifically to employ young women who speak Arabic, have an academic background in Islamic studies or similar and are therefore less prone to a reproduction of culturalistic logics of action. There are many ways for the EU to overcome persistent patterns in its external promotion of gender democracy. To regain the tremendous loss of credibility, however, restraint and respect for the variety of different opinions are required.

**Bibliography**

Agapiou-Josephides, K. et al 2012. *Enhancing EU-Action to Support Universal Standards For Women's Rights During Transition. Study requested by the European Parliament's Subcommittee on Human Rights.* EXPO/B/DROI/2011/24 November/2012 PE 457.119. [Online]. Available at: http://www.europarl.europa.eu/committees/en/ studiesdownload.html?language-Document=EN&file=79288 [accessed: 14 February 2013].
Amnesty International. 2012. *Egypt: A year after 'virginity tests', women victims of army violence still seek justice.* [Online]. Available at: http://www.amnesty.org/en/news/egypt-year-after-virginity-tests-women-victims-army-violence-still-seek-justice-2012-03-09 [accessed: 8 August 2012].

---

22    *More for more* is a new approach of positive conditionality within the renewed European Neighbourhood Policy (European Commission 2011).

23    Interview with Amal Basha, head of the Arab Sisters in Yemen, 27-11-2012 in Berlin. Although Yemen is not in the focus of this study, her voice as an Arab women's rights activist is important in the context of this argument.

Berriane, Y. 2011. Le Maroc au temps des femmes? La féminisation des associations locales en question. *Année du Maghreb* VII, 2011, CNRS Editions, 332-342.

Block, J. 2012. Frauenbewegungen in Ägypten. Der Arabische Frühling und säkular orientierte Frauenorganisationen. *Mediterranes*, 1/2012, 57-59.

Borkstett, I. 2012. *Gender-Diskurse in Politik und Gesellschaft.* Unpublished Master's Thesis, submitted in 2012 at the faculty of economic and social science, Helmut-Schmidt-Universtity/University of the German Federal Armed Forces Hamburg.

Brac de la Perrière, C. 1997. Die algerische Frauenbewegung zwischen Nationalismus und Islamismus, in *Feminismus, Islam, Nation. Frauenbewegungen im Maghreb, in Zentralasien und der Türkei,* edited by C. Schöning-Kalender, A. Neusel and M.M. Jansen. Frankfurt am Main: Campus Verlag, 167-184.

Chappell, L. 2004. *Contesting Women's Rights. Refereed paper presented to the Australasian Political Studies Association Conference, University of Adelaide, 29 September – 1 October 2004.* [Online]. Available at: http://www.adelaide. edu.au/apsa/ docs_papers/Others/Chappell.pdf [accessed: 25 June 2012].

Choluj, B. 2003. Zugänge zu Geschlechtergerechtigkeit in Ost und West, in *Grenzen Überwinden – Der EU-Erweiterungsprozess aus frauenpolitischer Sicht,* edited by Frauenakademie München. Frankenakademie Schloss Schney, 21– 23 February 2003.

Commission of the European Communities. 2007. *Communication from the Commission to the European Parliament and the Council. Gender Equality and Women Empowerment in Development Cooperation.* [Online]. Available at: http://eur-lex.europa.eu/LexUriServ/site/en/com/2007/-com2007_0100en01.pdf [accessed: 23 June 2012].

Coleman, I. 2011. *'Blue bra girl' rallies Egypt's women vs. oppression.* [Online]. Available at: http://edition.cnn.com/2011/12/22/opinion/coleman-women-egypt -protest/index.html [accessed: 9 August 2012].

EEAS. 2010. *EUROMED Partnership: Strengenthing the Role of Woman in Society. Multi-Annual Report 2006-2009.* [Online]. Available at: http://www. eeas.europa.eu/ euromed/women/docs/-multi_annual_report_2006-2009_en.pdf [accessed: 4 June 2012].

EEAS. 2012. *EU supports Women's Participation in Peacebuilding and Post-Conflict Planning.* [Online]. Available at: http://eeas.europa.eu/ifs/docs/2012 0201_pressrelease_eu-undp_en.pdf [accessed: 23 June 2012].

El-Hawary, H., F. Emam and K. Gemeinardt-Buschhardt 2012. *Women of the Tahrir Square – Secular and Religious Motivated Activists and the Constitution of a Democratic Society.* Conference paper. International Conference on: Realigning Power Geometries in the Arab World, Leipzig 24–26 February 2012.

Euro-Mediterranean Human Rights Network (ed.). 2009. *Gender Equality in the Euro-Mediterranean Region: From Plan to Action? Shadow Report on the Implementation of the Istanbul Plan of Action.* Copenhagen, October 2009.

EuroMeSCo (ed.). 2006. Women as Full Participants in the Euro-Mediterranean Community of Democratic States. *EuroMeSCo Annual Report 2006*. [Online]. Available at: http://www.euromesco.net/images/02.pdf [accessed: 24 August 2012].

Harders, C. 2011. *Gender Relations, Violence and Conflict Transformation*. [Online].Availableat:http://humansecuritygateway.com/documents/BERGHOF _GenderRelationsViolenceandConflictTransformation.pdf[accessed: 24 August 2012].

Hassan, R. 1997. Feministische Interpretation des Islams, in *Feminismus, Islam, Nation. Frauenbewegungen im Maghreb, in Zentralasien und der Türkei*, edited by C. Schöning-Kalender, A. Neusel and M.M. Jansen. Frankfurt am Main: Campus Verlag, 217-233.

Hassim, S. 2003. The Gender Pact and Democratic Consolidation: Institutionalizing Gender Equality in the South African State. *Feminist Studies*, 29(3) (Fall 2003), 505-528.

Hussein, A., E. Schmidt, A. Zorob 2012. Medien und die Revolution. Die Förderung von Geschäftsfrauen als Legitimierung der Regierung. *Mediterranes*, 1/2012, 62-64.

Jünemann, A. 2009. Zwei Schritte vor, einer zurück: Die Entwicklung der europäischen Mittelmeerpolitik von den ersten Assoziierungsabkommen bis zur Gründung einer 'Union für das Mittelmeer', in *Der Mittelmeerraum als Region*, edited by R. Hrbek and H. Marhold. Europäisches Zentrum für Föderalismus-Forschung Tübingen: Occasional Papers Nr. 35/2009, 26-59.

Jünemann, A. 2004. Civil Society and Transnational Non-Governmental Organizations in the Euro-Mediterranean Partnership, in *Civil Society in Democratization*, edited by P. Burnell and P. Calvert. London: Taylor & Francis, 206-224.

Kalin, I. 2009. Roots of Misperception. Euro-American Perceptions of Islam Before and After September 11, in *Islam. Fundamentalism and the Betreyal of Tradition*, edited by J. Jumbard. Bloomington, Indiana: World Wisdom Inc., 149-193.

Kelly, S. 2010. Hard-Won Progress And a Long Road Ahead: Women's Rights in the Middle East and North Africa, in *Women's Rights in the Middle East and North Africa. Progress Amid Resistance*, edited by S. Kelly and J. Breslin. New York: Freedom House, 1-14.

Kreile, R. 2009. Transformation und Gender im Nahen Osten, in *Der Nahe Osten im Umbruch. Zwischen Transformation und Autoritarismus*, edited by M. Beck et al. Wiesbaden: VS-Verlag für Sozialwissenschaften, 253-276.

Kynsilehto, A. and Melasuo, T. 2006. Gender Equality: A truly Euro-Mediterranean Concern? *Quaderns de la Mediterrània*, Issue 7/2006, 209-215.

Mashhour, A. 2005. Islamic Law and Gender Equality – Could There be a Common Ground? A Study of Divorce and Polygamy in Sharia Law and Contemporary Legislation in Tunisia and Egypt. *Human Rights Quarterly*, Vol. 17 (2), 265-296.

Mernissi, F. 2004. *Herrscherinnen unter dem Halbmond. Die verdrängte Macht der Frauen im Islam.* Freiburg: Herder-Verlag.

OECD Social Institutions and Gender Index (SIGI). 2012. *Region – Gender Equality in Middle East and North Africa.* [Online]. Available at: http://www.genderindex.org/ranking/ Middle%20East%20-and%20North%20Africa [accessed: 26 June 2012].

Pavlik, P. 2005. Equality without Gender: Implementation of the EU Initiative EQUAL in the Czech Republic, in *The Policy of Gender Equality in the European Union*, edited by A. Jünemann and C. Klement. Baden-Baden: Nomos Verlag, 146-156.

Qutb ash-Shaheed, S. 1951. *The America I have seen. In the Scale of Human Values.* [Online]. Available at: http://www.bandung2.co.uk/books/Files/Education /The%20America%20I%20-Have%20Seen%20-%20Sayyid%20Qutb.pdf [accessed: 26 June 2012].

Raouf Ezzat, H. 2012. *Women and the Interpretation of Islamic Sources.* [Online]. Available at: http://www.irfi.org/articles/articles_451_500/women_and_the_ interpretation_of.htm [accessed: 26 December 2012].

RDFL/IFE 2011: Joint statement of Assoziation Najdeh, RDFL, and IFE released in a workshop. '*Equality First: Promoting a Common Agenda for Equality between Women and Men through the Istanbul Process*', 17–18 December 2011 in Beirut, Lebanon.

El Saadawi, N. 2011. *Statement of the Egyptian Women's Union Cairo 1st March 2011.* [Online]. Available at: http://www.nawalsaadawi.net/index.php? option=com_content&view=article&id=127:-egyptunion&ca [accessed: 26 June 2012].

Said, E. 1979. *Orientalism.* New York: Vintage.

Sholkamy, H. 2012. Women Are Also Part of This Revolution, in *Arab Spring in Egypt. Revolution and Beyond*, edited by B. Korany and R. El-Mahdi. New York: American University in Cairo Press.

Siklova, J. 2005. Welcher Feminismus existiert im Postkommunismus? Ein deutsch-tschechischer Vergleich, in *The Policy of Gender Equality in the European Union*, edited by A. Jünemann and C. Klement. Baden-Baden: Nomos-Verlag, 165-172.

United Nations Development Programme, Arab Fund for Economic and Social Development. 2002. *Arab Human Development Report 2002. Creating Opportunities for Future Generations.* [Online]. Available at: http://www. arab-hdr.org/publications/other/ahdr/ ahdr2002e.pdf [accessed: 14 June 2012].

Chapter 4

# Learning to Cope: The Development of European Immigration Policies Concerning the Mediterranean Caught Between National and Supra-National Narratives

Peter Seeberg

## Introduction

The revolts in the MENA region summarised under the label of the 'Arab Spring' have challenged the European understanding of the Arab Mediterranean countries. Pragmatic EU support of the authoritarian leaders of for instance Tunisia and Egypt, as practised for decades, seems no longer to be a meaningful foreign policy strategy. In order to respond to the, in many ways, surprising developments of the so-called 'Arab Spring', the EU leaders have – half-heartedly – supported attempts by the Arab peoples of Tunisia, Egypt, Libya, Yemen, Syria, etc. to 'rock the casbah' (Goldstone 2011), yet without a clear foreign policy vision and without a European consensus. However, seen from the European side dealing with the phenomenon at the policy level is not only a question of breaking with the former autocrats and finding ways of working together with newly established governments, partly dominated by Islamists (Seeberg 2012). Apart from the political issues, a different item seemed to be on the agenda already from the beginning of 2011. There is an unofficial ambition behind the EU efforts to hold off a wave of Arab migration towards Europe, and one of the means is to provide sufficient economic incentive to stay home (Vinoceur 2011, Vesely 2011).

As mentioned in the New York Times, a poll in France pointed at a paradoxical, but easily understandable contradiction in the way in which the recent development in the Middle East has been perceived in Europe: 'While the events of the Arab Spring were presented positively by the media, most people were mainly worried that they would mean even more potential immigrants' (Vinoceur 2011). It seems that the European public is for supporting democratic progress in the Middle East, but sceptical about the consequences if they include an increasing number of immigrants. Migration is again becoming a sensitive issue in domestic politics within the EU member states.

Shortly after the Tunisian President Zine El Abidine Ben Ali had left office and gone into hiding in Saudi Arabia, Tunisian migrants started to arrive on the Italian

Island Lampedusa, within a few days counting a population of several thousand immigrants who were escaping turmoil in their country. Their arrival made the Italian government declare the immigration situation a humanitarian emergency and raise the issue at the EU level. Maybe the reaction, as discussed by Leonhard den Hertog, was exaggerated (den Hertog 2011), but once again the migration issue grasped the media headlines, emphasising the European ambivalence: on one side the European need for cheap manpower in the labour market, and on the other side the negative perspective of a Europe flooded by millions of Arabs and Africans. The incidents with the Tunisian migrants at Lampedusa were in both the media and the public discourse interpreted as a phenomenon which might threaten stability and security in the Mediterranean region (MWT 2011).

This chapter analyses how recent developments in Mediterranean migratory movements are changing not only the conditions for immigration and security policies of the EU states north of the Mediterranean but also the logics of action of EU decision makers reacting to a changing environment. It will deal with Mediterranean migration not only as a globalised, but also as a regional and local phenomenon, as well as considering the perspectives in European policies aiming at controlling and regulating migration movements, refugee flows and illegal migrants trying to reach European shores (Baldwin-Edwards 2005, Fargues 2008, Sørensen 2006).

Within recent decades new developments have taken place in the Mediterranean regarding migration movements and policy reactions to this important phenomenon, creating complex patterns of continued migration towards Europe, transit migration through southern and eastern Mediterranean states and trans-regional, globalised migration (Fargues 2004). At the same time increasingly restrictive immigration policies and both external and internal EU securitisation of immigrant groups seem to emphasise that security concerns in the Mediterranean are not only a question of external security and North-South issues, but also an issue of internal challenges in the involved states and transnational developments such as irregular migration, cross-border crime and transnational terrorism (Tabutin and Schoumaker, 2005, Baldwin-Edwards 2006). Given this situation the question arises if and how the events of the 'Arab Spring' induced changes in migration policies of EU member states? And whether it shaped the establishment of a coherent EU immigration policy and the relationship between national and supranational migratory policies?

## Migration, Security and the Logics of Action Approach – Theoretical Considerations

The complex character of the migration issue entailing a wide range of security aspects raises demands for further theoretical developments aiming at understanding important social phenomena beyond traditional state actors, organisations, institutions, etc (Hannay 2003, Collyer 2006, Huysmans 2006, Seeberg 2007). Security has become a key issue in EU policies (Laidi 2008, Youngs 2010, Pace and Seeberg 2010), and in connection with the institutional cooperation related to the Barcelona Process and the further development of European-Middle Eastern cooperation, the political narratives related to overall migratory movements, immigrant groups, ethnic minorities, etc have changed.

Before 9/11 the Islamist opposition in the Arab countries was seen in many European narratives as constituting a substantially important part of the political opposition to problematic regimes regarded as authoritarian by the EU. But as a result of the securitisation of Muslim immigrants in Europe and the pragmatic policies dealing with the authoritarian regimes in the Arab world (Seeberg 2010a, Seeberg 2010b), the EU has only reluctantly approached oppositional movements and parties in the countries south and east of the Mediterranean. With the Arab revolts of the year 2011 the conditions for this pragmatic European logic of action has changed.

The concept of securitisation is understood here within the framework of the so-called linguistic turn in International Relations theory as processes by which specific phenomena through speech acts are transformed into security issues, thereby legitimising extraordinary measures (Ciută 2009, Eriksson and Giacomello 2006, Kostakopoulou 2008). However, this chapter subscribes to a societal understanding of the securitisation process, where the study of securitisation not only requires a study of speech acts, but also of contextual factors, i.e. specific historical and institutional developments (Adamson 2006, Dijck 2006) – an important aspect of the Logics of Action approach (see below).

Studies about European immigration policies concerning the southern Mediterranean have often focused on 'fortress Europe', suggesting a more or less homogenous common European migration policy approach. This perception is being contested by the recent events concerning African and Arab immigrants heading towards Europe, as these migration movements have caused several unilateral actions by different EU member states. Taking these events and the broader context of the political upheavals in North Africa as a starting point, this chapter looks at disruptions within the EU immigration regime towards the southern Mediterranean states.

Applying the Logics of Action approach with a focus on political learning, the chapter analyses how adaptations of national immigration policies affect what so far can be seen as attempts to establish a common European migration policy. The notion of 'in-between-ness', as presented in the Introduction to this volume by Horst et al., is taken as a point of departure in an attempt to analyse the conditions for both EU migration policy and national migration policies as a dialectical process of political learning affecting both the national and the supranational narratives about migration and security. Horst et al. mention how 'the often lamented weak actorness of the EU is produced and reproduced by both its actors and its structures' and that the 'Logics of Action, then, is the analytical concept introduced to grasp exactly this "in-between" site of interplay between the two levels' (Horst et al. in this volume).

An important theoretical point of departure for this chapter is that because of the specific political learning process related to the Mediterranean cooperation and the given institutional development within the framework of the policy instruments at the disposal for the EU, the specific political practices tend to promote a pragmatic and consensus-based foreign policy. The Lisbon Treaty has moved important aspects of migration to majority voting and co-decision. This has consequences for the whole, broad range of migration issues which is dealt with in new policies developed recently within the EU system.

Since the launching of the European Security Strategy, 'A Secure Europe in a better World' in 2003 (EU-Commission 2003), which focuses on terrorism, weapons of mass destruction (WMD), regional conflicts, state failure and organised crime, the scope is widened considerably in the new EU initiatives. This can, for instance, be seen in 'The EU Internal Security Strategy in Action: five steps towards a more secure Europe' of November 2010 (EU Commission 2010), which, besides the state-oriented security issues, deals with a broader range of phenomena like human trafficking, drugs and arms trafficking, terrorism and radicalisation, cybercrime and illegal migration. As a result of the new developments, the EU is thus going through processes of political learning, where the institutions of the union seek to develop abilities at working with phenomena like this, adding new dimensions to the migration-security nexus.

This has for years been relevant for the EU in a broad foreign policy perspective, as shown by Cornelius Adebahr, who distinguishes between structural, procedural, operational and ideational mechanisms, which together create learning processes (Adebahr 2009). The challenges from the uprisings in 2011 are met by expressions in new EU documents which combine a focus on democratic transformation in the MENA region with introducing new means of dealing with migration, as is expressed in 'A new response to a changing neighbourhood', where it says that to support 'democratic transformation, Comprehensive Institution-Building programmes [...] will be set up: they will provide substantial expertise and financial support to build the capacity of key administrative bodies (customs, enforcement agencies, justice) and will be targeted in priority towards those institutions most needed to sustain democratization' (EU-HR 2011: 16-17).

To build a stronger partnership with people, the Commission will launch a 'dialogue on migration, mobility and security with e.g. Tunisia, Morocco and Egypt (as a first step towards a Mobility Partnership)' (EU-HR 2011: 17). This dialogue exemplifies procedural, operational and ideational answers to structural challenges in the Mediterranean and can be seen as expressions of political learning, the results of which lead to new organisational developments – in a dialectical process involving national as well as supranational levels. The actual dialogue on migration, mobility and security between the EU and the Arab states and the implementation of mobility partnerships, etc seem to be progressing at a slow pace, as documented in a Joint Staff Working Document under the EU Commission (EU Commission 2012). It will be part of the EU's logic of action to get accustomed to more binding forms of cooperation with Islamist parties and movements, which especially after the elections in 2011 and 2012 have become more or less dominant at the political scene in the southern Mediterranean States.

## Immigration and the Institutional Development of the EU

As demonstrated by Desmond Dinan, the development of the EU's foreign policy can be described as episodic (Dinan 2009). The changing of the treaties that constitute the foundation for the EU's foreign policy activities has taken place in a gradual process, often attached to a national context, where EU-sceptical populations in some member states have held up or postponed the development of the EU towards becoming an actual union with more explicit state-like features. This point emphasises, as mentioned in the Introduction to this volume, the co-determination of agents and structures, because the EU has to be seen as a hybrid that draws on both national and supranational logics of action. The EU is an almost federalist, state-like entity and even the foreign policy of the EU might have state-like characteristics, but the EU is hardly on its way to developing into a full-fledged state. As Dinan convincingly predicts, the EU will continue being an association of states which recognise the value of sharing sovereignty and resources within a limited spectrum of policy fields, but continue to see themselves as integrated parts of an international system, where the individual states retain responsibility for the main aspects of foreign policy, especially regarding security.

With the appointment of a political leader both as the High Representative of the Union for Foreign Affairs and Security Policy and as the Commission Vice-President, the idea was to create a stronger unity in EU foreign policy. At the same time and as part of the setup, the European External Action Service (EEAS) was supposed to provide an efficient organisation behind the new institutions and secure a stronger global impact. Furthermore the appointment of a President of the European Council (Herman van Rompuy) was intended to contribute to the Lisbon-based institutional structure, and together with José Manuel Barroso, the President of the Commission, and the High Representative Catherine Ashton, Herman van Rompuy was supposed to form a leadership with formal competencies sufficient for launching a new, more active EU on the international political scene. However, the development of the EEAS is not really in place yet and the surrounding world will still have to wait and see how this foreign policy instrument will develop. Added to that the latest agency built to enhance Euro-Mediterranean cooperation, the Union for the Mediterranean (UfM), has more or less stopped developing partly due to controversies related to the Arab-Israeli conflict (Seeberg 2010b, Schlumberger 2011).

The EEAS has proclaimed migration as one of the strategic priorities in the foreign policy relations of the EU and as a phenomenon which the EU systematically is 'placing on the agenda of its political, economic and social dialogues with third countries' (Europa 2008). Migration is thus, according to the official narrative of the EEAS, an issue placed in the centre of external relations on behalf of the new institutional set-up after Lisbon. The official EU material and homepages emphasise that migration in the context of the EEAS is to be understood as a multiplicity of phenomena ranging from overall relations between development and migration in Third World countries, irregular migration, human trafficking etc, to the question of integrating immigrants in industrialised countries. The (partly contradictory) discourses on migration all impact on the logics of action of the EU migration policies.

In a European Parliament Resolution related to the development of a common immigration policy, the relation between immigration and security appears in a number of contexts, which are relevant to briefly go through. The document is called 'A Common Immigration Policy for Europe' (Europa 2008), but has a broader scope, which includes the security dimension. This can be seen in the introduction, where both external and internal security is touched upon, but later in the document a whole section is devoted to the issue – under the heading 'Security and Immigration'. The structural composition of the document emphasises that the security dimension was thought of as being important when drawing it up. Besides a short introduction, the document consists of 92 paragraphs. The first 42 paragraphs, divided into two chapters, deal with General Considerations (1-10) and Prosperity and Immigration (11-42). The second part of the document consists of 50 paragraphs, of which the first chapter deals with Security and Migration (43-76) and the second and last chapter with Solidarity and Immigration (77-92). The chapter entitled Security and Migration, however, focuses on border management, irregular migration and returns, with a main focus on the common borders and other perspectives related to external security. The chapter Prosperity and Immigration contains a section which focuses on integration, but without explicit formulations related to security. However, it is clear from the chapter that integration is seen as an important activity in dealing with a reality where population ageing will lead to a situation which 'will become a reality in the medium term, with the working age population projected to fall possibly by almost 50 million by 2060; whereas immigration could act as an important stimulus to ensure good economic performance in the EU' (Europa 2008: 5). This situation will, expectedly, show a positive impact on the logics of action of EU immigration policies. Summing up, the document deals with an essential challenge for the EU, and even though the document is very general in its approach, it represents an important stage in the institutional development of the EU.

On 25 May 2011 Ashton, the High Representative of The Union, launched a new policy called 'A New Response to a Changing Neighbourhood' which takes up the challenges from the new developments in the Middle East (EU-HR 2011). On the EU homepage it is stated that, together with the countries in the Middle East, the 'EU would launch institution-building programmes, collaborate closely on migration, mobility and security and launch pilot programmes to support agricultural and rural development'. In the policy document more detailed information can be found which furthermore emphasises the relationship between migration and security seen from the European side.

The significant novelty about this is that it is produced in a context where the Lisbon Treaty has moved all aspects of migration policy to majority voting and co-decision (Luedtke 2009). The changing institutional settings are shaping the EU logics of action within the field of migration policy, meaning that it is becoming more and more difficult for the individual member states to uphold their right to maintain local practices in dealing with migration and integration of immigrants, which for some member states creates serious internal political conflicts. Adam Luedtke has analysed differences between Belgium, France and the UK as to the level of 'EU control' and concludes: 'when Lisbon takes effect, legal migration will lose its "special" status and become a "normal" area of EU law' (Luedtke 2009: 21). This might be the case. However, recent developments in EU member states where EU scepticism is widespread, for instance in Austria, Denmark and Ireland, demonstrate that this process will tend to be rather long-lasting (Reyneri and Fullin 2010), since in some of the EU member states negative attitudes towards the EU are linked with anti-immigration positions in right-wing parties and movements. The recent development in the Middle East and the European intervention in Libya via NATO might be popular amongst the European public, but – as emphasised above – a development that 'ignites' migration flows towards European coasts would probably change this. The Arab revolts have revitalised the securitisation of migration and thereby strengthened the pragmatic logics of action among EU decision makers.

The security threats as they are perceived in the EU constitute a broad range of phenomena, which include more non-state related security issues like migration, energy and resource security, climate change, non-proliferation, combating international terrorism, trans-border organised crime and the fight against drugs (EU-HR 2011: 6). Ole Wæver and others have suggested the concept of 'non-traditional security' to cover a complex range of phenomena which do not deal with security defined in traditional geopolitical terms and confined to relations between nation-states, deterrence, the balance of power, and military strategy (Wæver et al. 1998, Williams 2003, Floyd 2007). The important point is that non-traditional security issues or phenomena might represent just as challenging problems as questions related to state power and at the same time, because of their rather intangible character, might be more difficult to deal with.

It is not unusual that the EU tends to solve problems by institution building. The Lisbon Treaty represents in itself an attempt to strengthen the EU foreign policy apparatus, so that the cooperation with the neighbouring countries can be broadened to cover a more comprehensive range of issues in an integrated and more effective manner. It is stated in the new policy that the reform process in the Middle East is taking place differently from one country to another, but that certain elements are required to secure a strong and lasting commitment to what is termed a 'deep and sustainable democracy'. This is then, still in the same document, defined as free and fair elections, freedom of association, rule of law and fight against corruption plus a 'security and law enforcement sector reform (including the police) and the establishment of democratic control over armed and security forces' (EU-HR 2011: 3).

As hinted at by Kerstin Rosenow, it seems that the attempts at constructing a common European migration policy can be seen as a prerequisite for a common EU integration policy (Rosenow 2009). She furthermore claims that the continued existence of a varied multitude of European integration schemes have contributed to slow progress regarding a possible harmonisation of the integration policies within the EU. The development of instruments aimed at controlling and steering migration towards Europe is also for that reason an important part of the development of European institutions. Understanding the recent changes in European practices might therefore benefit from an approach that focuses on the 'in-between' level, where actors and structures collide and negotiate institutional and policy developments.

## Migration Policy Between National and Supranational Narratives

Luedtke mentions that individual EU member states might tend to securitise migration as a result of the fact that they react based on specific, negative experiences in the given state, whereas common policies formulated in Brussels tend to be more open and tolerant, apparently based on more principled positions. Luedtke explains this by referring to the fact that 'Eurocrats are free to take this pro-immigrant line because they do not face direct electoral pressure in the way that national officials do' (Luedtke 2009: 49). So if the actual narratives are analysed the differences will be obvious. The officials in Brussels are more sympathetic to the rights and freedoms of non-EU citizens than is the case in the member states, where soft migration policies are a 'no-go area' for politicians, who care about their own political future. In other words the 'Eurocrats' follow a logic of action that differs from national decision makers in the sense that the built-in political control at the national level is partly suspended at the supranational level.

Luedtke's argument mainly takes its point of departure in the debates related to the integration of immigrants in the European states and thereby to the question of inner security in the EU. A parallel argument can be brought forward related to the outer security, where there is a gap between the official EU position and the actual practices in several of the EU member states. It should be mentioned that the issue is not without problematic political implications, as demonstrated by Christina Boswell (Boswell 2007).

Boswell points at securitisation of immigration as an, in some cases, problematic strategy for European states and takes the recent practice where the EU has increasingly been 'outsourcing' various areas of migration control and refugee protection to countries in regions of origin. Her argument is that this outsourcing of the implementation of immigration policies to the source countries can be seen as a successful securitisation (Boswell 2007). This can be explained by referring to the reality, that when 'leaving' immigration and integration policies to the supranational level the individual EU member states are able to avoid democratic and public scrutiny, which makes it difficult for the media and the political opposition in the given member state to involve public protest. The fact that other important non-state actors like for instance NATO also consider migration as an important security issue adds to the 'institutional alienation' of national migration policies.[1] Regardless of the circumstances: the built-in democratic deficit in the EU system will in this case internally legitimise a securitisation of immigration and integration policies in the EU.

Several scholars have demonstrated that various aspects of European migration policies are constructed in a security context (Huysmanns 2000, 2006, Seeberg 2007, Tocci and Cassarino 2011). The concept of securitisation has been used in connection with analysis of different kinds of migration, maybe most frequently illegal migration. The illegality in itself makes this almost self-evident. In an article from 2000 Jef Huysmans claims that migration has become a meta-issue, and that it 'has become a powerful theme through which functionally differentiated policy problems, such as identity control and visa policy, asylum applications, integration of immigrants, distribution of social entitlements, and the management of cultural diversity are connected and traversed' (Huysmans 2000: 763). Huysmans argues that the development of common migration policies is embedded in societal and political processes that articulate an endangered society and that the Europeanisation of migration policies thus securitises migration by integrating migration policy into an internal migration security framework, which partly feeds into a negative politicisation of immigrants, asylum seekers and refugees (Huysmans 2006). As mentioned by Nathalia Tocci and Jean-Pierre Cassarino, the 'fear of terrorism, political Islam, smuggling and organised crime, unauthorised migration and the wider spill-over effects of instability has induced most Europeans, leaders and publics alike, to deepen a policy of containment in recent years' (Tocci and Cassarino 2011: 22). These phenomena together constitute the background for the securitisation of immigrants and migration in the EU member states.

The process of securitisation of migration has both an external and an internal dimension, which in many ways are interconnected. The tightening of the external borders is followed by a parallel tendency to opt for more aggressive means of integrating immigrants into the European societies – leading to a tendency to give up on multiculturalism or maybe even pronounce it as a failure (Triadafilopoulos 2011). Such new ways of dealing with immigrants arriving in Europe can be described as 'civic integrationism' and represent, according to Triadafilopoulos, 'not simply a new brand of old-style xenophobia, but rather a self consciously liberal response to the challenges of cultural pluralization that seeks to distinguish

---

1   As for instance expressed in an interview by the author with a NATO officer, NATO Headquarters, Brussels, 2008: 'Let me put it this way, clearly NATO, or rather the member states of NATO, are quite concerned with the questions of immigration, most NATO countries are also European Union members [...].'

itself from its primary competitor, liberal multiculturalism' (Triadafilopoulos 2011: 863).

A different interpretation might take its point of departure in the EU and its changing institutional development, including the gradual establishment of the free movement of labour that is a result of the Single European Act and the implementation of the Schengen Agreement with its internally open borders in the EU. With this development the external borders become more important, as shown by Aderanti Adepoju et al. (Adepoju et al. 2010). There is a logical interconnectedness between internal liberalisation and external de-liberalisation and this process is part of the political learning, which the EU has been going through within the last decades. And as a result of that development it gradually becomes obvious 'that there is a need to establish a common EU immigration policy to replace fragmented and inconsistent national regimes' (Adepoju et al. 2010: 43).

## Euro-Mediterranean Migration and the Changing Political Scene

As emphasised by Stephen Castles and Mark J. Miller in their classic textbook 'The Age of Migration' the Middle East contains all the relevant conditions for producing migrants. It is 'an area where enormous political, cultural and economic diversity has resulted in many varied types of migration and mobility' (Castles and Miller 2009: 159). Middle Eastern migration is internal, meaning that it takes place behind borders. It is also regional – a large number of Syrians work in Lebanon (the local perspective) as do a large number of Syrians in the Gulf (the interregional perspective) (Ghoneim 2010). The largest population movements related to the Middle East, however, are trans-regional movements, first of all towards Europe, as shown already in the 1980s by Fred Halliday (Halliday 1984: 30), and, as demonstrated by Philippe Fargues, these movements have since then gradually increased and until recently seemed to be growing in relatively stable patterns (Fargues 2009: 19).

As mentioned in the introduction of this chapter a number of research projects have been documenting the migratory movements in the Mediterranean region. Taking the Middle East and its relations to the EU as a starting point it can be claimed that the political and institutional developments are creating huge challenges for the attempts at cooperation. On one side the complex challenges in the Middle East, not the least in relation to the Arab-Israeli conflict and the war in Iraq, have led to pragmatic logics of action in European foreign policy towards the MENA-region (Seeberg 2010b). On the other side the EU is experiencing a continuously slow process of its own institutional development, which only recently has seen the Lisbon Treaty beginning to materialise; a development, which in itself is leading to pragmatism as the dominant logics of action within EU Mediterranean policies.

In understanding migration as an important issue in a security context the role of transnational networks becomes highly relevant. Different phenomena attached to migration processes like chain migration related to family reunion, migration networks (be they official, semi-official or clandestine), or ethnic diasporas all constitute examples of transnational social formations. But also more problematic phenomena like human trafficking or illegal migration activities organised by people smugglers can be seen as manifestations of transnationalism. With the tendency to securitise migration movements and with the growing focus on radical Islamist organisations in the last decade, the interconnectedness between security and migration is developing new dimensions in the narratives related to transnational social movements in the Mediterranean.

For obvious reasons it is rather difficult to analyse, but most probably the emphasis on transnationalism should not be exaggerated, since it is possible to find both relatively stable and regular migratory movements and more individualised, arbitrary migration processes. A number of migration processes take place at random and have accidental character; often representing what might be possible rather than consciously planned long journeys. The migrant – if not a work migrant on a contract – will tend to spend a long time, with several 'stops' on the way, before he or she ends in a specific location where it is possible to earn a living, and often the final destination might be far from what was anticipated at the beginning of the journey. The accidental character of (a part of) the migration processes contributes to the security aspect attached to them. And from the receiving states this issue adds dimensions to the difficulties in dealing with the question, whether the immigrants are clandestine and explicitly unwanted or just 'officially unwanted' but, as shown by Luedtke, in practice an expression of a *de facto* policy of labour migration, as in Spain in the last decades (Luedtke 2009: 16).

It is an interesting irony, as demonstrated by Ahmet İçduygu, that 'while most of the southern European countries on the Mediterranean shores together with other EU countries tend to be advocating or actually adopting a range of restrictive controls against the incoming migrant flows, their economies are able to absorb thousands of irregular migrants without any unbearable confrontation' (İçduygu 2007: 142). The important point here is that in the actual European reality it is of course not only a question of absorbing irregular migrants, but of absorbing migrants in a broader sense. The southern European economies are in some areas hardly able to function without an influx of a cheap labour force from other continents, first of all from Northern Africa, but also from other regions of the world (Baldwin-Edwards 2006). And gradually this reality is spreading to the rest of Europe in the sense that a growing part of the unskilled European labour market is being dominated by immigrant workers (Kogan 2006, Blume et al. 2009).

Europe is importing a labour force which Europe itself no longer is able to provide due to ageing. The EU is experiencing radical changes in its demographic composition, which makes it necessary to implement new strategies. Therefore the EU has taken up competition with the US in attracting skilled workers. An example of this is the programme launched by the European Commission in 2009 called the 'blue card' intending to lure highly skilled third-country migrants to the European economies.[2] But as a matter of fact this process started many years earlier. A shrinking European labour force has for decades been balanced off by immigration resulting in a process of mutual accommodation, on one side by the European host societies and on the other side by the immigrants arriving in Europe (Hooghe et al. 2008, Castles and Miller 2009, Fargues 2009). According to a UN migration analysis, the EU currently integrates two million new migrants a year – a figure that is likely to increase, as demonstrated by several migration trend analyses, for instance the UN overviews.[3] It should be emphasised, however, that this does not mean that attempts at preventing specific groups from arriving in Europe have been brought to a halt (Carling 2007).

Traditionally the challenge has been met by the EU member states with different national integration strategies, but over time this has changed, so that a gradual establishing of supranational immigration policies is taking place, which also contain an integration dimension. One of the EU homepages is called 'Towards a common European Union immigration policy'[4] and even though there might be a long way ahead before the EU will reach this goal, there is no doubt that steps on the way have been taken, so that immigration and integration policies at the national level are gradually being replaced by common EU policies. Still the concrete integration activities take place locally and therefore will have a tendency to reflect national strategies and concrete practices developed over the last decades (Joppke 2010).

The different national integration strategies of course have to do with different conditions as described, for instance, by Göran Larsson et al. in their analysis of minorities with Islamic background in Scandinavia and the Baltic states and discussed in a review of their work (Larsson 2009, Seeberg 2011). Similar realities can be seen in the context of Greece and Italy (Triadafilopoulos 2011). Different ideological and political traditions have contributed to the well-known integration paradigms that characterise national and/or regional discourses and integration practices within Europe.

Rob Euwals et al. compare the conditions for Turkish immigrants in Germany and the Netherlands and demonstrate that a convergence has taken place bringing the two neighbouring countries closer together regarding integration policies: 'While Germany became less restrictive with respect to family reunification and family formation, the Netherlands became more restrictive [...] From 2003 onwards Dutch naturalization policy started to become stricter' (Euwals et al. 2010: 520-522). However, Euwals et al. do not seek to explain the demonstrated changes by pointing at a supranational development at the EU level. Other analyses have

---

2    See European Council press release. Brussels, 25 May 2009: Great News: European Council adopts EU Blue Card!

3    See for instance United Nations: Trends in Total Migration Stock: The 2005 Revision. UN 2006. For a highly interesting comment to this, see Koser 2008.

4    http://ec.europa.eu/home-affairs/policies/immigration/immigration_intro_en.htm.

also shown the same tendencies at convergence between the EU member states regarding immigration and integration policies and practices – and how these have been exposed to an increased securitisation (Geddes 2003).

The political reactions to the 'Arab Spring' at the EU level have been followed by a rather differentiated pattern of behaviour by the member states. The new EU foreign policy setup, established on the basis of the Lisbon Treaty, has thus not decisively altered the status of the EU as an actor, which is characterised by the fact that the member states more or less perceive themselves as independent states pursuing their own foreign and security policy. The 'Arab Spring' is adding new dimensions to the role migration is playing in Mediterranean cooperation in the sense that what used to be a rather stable relationship between the EU and the authoritarian regimes of the Middle East is gradually changing into a new, dynamic and unknown reality which seems difficult to predict and which might have serious consequences for the Mediterranean security environment.

The unrest and uprisings in the spring of 2011 and 2012 have thus contributed to uncertainty in the EU linked to the migration pressure from non-European Mediterranean states. The phenomenon is no novelty and has a complex historical background and character. The actual migration towards Europe has for decades consisted of ordinary work migration, where this might be possible, but also illegal migration and different forms of irregular migration, human smuggling and migration related to organised crime. All forms of migration are developing transnational networks which emphasise the complexity of the issue – and constitute an important part of the reason for the focus on security related to the migration phenomenon on both sides of the Mediterranean. In this sense the security aspects resulted in the construction of an informal alliance between authoritarian MENA states on one side and the EU on the other, with consequences for the foreign policy and security strategies. As pointed out by Roberto Aliboni and Fouad M. Ammor, the EU and the Arab states have over the years developed a growing, yet mostly unspoken, consensus across the Mediterranean related to the securitisation of oppositional groups in the Arab world (Aliboni and Ammor 2009).

The changing Middle Eastern political scene leads to a potential erosion of this consensus and possible informal alliance, which impacts on the logics of action of EU policies. If the weak, but stable and resilient authoritarian states are no longer providers of stability, law and order in the MENA region, the EU will have to consider if it is more appropriate to support the groups creating the unrest in 2011 and 2012 in the Middle Eastern states. For the EU this is and will, probably for years ahead, constitute a complex and difficult political learning process, which has already started.

## Conclusion

It has been the main ambition of this chapter to analyse how the development of the relation between migration and security in a Mediterranean setting establishes a dialectical political learning process which has important consequences for the development of the logics of action of EU migration policies related to the Middle East and for the national immigration policies of the EU member states. As shown, the challenges related to the 'Arab Spring' have contributed to this by creating more complex preconditions for European decision making.

The Lisbon Treaty and its gradual implementation do not seem to lead to radical changes in this pattern. The EU is still to be characterised as an actor whose member states more or less perceive themselves as independent states pursuing their own immigration and integration policies. And regarding integration policies there is a contradiction between rather intolerant local practices in some of the EU member states and more accommodating ideological formulations from the 'Eurocrats' – not having critical voters to face. To this regard one can speak of a certain persistence concerning the framework of European migration policy that was not fundamentally altered by the 'Arab Spring'.

At the same time, the 'Arab Spring' may also trigger important changes within the Euro-Mediterranean political space regarding migration issues. As mentioned the focus on security for years resulted in the construction of an informal alliance between authoritarian MENA states on one side and the EU on the other with consequences for the migration policy and security strategies. However, this pattern might be broken and the years to come will probably see an erosion of the cooperation and consensus between the European and Middle Eastern states founded on the logics of action of a pragmatic realism based policy from the EU side. The fact that migration has become *high politics* and constitutes an important part of foreign and security policies, contributes to making it a more complex issue. This is because it opens a possibility for a securitisation of the migration issue at the national level, where mechanisms of inclusion and exclusion are the result of political processes dealing with the challenges related to the historical development of European-Middle Eastern relations.

The chapter has attempted to demonstrate how the EU is going through political learning processes, where the institutional structures of the EU seek to develop abilities in working with non-traditional security issues like migration, environmental issues, and combating international terrorism, trans-border organised crime, etc. This highly complex field in itself calls for new institutional frameworks and the chapter thus showed how political learning on the part of the EU is reflected in the official documents issued by different EU institutions from 2004, when the European Neighbourhood Policy was launched to the recent situation, in which the EU is seeking to find answers to the challenges related to the 'Arab Spring'.

The intraregional interaction is influenced by the Arab uprisings, and the rather stable migration patterns which we have been seen for decades in the Mediterranean seem gradually to be replaced by new dynamics and unpredictable tendencies related to the local conflicts and unrest. The Tunisian refugees and migrants reaching Lampedusa in the early months of 2011 were the first representing the new tendencies, followed by other forced migrants from Libya (or transit migrants from Africa leaving Libya). The Syrian refugees entering the neighbouring states and Europe represent another part of the complex reality, and it is rather unlikely that they will be the only forced migrants in the Middle East resulting from the dramatic events in 2011 and 2012.

The EU has followed the logics of action of its traditional political behaviour and issued a new policy, 'A New Response to a Changing Neighbourhood', which mostly has the character of general declarations of intent. As shown the policy is a product of a situation in which the Lisbon Treaty is gradually being implemented at the same time as the EU is experiencing dramatic and unforeseen changes in its neighbourhood. The recent development in the Middle East and the NATO intervention in Libya were positively received in the European media, but – as mentioned – a development where migration flows towards Europe increase would probably change this. A changing EU is learning to cope with a new Middle Eastern reality both as to the migration phenomenon and in a broader political perspective. The pragmatic supranational narratives of the EU have so far not changed, but the challenges of the Arab revolts could easily lead to situations, where national(-istic) European narratives will again dominate the European public sphere.

## Bibliography

Adamson, F.B. 2006. Crossing Borders. International Migration and National Security. *International Security*, 31, 165-199.

Adebahr, C. 2009. *Learning and Change in European Foreign Policy. The Case of EU Special Representatives*. Baden-Baden: Nomos.

Adepoju, A., F. Van Noorloos and A. Zoomers 2010. Europe's Migration Agreements with Migrant-Sending Countries in the Global South: A Critical Review. *International Migration*, 48, 42-75.

Aliboni, R. and F.M. Ammor. 2009. Under the Shadow of 'Barcelona': From the EMP to the Union for the Mediterranean. *EuroMesco Paper*, January 2009, 1-34.

Baldwin-Edwards, M. 2005. *Migration in the Middle Eastern Mediterranean*. A Regional Study prepared for the Global Commission on International Migration. Athens: Mediterranean Migration Observatory. University Research Institute for Urban Environment and Human Resources, Panteion University.

Baldwin-Edwards, M. 2006. 'Between a Rock & a Hard Place': North Africa as a Region of Emigration, Immigration & Transit Migration. *Review of African Political Economy*, 108, 311-324.

Blume, K., M. Ejrnæs, H.S. Nielsen and A. Würtz 2009. Labor Market Transitions of Immigrants with Emphasis on Marginalization and Self-Employment. *Journal of Population Economics*, 22, 881-908.

Boswell, C. 2007. The Securitisation of Migration: A Risky Strategy for European States. *DIIS Brief*. Copenhagen: Danish Institute for International Studies.

Buzan, B., J. de Wilde and O. Wæver 1998. *Security. A New Framework for Analysis*. Boulder (Col.), Lynne Rienner Publishers.

Carling, J. 2007. European Strategies for Reducing 'Unwanted' Immigration. *DIIS Brief*. Copenhagen: Danish Institute for International Studies.

Castles, S. and M. Miller. 2009. *The Age of Migration. International Population Movements in the Modern World*. London, Macmillan.

Ciuta, F. 2009. Security and the Problem of Context: A Hermeneutical Critique of Securitisation Theory Security and the Problem of Context. *Review of International Studies*, 35, 301-326.

Collyer, M. 2006. Migrants, Migration and the Security Paradigm: Constraints and Opportunities. *Mediterranean Politics*, 11, 255-270.

Den Hertog, L. 2011. Revolutions and their immigrants: EU's response. Brussels: Centre for European Policy Studies.

Dijck, D.V. 2006. Is the EU policy on illegal immigration securitized? Yes of course! A study into the dynamics of institutionalised securitization. *3rd Pan-European Conference on EU Politics*. Istanbul.

Dinan, D. 2009. Saving the Lisbon Treaty: An Irish Solution to a European Problem. *Journal of Common Market Studies*, 47, 113-132.

Eriksson, J. and G. Giacomello. 2006. The Information Revolution, Security, and International Relations: (IR) Relevant Theory? *International Political Science Review*, 27, 221-244.

EU Commission. 2003. *A secure Europe in a better world* [online]. Available from: http://www.consilium.europa.eu/uedocs/cmsUpload/78367.pdf [Accessed: 1 August 2012].

EU Commision. 2010. *The EU Internal Security Strategy in Action: Five steps towards a more secure Europe* [online]. Available from: http://ec.europa.eu/commission_2010-2014/malmstrom/archive/-internal_security_strategy_in_action_en.pdf [accessed: 1 August 2012].

EU Commission. 2012. *Partnership for Democracy and Shared Prosperity: Report on activities in 2011 and Roadmap for future action* [online]. Available from: http://ec.europa.eu/world/-enp/docs/2012_enp_pack/pship_democracy_report_roadmap_en.pdf [accessed: 1 August 2012].

EU-HR. 2011. *A New Response to a Changing Neighbourhood* [online]. Available from: http://ec.europa.eu/world/enp/pdf/com_11_303_en.pdf [Accessed 1 August 2012].

Europa. 2008. *A Common Immigration Policy for Europe* [online]. Available from: http://europa.eu/-rapid/pressReleasesAction.do?reference=MEMO/08/402 [accessed: 1 August 2012].

Euwals, R., J. Dagevos and and H. Roodenburg 2010. Citizenship and Labor Market Position: Turkish Immigrants in Germany and the Netherlands. *International Migration Review*, 44, 513-538.

Fargues, P. 2004. Arab Migration to Europe: Trends and Policies. *International Migration Review*, 38, 1348-1371.

Fargues, P. 2008. *Emerging Demographic Patterns across the Mediterranean and their Implications for Migration through 2030*. Transatlantic Council on Migration, 2008 New York. Migration Policy Institute.

Fargues, P. 2009. *Mediterranean Migration 2008-2009 Report*. San Domenico di Fiesole: Robert Schumann Centre for Advanced Studies, European University Institute.

Floyd, R. 2007. Towards a Consequentialist Evaluation of Security: Bringing Together the Copenhagen and the Welsh Schools of Security Studies. *Review of International Studies*, 33, 327-350.

Geddes, A. 2003. *The Politics of Migration and Immigration in Europe*. London: Sage.

Ghoneim, A.F. 2010. Labour migration for decent work, economic growth and development in Egypt. *International Migration Papers*. Geneva: International Labour Office.

Goldstone, J.A. 2011. Understanding the Revolutions of 2011. Weakness and Resilience in Middle Eastern Autocracies. *Foreign Affairs*, 90, 8-17.

Hallidya, F. 1984. Labor Migration in the Arab World. *Middle East Report*, 123, 3-10, 30.

Hannay, D. 2003. Strengthening Europe's Role in World affairs: Foreign Policy, Security and Immigration. *European Foreign Affairs Rewiev*, 8, 365-368.

Hooghe, M., A. Trappers, B. Meuleman and T. Reeskens 2008. Migration to European Countries: A Structural Explanation of Patterns, 1980-2004. *International Migration Review*, 42, 476-504.

Huysmans, J. 2000. The European Union and the Securitization of Migration. *Journal of Common Market Studies*, 38, 751-777.

Huysmans, J. 2006. *The Politics of Insecurity: Fear, Migration and Asylum in the EU*. Oxon: Routledge.

İçduygu, A. 2007. The Politics of Irregular Migratory Flows in the Mediterranean Basin: Economy, Mobility and 'Illegality'. *Mediterranean Politics*, 12, 141-162.

Joppke, C. 2010. *Citizenship and Immigration*. Cambridge: Polity Press.

Kogan, I. 2006. Labor Markets and Economic Incorporation among Recent Immigrants in Europe. *Social Forces*, 85, 697-721.

Koser, K. 2008. *Dimensions and Dynamics of Contemporary International Migration*. Conference Paper. 'Workers without borders: Rethinking economic migration'. Maastricht Graduate School of Governance, 18 March 2008.

Kostakopoulou, D. 2008. How to Do Things with Security Post 9/11. *Oxford Journal of Legal Studies*, 28, 317-342.

Laidi, Z. (ed.) 2008. *EU Foreign Policy in a Globalized World. Normative power and social preferences*. Abingdon and New York: Routledge.

Larsson, G. (ed.) 2009. *Islam in the Nordic and Baltic Countries*, Abingdon and New York: Routledge.

Luedtke, A. 2009. Uncovering European Union Immigration Legislation: Policy Dynamics and Outcomes. *International Migration*, 49.

MWT. 2011. Tunisian migrants of Lampedusa: France is shivering. *Masr wa Touness* [Online]. Available from: http://masrwatouness.wordpress.com/2011/04/24/tunisian-migrants-of-lampedusa-france-is-shivering/ [Accessed 1 August 2012].

Pace, M. and P. Seeberg 2010. *The European Union's Democratization Agenda in the Mediterranean.* Abingdon and New York: Routledge.

Reyneri, E. and G. Fullin, 2010. Labour Market Penalties of New Immigrants in New and Old Receiving West European Countries. *International Migration,* 49, 31-57.

Rosenow, K. 2009. The Europeanization of Integration Policies. *International Migration,* 47, 133-159.

Schlumberger, O. 2011. The Ties that do not Bind: The Union for the Mediterranean and the Future of Euro-Arab Relations. *Mediterranean Politics,* 16, 135-153.

Seeberg, P. 2007. 'Unity in Diversity', security and migration. The Changing European Foreign Policy and Security Agenda in the Mediterranean, in *EU and the Mediterranean. Foreign Policy and Security,* edited by P. Seeberg. Odense: University Press of Southern Denmark.

Seeberg, P. 2010a. European Neighbourhood Policy, post-normativity and pragmatism. *European Foreign Affairs Review,* 15, 663-679.

Seeberg, P. 2010b. Union for the Mediterranean – pragmatic multilateralism and the de-politicization of European-Middle Eastern relations. *Middle East Critique,* 19, 287-302.

Seeberg, P. 2011. Review of *Islam in the Nordic and Baltic Countries,* edited by Göran Larsson (London and New York: Routledge, 2009), *Journal of Islamic Studies,* 22, 110-114.

Seeberg, P. 2012. Is an Islamist Democracy emerging in North Africa? Its contours and objectives, a view from the North *EuroMeSCo Brief* [Online]. Available at: http://www.euromesco.net/images/-briefs/euromescobrief42.pdf [accessed: 10 February 2013].

Sørensen, N.N. (ed.) 2006. *Mediterranean Transit Migration.* Copenhagen: Danish Institute for International Studies.

Tabutin, D. and B. Schoumaker. 2005. The Demography of the Arab World and the Middle East from the 1950s to the 2000s. A Survey of Changes and a Statistical Assessment. *Population,* 5/6, 505-591.

Tocci, N. and J-P. Cassarino. 2011. Rethinking the EU's Mediterranean Politics Post 9/11. *IAI Working Papers,* 11.

Triadafilopoulos, T. 2011. Illiberal Means to Liberal Ends? Understanding Recent Immigrant Integration Policies in Europe. *Journal of Ethnic and Migration Studies,* 37, 861-880.

Vesely, M. 2011. Why is the West bombing Libya? *The Middle East.* May 2011, 20-21.

Vinoceur, J. 2011. Issue of Arab Spring Migrants to Cast Shadow on G-8 Talks. *New York Times,* 16 May.

Williams, M.C. 2003. Words, Images, Enemies: Securitization and International Politics. *International Studies Quarterly*, 47, 511-531.

Youngs, R. 2010. *The EU's Role in World Politics. A retreat from liberal internationalism*. London and New York: Routledge.

# Chapter 5

# Free Trade, Development and Authoritarianism in a Rentier Economy: Intentions and Reality of the EU's Logic of Action in Algeria[1]

Jakob Horst

## Introduction

'In the current situation of instability in the region, Algeria appears as a factor of stability', declared Laura Baeza, then head of the EU Commission Delegation in Algiers in August 2012 (El Watan 2012, author's translation). In this chapter it is argued that the EU's policy approach within the Euro-Mediterranean Partnership (EMP) was and is shaped by a specific logic of action that is suitable to support this 'stability' by strengthening the political economy environment in the Algerian rentier state which functions as a stabilising force for authoritarian government. Although the 'Arab Spring' puts into question the EU's role in the Middle East and North Africa (MENA) and lots of ink was spilled over the need to 'adapt' the EU's foreign policy approach to its southern neighbouring countries (Behr 2011, European Commission and High Representative 2011, Gillespie 2011), there are until now no signs of major adjustments affecting the core of EU-Algerian relations.

Since 1995 the EU-MENA relations are institutionalised through the multilateral framework of the Euro-Mediterranean Partnership (EMP). Even though the EMP's framework was refined and further developed by other EU induced initiatives like the European Neighbourhood Policy (ENP) and, more recently, the Union for the Mediterranean (UfM), the EMP, also after the 'Arab Spring', remains to be an important institutional framework. This is due specifically to the bilateral association agreements concluded in this context, that constitute the only legally binding agreements signed by both sides.

1 I would like to thank Delf Rothe and Annette Jünemann for the valuable comments on earlier drafts of this article. Furthermore I would like to thank Ahcène Amarouche, Nordine Grim and the Friedrich Ebert Foundation in Algiers for their support. This article is based on my research project on economic liberalisation within the EMP-association agreement and its impact on authoritarian rule in Algeria.

Applying the Logics of Action approach outlined in the introduction of this book the chapter conceptualises the implementation of the Euro-Mediterranean trade regime through the association agreement with Algeria as an intraregional political process with a purposeful objective (development, democratisation) but with unintended side effects (strengthening factors of authoritarianism). By combining the Logics of Action approach with the understanding of the EU's international role as a 'structural power' the chapter transcends the understanding of the European Union as a purely 'normative' international actor and the binary conception of the democratic north spreading its 'mode of society' to the south.

The chapter is structured as follows: First, I will explain the integration of the structural power concept within the Logics of Action framework. Second, I will focus on the EU's logic of action within the Euro-Mediterranean Partnership. The third section deals with the specific socio-economic and political context in Algeria and in the fourth section I will analyse the (unintended) effects of the EU's logic of action in Algeria. The fifth section identifies persistent logics that explain Algeria's 'immunity' regarding the wave of political upheavals and deals with the question why the EU's policy approach toward Algeria has not changed after or during the 'Arab Spring'. Finally, in the last section, the results of this chapter will be summarised, leading to open questions for further research.

## Enriching Logics of Action: The EU as a Structural Power

As mentioned in the introductory chapter of this book, the Logics of Action approach emphasises that political processes are shaped by the co-determination of actors and structures and that they cannot be explained by universal causal laws. This contribution conceptualises the Euro-Algerian relations (with a special focus on trade policies) as a political process that is shaped by specific logics of the actors involved, but also by specific structual factors affecting these logics of action and the political process itself. For the purposes of this chapter, it is useful to further enrich the Logics of Action approach by including some additional theoretical elements. To specify the above mentioned co-determination between actors and structures in analysing a political process I propose to include some ideas of Susan Stranges' concept of structural power in order to build a better understanding of the EU's role as an international actor in the Mediterranean.

Today it is widely accepted that the European Union can be characterised as an international actor (Schumacher 2005). However, what is still contested, is the question what kind of international actor the European Union is and how it should be conceptualised. Since the beginning the discussion on the EU's international actorness it was mostly seen as a somehow peaceful and 'docile' actor (Pace 2007). Specifically Ian Manners' concept of the EU as a 'normative power' was the object of controversial debates in the last years. Manners assumed that the EU should be understood as an international actor who is able to 'shape the conceptions of normal' of other actors/states (Manners 2002: 240). Manners emphasises that the

EU, as a result of its own historical experience, developed a genuine normative character that also affects the goals and instruments of its external policy. The EU's external policy does not aim only at shaping the rational calculations of other international actors by applying threats or incentives, but tends to modify the basic values itself that constitute the fundament of other actors actions. Manners argued that the norms and values diffused by the EU's external policy (democracy, rule of law, human rights …) are principally universalistic.

However, other authors contested this conception of the EU's international role.[2] Patrick Holden argued that the normative power concept neglects the relevance of interest driven politics and more material configurations of power. At the same time classical realist concepts of power are not adequate either to analyse the external action of the EU (Holden 2009). Instead, Holden assumes that 'normative considerations in EU foreign policy are interacting with and are shaped by self-interest considerations' (Holden 2009: 10). Essentially this concept aims at questioning the normative power approach. In doing so, however, it does not exclude the possibility that the EU's foreign policy actions imply some sort of 'norm spreading', but proposes to conceive these processes also as part of the assertion of political and material interests.

Holden thereby refers to the structural power concept by Susan Strange who defined structural power as 'the power to shape and determine the structures of the global political economy within which other states, their political institutions and their economic enterprises have to operate' (Strange 1988: 24-25). Strange contrasted this conception of structural power with the traditional idea of 'relational power', which was mostly described as the capacity of one actor A to enforce its will opposite to another actor B against the will of the latter. Instead the concept of structural power focuses on the ability of an actor to shape 'the rules of the game', that is to shape the institutional setting within which social (and political) processes take place. At the same time Strange's concept of structural power allows for an understanding of power as purely a property of social relations. On this second level structural power goes more in the direction of Foucault's notion of 'productive power' (Foucault 1995), where power is not a possession or 'resource' of actors, nor necessarily takes a repressive form. However, Strange's concept is distinct from Foucault's model because it implies a certain 'directedness' of power as a property of social relations, i.e. it can produce winners and losers. Another important point of this second level of structural power is its potential 'unintendedness'. Whereas on the first level structural power is understood as something to be 'used' intentionally in order to shape institutional settings in

---

2  Pace (2007) for example focus on the *construction* of this specific understanding of the EU's foreign policy character. Smith (2005) criticises the overall concept of the 'civil' character of the EU's policies abroad. And Bicchi (2006) contrasts the normative power model with sociological institutionalism. Drawing on the concept of role-theory, Jünemann (2010) explains the erosion of the EU's identity as a civilian power with a changing security paradigm after 9/11.

compliance with specific interests, on the second level Strange emphasises the possibility that structural power produces effects without having been intended or even realised by the actor 'possessing' this structural power.

When we look at the specific case of the EU's trade regime in the Mediterranean we can identify similar patterns. While the EU tries to widen its export market in order to ensure economic prosperity within its own borders this policy is accompanied by a developmentalist discourse emphasising the need for southern Mediterranean countries to open their economies in order to gain access to the world economy and to profit from comparative advantages and technology transfers coming with foreign direct investments. This chapter shows that the EU's trade policy, at the same time, produces unintended effects that can be ascribed basically to the EU's structural power within the Euro-Mediterranean political space.

Moreover the understanding of the EU as a structural power fits well with the specific assumptions of the Logics of Action approach as the structural power concept obviously accounts for the importance of structural factors but escapes from deploying a tautological structuralism and thereby keeps in mind the co-determination of actors and structures. The added value in combining the structural power concept with the Logic of Action approach lies in the possibility to reveal the logics of action that have driven the developmental bias of the EU's policy and therefore shaped also its understanding of 'democracy promotion'. Furthermore the structural power approach breaks with the long dominant narrative of the EU as a purely normative international actor spreading universal values across third countries in the southern Mediterranean and elsewhere.

## Explaining the EU's Logic of Action in the Mediterranean: Development and Democratisation through Liberal Economic Reforms

The foundation of the Euro-Mediterranean Partnership in 1995 that for the first time institutionalised Euro-Med relations on a multilateral level has to be seen within the specific international political and ideational context at the end of the 1980s and the beginning of the 1990s. Particularly important to understand the specific logic behind the EU's emerging Mediterranean policy is the fundamentally changing international security environment at that time. The breakdown of the Soviet Union and the end of the bipolar constellation of the international system changed European security calculations and more 'soft' security issues came to the fore. In accordance with such an 'extended' security perception certain issues, specifically migration, pushed to the centre of attention (Bicchi 2007) within Europe's Mediterranean policy. Then European Commission President Jacques Delors emphasised in a speech in 1992 that most countries in the southern Mediterranean struggled with problems of 'security and migratory pressure' and that there was an urgent need for action on the EU's side (European Commission 1992: 10).[3] The fear of political fundamentalism and terrorism played an important role within the process of 'securitising' migration in the Euro-Mediterranean context. European debates perceived Islamic fundamentalists as a potential threat not only for the autocratic – although western-friendly – regimes in the southern Mediterranean, but also as creating a dangerous 'fifth column' of radical Muslims within European countries (Bicchi 2007: 141).[4] All in all, the southern Mediterranean countries in the beginning of the 1990s were seen as constituting a neighbouring space of risk and danger whose problems had to be addressed by the EU in order to assert its own security interests.

The answer to these challenges at Europe's 'southern flank' was the EMP, which initially was conceptualised as a 'region building' project aimed at reducing the 'gap' between the northern and the southern side of the Mediterranean. Eventually, the aim was to create a common Euro-Mediterranean space of prosperity and security, as was emphasised in the EMP's founding document. In accordance with such a holistic approach the EMP's multilateral cooperation framework included a political, an economic, and a socio-cultural dimension (the three so called 'baskets') (Barcelona Declaration 1995).

However, it quickly became clear that the multilateral political level of the EMP was doomed to fail mainly because of the ongoing Israeli-Palestinian conflict and the definite failure of the peace process after the emergence of the second Intifada in 2000. As a result the bilateral association agreements, that the EU signed one by one with all EMP partner countries[5] became the actual institutional basis of the EMP (Barbé and Herranz Surrallés 2010: 129-130). In addition to this, preference of the bilateral over the multilateral level the second (economic) 'basket' attained a predominant position within the EMP's cooperation framework and constitutes also the cornerstone of the bilateral association agreements. The focus on the economic sphere was not only due to an eligible concern about troubles in the political field triggered by the Arab-Israeli conflict. Rather it is the overall conception of the EMP that inherently puts a special emphasis on economic issues (Jünemann 1999, Martin 2007). If one looks at the association agreement with Algeria, which was signed in 2002 and came into force in September 2005, more

---

3    See the contribution of Peter Seeberg in this book.

4    Not least the events in Algeria since the military coup in the end of 1991 and the following cruel conflict between armed Islamic groups and the military junta, together with the GIA-bombings in France contributed to the European sentiment of being threatened by an insecure unstable southern neighbourhood.

5    Tunisia was the first country to sign an association agreement in 1995, followed successively by Israel, Morocco, Lebanon, Jordan, Egypt and Algeria. The Palestinian Authority signed an interim association agreement in 1997, Turkey established a customs union with the EU in 1995 and Syria's association agreement was initialised in 2004 but not yet ratified.

than two-thirds of the treaty text of 90 pages deal with commercial measures and economic and financial cooperation issues.

The objectives of the second basket were stated as 'the acceleration of the pace of sustainable socio-economic development' and the 'improvement of living conditions of their [the contracting parties, JH] populations, increase in the employment level and reduction in the development gap in the Euro-Mediterranean region' (Barcelona Declaration 1995: 127). To fulfil these ambitious goals the EU established two main instruments. First, the implementation of a Euro-Mediterranean Free Trade Area (EMFTA) was meant to strengthen economic growth by reducing prices of imported goods and a reallocation of capital and labour in the most effective industrial sectors within the respective economies. Second, the EU intensified financial cooperation measures through the MEDA funds (in 2007 MEDA was replaced by the European Neighbourhood and Partnership Instrument, ENPI). Part of the economic focus of the EMP was the European idea that the economies (and societies overall) of the southern Mediterranean states had to be 'modernised' in order to address the potential threats sparked by high unemployment rates, economic hardship and demographic pressures. The link between economic cooperation, liberalisation, overall modernisation and security is well clarified in a statement by Eberhard Rhein, who, between 1986-1996, was responsible for the EU Commission's policy toward the MENA countries:

> The security threats in the MED, as perceived by the EU are not military ones, neither today nor in the next 10-20 years […]. The real threats derive from increasing population, inability to employ the growing numbers of young people, illegal immigration, persistent poverty, environmental hazards, water scarcity, food shortages, urban chaos etc. Therefore, the response to the risks has to be primarily of a socio-economic nature. Europe has to 'shake up' the MED societies in such a way that they are better able to face the challenges of the next century. They need […] to undergo profound system changes. (cited in Weiss 2002: 12)

In the minds of its intellectual founders the EMP was expected to initiate and structure these deep systematic changes. The implementation of the EMFTA played a crucial role in this scenario. Three years after the initial conference in Barcelona Rhein emphasised that 'trade, free trade to be precise, is […] an essential instrument to provoke necessary changes on the side of Europe's Mediterranean partners' (Rhein 1998: 166). Thus, the implementation of the EMFTA and its accompanying measures were explicitly seen as instruments to trigger comprehensive socio-economic changes within the southern Mediterranean partner countries. On the economic level the EU expected that with the cancellation of customs duties trade would increase and all participating countries would profit from the realisation of comparative advantages and overall economic growth. Because of increased competition of European import-products it was furthermore expected that positive effects for the efficiency and productivity of southern

Mediterranean economies would materialise and that capital would concentrate within internationally competitive sectors (Evans 1993, Hunt 2005). With such a reallocation of capital and other production factors EU policy makers counted on an increasing employment level due to job creation in newly emerging export sectors.

But the results expected from the EMP went beyond the economic sphere. As mentioned in the beginning of this chapter the comprehensive modernisation and development process was expected to trigger 'spill over effects' to the political sphere, fostering political opening and liberalisation. 'In designing the Barcelona process, the EU's philosophy was that economic and political objectives were symbiotic: economic reform would bring in its wake political reform, which would give a further boost to economic performance, the latter helping to stem any potential for unsustainable levels of migration and thereby enhancing security objectives' (Youngs 1999: 17). However, this developmentalist approach to democracy promotion was and is not surprising, considering long dominant European fears about the consequences of abrupt political changes bringing to the fore fundamentalist (i.e. islamist) governments.[6] Thus, the EU, contrary to the US policy in the last decade, adopted an incrementalist approach to democracy building. It presumed that moderate pressure on governments to enact liberal economic reforms and economic incentives would slowly but irreversibly reduce the power of authoritarian modes of governance (Dillman 2002).

The question why the EU adopted this developmentalist-modernisation logic of action concerning its external policy – not only in its southern Mediterranean neighbourhood – can be addressed from different angles. Monar, for example, chose a technical explanation and affiliates the dominance of economic elements within the EMP with an inherent tendency of the EU's institutional structure to produce more decisions concerning economic policy, due to the dominance of the 'communitarised' areas of trade policy and development cooperation (Monar 1999: 79). While this assumption is certainly true one should go beyond purely technical explanations and explore the deeper reasons for the EU's economistic-modernisation bias toward third countries and to the southern Mediterranean states specifically.

The Logics of Action approach offers a valuable theoretical basis to deal with this question because it allows a deeper understanding of specific factors shaping the EU's logic of action within the Euro-Mediterranean political space to be built. The two factors that are specifically important in this context are *identity* and *power*. First, it is argued with Bicchi (2006) that the EU's logic of action within the Euro-Mediterranean political space can be described as following an 'our-size-fits-all'-imagination: Essentially the European integration process, based on the functional cooperation in the economic sphere, is mirrored in the overall

---

6   Also here the Algerian case played a major role, considering the European perception, that the opening of the political sphere went 'too fast' and produced the undesirable result of the FIS's election victory in 1991.

economistic-modernising bias of the EMP. This means that there certainly is a 'normative' element in the EU's logic of action, claiming the dispersion of a set of norms and values which are seen to represent the specific European heritage and which are estimated to be able to trigger a 'repetition' of the European experience within other world regions. This ideational agenda of 'Europeanization' (Lavenex and Schimmelfennig 2009) materialises in specific political instruments like the EMFTA. However, in order to build a better understanding of the impacts of the EU's logic of action it is necessary, second, to integrate the above-mentioned understanding of the EU's role as a structural power. This is particularly important when we look at the impact of the EU's logic of action within the context of specific southern neighbouring countries like Algeria and focus on the *unintended* effects of the EU's structural power. In the following sections I will analyse the specific Algerian national context and the impact of the EU's logic of action within this specific setting.

## The Algerian Context: Development and Authoritarianism in a Rentier Economy

After its independence in 1962 Algeria established a state-centred economy that essentially followed the socialist model of the Soviet Union. A state-financed public industrial sector should serve as the cornerstone of the Algerian 'capitalisme d'état'. The Algerian state – after having gained political independence from France – was seen as the only actor capable of managing the development and industrialisation of the Algerian economy and thereby to gain also economic independence (Raffinot and Jacquemot 1977). The crucial moment of the Algerian postcolonial development process came in the year 1971, when President Houari Boumediène nationalised the industrial sector of hydrocarbons (HC). With the income generated by the state-controlled HC exports the Algerian government launched a development programme that was expected to transform Algeria in a short timeframe from an agrarian into a modern industrialised society. The works of the French economist Destanne de Bernis[7] who advised focusing on so-called 'industrialising industries' to push-start an internal development dynamic (Destanne de Bernis 1971) played a central role within the Algerian development strategy of the 1970s. The development of these heavy industries (steel, mechanics and electrics, chemicals) through public investment was expected to trigger the development of all other productive industrial sectors and incite technological progress.

---

7   Gérard Destanne de Bernis, who lived and taught in Algeria during the first years of independence, was a student of the French economist François Perroux, whose work was highly influential for the state-centred development models in the postcolonial period in the 1960s and 1970s.

In the first decade after its independence the Algerian development project was seen as a role model and the country experienced one of the highest growth rates in the 'third world' (the average Algerian growth rate between 1965-1980 was 7.5 per cent). However, the state-financed industrial sector remained mostly unproductive and depended strongly on foreign imports – mainly technology and machines – without being able to export own products. Thus, during the 1970s two disconnected economic sectors emerged in Algeria: On the one side the public-financed interior industrial sector with its large state-owned enterprises. On the other side the rapidly growing export sector that nearly exclusively relied on oil and gas (Talahite 2002). One of the paradoxal effects of this industrialising strategy was, that the growing surpluses obtained by exporting oil and gas (specifically after the oil price choc of 1973) were mainly used to further extend the HC industry itself. 'By that fact Algeria experienced a radical change of the mode of insertion of its economy into the international system of division of labour; a change, that ultimately was not in its favour' (Amarouche 2004: 201, author's translation). After the relative formal success of this state-centred development strategy during the second half of the 1960s and the 1970s, the country faced serious difficulties after the world oil price collapsed in 1986.[8] Algeria's external revenues dropped by 55 per cent in only one year and pushed the country into an economic downward spiral until it had to accept the first IMF structural adjustment programme in 1994.

Today Algeria's heavy dependence on the HC sector is unchanged. More than three quarters of the state income has its source in this sector (Djoufelkit 2008), nearly 99 per cent of Algerian exports are natural resources (oil and gas) or petrochemical products and half of the Algerian GDP growth depends on this sector (Benabdallah 2009). A result of this domination of the HC sector and the neglect of other industrial branches is that since the 1980s Algeria witnessed a deindustrialisation process and a constant shrinking of the public manufacturing sector (Bouzidi 2008). In 2006 public manufacturing contributed only 7 per cent to the GDP (in comparison to 15 per cent in the middle of the 1980s) and the industrial sectors outside the HC sector contribute only marginally to overall economic growth (Benabdallah 2009: 93). At the same time the tentatively emerging private sector was not able to offset this process. As a result Algeria shows the typical partition of an economy afflicted with 'dutch disease':[9] a booming export sector based on the HC recourses, an important sector of non changeable goods and a shrinking sector

---

8    Already since 1982 worldwide demand for oil declined, especially for the OPEC countries, because new producing countries like Mexico and Norway pushed in the market. By 1986 the oil price dropped to less than 10 USD per Barrel (from more than 40 USD in 1980) (Lowi 2009).

9    The term designates the phenomenon that the high export share of a specific product (often HC) leads to an appreciation of the real exchange rate and thereby harms the manufacturing sector, because its exports become more expensive. Admittedly the Algerian case differs from the typical dutch disease effect, because the Algerian Dinar underwent no significant re-evaluation in recent years. Consequently one could argue that

of changeable goods (industries other than HC). As a result today Algeria faces a sort of dilemma: On the one side the absolute necessity of a reindustrialisation to diversify the Algerian economy and to overcome the structural dependence on the HC rent (with its implications regarding the vulnerability to external price shocks) can be hardly imagined without referring to public investments and a state-led reindustrialisation programme. On the other hand such a strategy would perpetuate mechanisms that led to the delicate situation in the first place. 'Relying on the rent for the venture of economic development is a paradox in itself' (Benabdallah 2009: 96, author's translation).

Besides the negative effects that the predominance of the HC rent had on the Algerian development process since the 1970s, the country is also an ideal type example of how the resource abundance helped to develop and maintain authoritarian political structures. Although Algeria in 1989 witnessed a significant change within its political system with the establishment of a multiparty system and a series of communal, legislative and presidential elections the rules of political decision making remain opaque, the parliament has no substantial role in the legislative process and especially the control over the HC rent is not subject to any democratic control whatsoever (Lowi 2009). Basically, since independence in 1962, changes within the political power structure of the country were more a function of the struggles between different segments within the state elite than of the people choosing its representatives (Ouaissa 2005, Werenfels 2007).

The role of the externally generated rent for stabilizing the authoritarian political structures in Algeria can be described as twofold. First, one can observe the typical features of what Luciani (1990) called the 'allocative state'. In contrast to a 'productive' state, the allocative state is widely independent from the national economy and is able to free itself from taxing its citizens and thereby becomes less accountable. Besides this basic structural feature of the rentier state a second stabilising factor for authoritarian political structures is the ability of the state to regulate the distribution of rents and – if necessary – to coopt specific social or political groups in order to mitigate political or social protest. This last feature of allocative rentier states became specifically obvious in Algeria during the first half of 2011, when the Algerian authorities reacted to emerging protest movements inspired by the events in neighbouring Tunisia. When in the beginning of January 2011 major riots blazed in disadvantaged urban neighbourhoods all over the country and notably in the capital Algiers the Algerian regime instantly took back a decision of cancelling the subsidies for important staple foods like oil and flour.[10]

---

Algeria indicated the same symptoms of the dutch disease, but without showing the same underlying mechanisms. See for example Bellal (2011).

10   Another example of mitigating socio-political contestation were the salary increases for the 'gardes communaux', a special police force established in the 1990s whose members blocked public places in the centre of the capital for several days in April 2011. These measures were flanked by overall increases in public spending for public servants' salaries, housing and youth employment programmes (Mattes 2012).

Bearing in mind the stabilising factor of the HC rent for authoritarian governance in Algeria one important question is whether the EMFTA implementation is likely to shape the income structure of the Algerian state and potentially contributes to a decrease of the HC rent within the state budget.

## Effects of the EU's Logic of Action in Algeria

As explained above the EMFTA that originally was planned to be established by the year 2010 was expected to have several effects in the MENA countries of which the EU estimated a modernisation and restructuring of the respective economies and a political 'spill over' respectively. However, the implementation of the EMFTA depends on the entry into force of the individual bilateral association agreements.[11] In each association agreement the cut down of tariffs on goods is usually framed within a period of 12 years after the entry into force of the agreement. Algeria is a relative 'late comer' concerning trade liberalisation within the EMP-framework since its association agreement was signed only in 2002.[12] Its implementation and also other free trade agreements (like the admission to the Great Arab Free Trade Area, GAFTA) has led some scholars to refer to the Algerian example as a 'big bang' scenario (Hedir 2003) concerning trade liberalisation, referring to the fact that the opening took place prior to the completion of an adequate restructuring and reform of the Algerian industrial sector. In contrast to the cooperation agreement that Algeria signed in 1976 the association agreement applies a logic of 'reciprocity'. Because Algerian industrial goods already gained free access to the European market in the 1976 agreement the association agreement solely contains the opening of the Algerian market for European goods (and services). Looking on Algeria's external trade structure it becomes obvious that the country is deeply connected to and highly dependant on the European market. In 2011 over 52 per cent of Algerian Imports came from the EU and over 50 per cent of Algeria's exports (of which 97.19 per cent were HC) went to EU countries (Ministère de Finance 2012). This interdependency illustrates well the structural power of the EU within the Euro-Mediterranean political space in general and towards Algeria specifically. In theoretical terms: The EU's logic of action – to foster free trade as an instrument to trigger 'modernisation' and political opening – as well as its unintended effects could be neglected if the EU's structural power would not be so strong.

Until now there are no extensive quantitative studies dealing with the impact of free trade implementation within the Algerian association agreement. The

---

11   In fact the EMFTA does not constitute a full-fledged Free Trade Area, since it applies only to the trade rules between the European Union (common market) on the one side and the individual MENA countries on the other side.

12   The Association Agreements with Tunisia and Morocco were signed in 1995 and 1996 and came into force in March 1998 and March 2000 respectively.

European Union, through EuropAid, indeed commissioned a report dealing with the implementation of the association agreement in Algeria (Nancy et al. 2009). This document however does not go into greater detail concerning structural effects for the Algerian industrial sector but mainly focuses on the development of actual trade flows. Therefore my study mainly relies on expert interviews conducted in Algiers in March and April 2011.

The question of the impact that the trade liberalisation and the cut down of tariffs within the framework of the EMP's association agreement is going to produce in the fragile Algerian economic context described above, is quite well answered by a statement of an Algerian economist, who stressed that the problem with the implementation of the association agreement 'is not about the loss of some Billion Dinars of custom duties, its about that we are losing our economy'.[13] Most interlocutors in Algiers criticized the focus of many studies dealing with the question of effects of free trade implementation solely with regard to the loss of customs duties.[14] Algerian economist Youcef Benabdallah emphasised that the cut down of tariffs is going to have the negative effect of 'probably amplifying the process of de- industrialisation' in Algeria (Benabdallah 2008: 307, own translation). The Algerian private sector is until now not able to replace the shrinking public industrial sector and create growth outside the HC sector. The biggest part of the private sector in Algeria (97 per cent) is constituted of small size enterprises employing less than 10 people. Most of these enterprises are active in the sector of non-changeable goods as services and the public construction sector. This is not least the result of trying to avoid external competition that is expected to intensify with the further implementation of the association agreement. Beside this effect another option for those enterprises is to avoid the formal economy altogether and continue business activities within the 'shadow' economy. Furthermore the assumed effects of improved efficiency, reallocation and growth in prospering labour-intensive export-orientated sectors is largely exaggerated if one considers – as was pointed out before – that Algeria already has a customs-free access to the European market since the 1970s within the framework of the cooperation agreements of the 'Global Mediterranean Policy'.[15]

Algerian authorities are more and more aware of the potential consequences of growing external competition. In the end of 2010 during the fifth association

---

13    Interview with Algerian economist, 23 March 2011, Algiers. Own Translation.

14    See for example Hoekman (1998). In April 2012 Algerian industrial minister Mohamed Benmeradi declared that Algeria has already lost about 3 Billion US dollars due to decreasing custom duties. However, the question of state revenue losses as a result of tariff cuts is more serious for countries that cannot rely on HC rents (as, for example, Tunisia or Morocco).

15    This policy framework, launched in 1972, was the Community's first comprehensive approach towards the Southern Mediterranean neighbourhood. It consisted of bilateral trade and aid agreements and had no multilateral dimension. Member countries gained a customs-free access for industrial products.

council[16] meeting Algeria officially requested a three year prorogation of the tariff cut schedule that originally was planned to be completed by 2017 (Korso 2011). Until July 2012 there have been eight rounds of negotiations concerning the Algerian request during which significant discord between the Algerian and the European side became apparent.[17] The Algerian side was specifically concerned about certain manufacturing sectors like textiles and electronics, whose products it wanted to be excluded of the tariffs reduction process.[18] Finally, in the end of August 2012 Algerian trade minister Mustapha Benbada announced that the negotiations were completed and Algeria obtained a three year prorogation of the final implementation of the Euro-Algerian free trade zone. In detail the new accord that came into power on 1 September 2012 refers to two lists of industrial products that originally would have been the object of a complete tariff abrogation in September 2012 and September 2017 respectively.[19]

Theoretically the prorogation of the tariff cuts schedule for specific products should allow the Algerian side to gain more time necessary for preparing Algerian enterprises to face European competition. However, Algerian observers of the negotiation process are highly sceptical about whether these measures will suffice to counter the effects of the EMFTA implementation (Lamriben 2011). To prepare Algerian companies with respect to the external opening the Algerian government in May 2010 additionally put up a 'programme de mise-à-niveau' (support programme) for 20,000 small- and medium-sized enterprises equipped with 386 billion Algerian Dinar (around 4 billion Euro). Yet, this programme seems to have some difficulties to take off because of bureaucratic hindrances[20] and many observers within Algerian academic and business circles estimate

---

16    The association council, which was established by the association agreement (Art. 92) deals with general questions of the agreements implementation and should meet once a year on ministerial level (Council 2002: 79).

17    At the 6th association council meeting in June 2011 the negotiation process was almost cancelled entirely because the European side refused to accept the Algerian propositions (Wafi 2011).

18    This demand was in accordance with the guidelines of the association agreement, which in its article 11 allows for 'exceptional measures' to be taken in the form of increases or reintroduction of customs duties for 'infant industries'. However, these measures can be applied for a maximum period of 3 years and should not affect more than 15 per cent of overall imported industrial products from the EU.

19    Overall there are three lists of products annexed to the association agreement. The tariffs for the products of the first list were already reduced to zero with the coming into force of the association agreement in 2005. 82 of the 1058 products on the first list were chosen for a partly reestablishment of customs and will be completely liberated only in 2016. Out of the second list the tariff cuts of 174 products will be postponed for 3 years and finalised only in 2020 (APS 2012).

20    Interview with European Commission Delegation representative, 29 March 2011, Algiers.

these measures as coming 'far too late'.[21] Together with the highly controversial measures of the 'loi de finance' (supplementary budget) of 2009[22] these somehow bustling provisions indicate the intention of the Algerian government to dam up the growing imports from the EU which increased by nearly 19 per cent from 20.7 billion US Dollars in 2010 to 24.5 billion in 2011 (Ministère de Finance 2012) and searching for some strategy of dealing with the consequences of the EMFTA implementation.

Taking into account these developments it is more than questionable that the EMFTA is going to have a positive effect on the structure of state income in Algeria and its rentier state character as one of the central concerns when it comes to the question of the political economy fundaments of authoritarian rule. Rather one could argue that, if external economic opening occurs in a rentier economy context such as the Algerian, where the private sector is heavily underdeveloped and the public manufacturing industry is not in the position to compete internationally, trade liberalisation and the external opening of the economy could produce the exact contrary effects. In such a context trade liberalisation is likely to further strengthen the structural dependence on external rents and precisely not diversify the income structure of the state by increasing the relative proportion of tax income.[23] Consequently, one can argue that the EU's structural power as the main trading partner for Algeria (and the Maghreb countries as a whole) is likely to produce results that contradict the EU's normative claims emphasised within the context of the EMP (Darbouche 2008).

## Algeria and the 'Arab Spring': Persistent Logics

Algeria revealed a certain 'immunity' regarding the wave of political upheavals that ran through several Arab countries since the beginning of 2011. Even if Algeria also witnessed different sorts of protests – beginning with large scale riots spreading to all major cities in the beginning of January 2011 – most observers described the country as constituting an exception within its revolutionary international environment (Achy 2012, Entelis 2011, Zoubir 2011). Nevertheless, also in Algeria social protests are a daily phenomenon, and not only since 2011. These protest movements, however, mostly do not take an explicitly political

---

21    Interview with Algerian economist, 23 March 2011, Algiers.

22    The two major controversial points within the 'LFC 2009' were an obligation for importers to use a 'crédit documentaire' as the only possible way to pay suppliers and the provision that every FDI-project had to have at least a 51 per cent share of an Algerian investor.

23    Some observers in Algeria even see a trend of 'défiscalisation': Because of the overall comfortable macro-economic situation and the rising income based on high energy-prices, the state is more and more likely to cut down taxes not related to the HC sector (Benabdallah 2008).

stance but claim an improvement of living conditions within the existing political system without putting into question the system itself. During the year 2011 there were dozens of different professional groupings (teachers, medics and even the police) protesting in the capital Algiers for better payment or an improvement of their working conditions. An overall change of the political regime or claims for particular political figures to step down were rarely part of their claims.[24]

Many scholars of the 'Arab Spring' have emphasised the economic aspects of the protest movements and revolutions that shattered the southern Mediterranean countries since the beginning of 2011 (Malik and Awadallah 2011, Murphy 2011, Springborg 2011). Although economic hardship was not the only or even the main motivation for protesters to go on the streets, it is indisputable that it contributed to the demonstrator's claims for social justice, dignity and freedom. Liberal economic reforms that in many cases went hand in hand with authoritarian and repressive forms of governance[25] were often described as playing an important role in increasing economic inequality and hardship for large parts of the population (Beinin 2009, Catusse 2008, Pioppi and Guazzone 2009). With the 'Arab Spring' it also became clear that liberal economic reforms – the way they were implemented for example in Tunisia and Egypt – contributed to political change only to the degree they offered a possibility for ruling elites to shift patronage networks towards the private sector, marginalising large parts of the population and thereby finally nourished the frustration that prompted the protests culminating in revolutionary events. Thus the 'Arab Spring' also poses new questions about the underlying causes of the development stalemate in the southern Mediterranean countries and their impact on the chances of using the revolutionary moment for building more balanced and equitable systems of governance.

Bearing in mind the previous section it becomes clear that the European Union's broader policy approach toward Algeria did not change during or as a consequence of the 'Arab Spring'. Although Algeria managed to achieve a rescheduling of tariff cuts for some product lines, the overall logic of action of inciting economic modernisation through the implementation of the EMFTA was not put into question. In a broader context this also becomes clear when one looks at the first policy reassessments of the EU during the 'Arab Spring'. The *Partnership for Democracy and Shared Prosperity with the Southern Mediterranean* (European Commission 2011) emphasised the need to 'accelerate the conclusion and EU approval of trade liberalisation agreements' and that the 'common objective which has been agreed in both regional and bilateral discussions with Southern Mediterranean partners is the establishment of Deep and Comprehensive Free Trade Areas' (European

---

24   The Algerian independent students' movement and smaller human rights groups were the only protest groups that included such claims in their public demonstrations.

25   Thus Tunisia under Ben Ali was often considered to be an economic 'success story' (Pfeifer 1999).

Commission 2011: 9).[26] As Teti points out, the first reactions of the EU to the upheavals in the several southern Mediterranean countries 'rather represents an intensification of – rather than a qualitative change in – the EU's pre 2011 commitment to free trade as a pathway to development and social justice' (Teti 2012: 278).

The critique of *neoliberalism* was unquestionably overstrained in the past and Malik and Awadallah (2011) certainly have a point when they claim that the absence of an efficient independent private sector is a problem in many countries of the region (and specifically in Algeria). However, the EU's logic of action of modernisation through economic opening is highly unlikely to contribute to the emergence of an efficient and independent private sector. Rather it will contribute to a limitation of possibilities to build a functioning manufacturing industrial sector in Algeria. The urgently needed diversification of the Algerian export sector in order to decrease the dependence on HC rents is unlikely to be supported by the EMFTA. Overall it became clear in the last 17 years since the beginning of the EMP that the EU's logic of action in the Mediterranean rather contributed to the aggravation of specific structural economic problems instead of being part of a solution for these problems. That said it is also questionable whether this policy is suitable with regard to the officially declared aims of the EMP. The European belief that smoothly managed economic opening would produce spillover effects to the political sphere by creating an economically and politically self confident and demanding new middle class has had to be abandoned.[27] During the 'Arab Spring' it was not well integrated economically prosperous entrepreneurs who claimed their part in political decision making,[28] it was structurally marginalised fractions of society. This diagnosis likewise questions the EU's security calculations. Liberal economic reforms appeared to rather increase socio-economic tensions than contributing to an overall improvement of living conditions and social peace.


## Conclusion

This chapter aimed at analysing the EU's logic of action toward its southern neighbouring state Algeria with a special emphasis on Euro-Algerian trade relations. It showed that the EU's policy approach towards the southern Mediterranean countries is shaped by a specific logic of action rooted in the EU's

---

26   Interestingly enough the document speaks of 'free trade areas' (plural), indicating the EU's will to maintain its own 'hub'-position within the Euro-Mediterranean trade regime.

27   On the role of middle classes during the 'Arab Spring' see the contribution of Rachid Ouaissa in this book.

28   In Egypt for example many 'business men' closely affiliated to the regime obviously feared losing their privileged positions and countered the claims of protesters (Abdel-Baki 2012).

identity and self understanding that is likely to bring on some unintended effects. On the theoretical level this diagnosis puts into question the conceptualisation of the EU as a normative power. The concept of normative power is perhaps able to describe the influence of identity patterns on the conceptualisation of foreign policy. But it reaches its limits when it comes to the question of the actual impacts of this policy in third countries. Instead, in order to fully understand the impact of the EU's normative approach, one has to look on the actual logic of action of the international actor EU. By complementing the Logics of Action framework with the structural power concept, this chapter shed light on the unintended effects of the EU's policy approach that put into question the EU's ambitions of external development, overall modernisation and democratisation.

Furthermore the chapter illustrated that the EU's logic of action was not significantly altered by the events of the 'Arab Spring'. Recent developments within the negotiations regarding the legal framework of EU-Algerian trade relations that took place in 2011 and 2012 elucidates that there are noticeable worries on the Algerian side about potential future effects of the further implementation of the EMFTA regarding the possibilities of developing a functioning diversified industrial sector in the country. The slight adaptation of the tariff cut schedule, however, does not change the overall EU approach. Thus the EU's logic of action in this policy field can serve as an example for a persistent pattern within the Euro-Mediterranean political space amidst the profound political changes in the region since the beginning of 2011. This diagnosis of persistence in the EU's logic of action could also serve as a starting point for future research. A central question should focus on why the EU's approach shows this sort of persistence, despite its negative effects concerning the development opportunities of the country and its overall questionable results concerning expected political spillovers.

## Bibliography

Abdel-Baki, M.A. 2012. Coalitions within the Egyptian Banking Sector: Catalysts of the Popular Revolution. *Business and Politics*, 14(1), Article 5.

Achy, L. 2012. Algeria Avoids the Arab Spring? *Carnegie Endowment* [Online, 31 May].Availableat:http://carnegieendowment.org/2012/05/31/algeria-avoids-arab-spring [accessed: 13 August 2012]

Amarouche, A. 2004. *Libéralisation économique et problèmes de la transition en Algérie*. Lyon: Université Lumière Lyon II.

APS. 2012. Le nouveau schema du démantèlement tarifaire Algérie-UE. *Algérie Presse Service*. 28 May 2012.

Barcelona Declaration. 1995. Adopted at the Euro-Mediterranean Conference, 27 and 28 November 1995.

Barbé, E. and A. Herranz Surrallés. 2010. Dynamics of Convergence and Differentiation in Euro-Mediterranean Relations: Towards Flexible Region-Building or Fragmentation? *Mediterranean Politics*, 15(2), 129-147.

Behr, T. 2011. *Europe and the Arab World: Towards a Principled Partnership.* Munich: Ludwig-Maximilians-Universität.

Beinin, J. 2009. Neo-Liberal Structural Adjustment, Political Demobilisation and Neo-Authoritarianism in Egypt. In *The Arab State and Neo-Liberal Globalization*, edited by L. Guazzone and D. Pioppi. Reading: Ithaca Press, 19-46.

Bellal, S. 2011. La crise du régime rentier d'accumulation en Algérie. *Revue de la régulation, Capitalisme, Institutions, Pouvoir* (2), Algiers.

Benabdallah, Y. 2008. *L'Algérie Face à la Mondialisation.* Algiers: Friedrich Ebert Stiftung.

Benabdallah, Y. 2009. L'économie algérienne entre réformes et ouverture: quelle priorité? In *Le Maghreb face aux defies de l'ouverture en Méditerranée*, edited by L. Abdelmalki et al. Paris: L'Harmattan, 305-331.

Bicchi, F. 2007. *European foreign policy making toward the Mediterranean.* Basingstoke: Palgrave Macmillan.

Bicchi, F. 2006. 'Our Size Fits All': normative power Europe and the Mediterranean. *Journal of European Public Policy*, 13(2), 286-303.

Bouzidi, A. 2008. *Industrialisation et Industrie en Algérie.* Algiers: Friedrich Ebert Stiftung.

Catusse, M. 2008. *Le temps des entrepreneurs? Politique et transformation du capitalism au Maroc.* Paris: Maisonneuve & Larose.

Council. 2002. Council of the European Union. *Euro-Mediterranean agreement establishing an association agreement between the European Community and its member states, of the one part, and the People's Democratic Republic of Algeria, of the other part.* Brussels, 12 April 2002.

Darbouche, H. 2008. EU Trade Policy towards North Africa, 1995-2007: Status Quo Intended. In *Who is a Normative Foreign Policy Actor? The European Union and its Global Partners*, edited by N. Tocci, Brussels: Center for European Policy, 57-61.

Destanne de Bernis, G. 1971. Industries Industrialisantes et les options algériennes. *Revue Tiers-Monde* (Juillet-Septembre), 545-563.

Dillman, B. 2002. International Markets and partial Reforms in North Africa: What Impact on Democratization? *Democratization*, 9(1), 63-86.

Djoufelkit, H. 2008. *Rente, développement du secteur productif et croissance en Algérie.* Document de Travail No. 64. Paris: Agence Française de Développement.

El Watan. 2012. 'L'Algérie est maintenant beaucoup plus écoutée par l'Europe'. *El Watan.* 30. August 2012.

Entelis, J.P. 2011. Algeria: democracy denied, and revived? *Journal of North African Studies*, 16(4), 653–678.

European Commission. 1992. COM(92)2000, *From the Single Act to Maastricht and beyond: The means to match our ambitions.* Address by Jacques Delors, President of the Commission, to the European Parliament.

European Commission. 2011. European Commission and High Representative of the EU for Foreign Affairs and Security Policy, *A Partnership for Democracy and Shared Prosperity with the Southern Mediterranean,* COM(2011) 200 final. 8 March 2011.

European Commission and High Representative of The Union For Foreign Affairs And Security Policy. 2011. *A New Response to a Changing Neighbourhood A review of European Neighbourhood Policy,* COM(2011) 303 final. 25 May 2011.

Evans, D. 1993. Visible and invisible hands in trade policy reform. In *States or markets? Neo-liberalism and the development policy debate,* edited by C. Colclough and J. Manor. Oxford: Oxford University Press, 48-77.

Foucault, M. 1995. *Discipline & Punish: The Birth of the Prison.* New York: Knopf Doubleday.

Gillespie, R. 2011. *Europe and its Arab Neighbors: New Wine in Old Skins* [Online]. Available at: http://carnegieendowment.org/2011/06/15/europe-and-its-arab-neighbors-new-wine-in-old-skins [accessed: 23 July 2012].

Hedir, M. 2003. *L'économie algérienne à l'épreuve de l'OMC.* Algier: Edition Anep.

Hoekman, B. 1998. Free trade agreements in the Mediterranean: a regional path towards liberalisation. *Journal of North African Studies,* 3(2), 89-104.

Holden, P. 2009. *In search of structural power: EU aid policy as a global political instrument.* Farnham: Ashgate.

Hunt, D. 2005. Implications of the Free Trade Agreements between the EU and the Maghrib Economies for Employment in the Latter, Given Current Trends in the North African Exports: Cline's Fallacy of Composition Revisited. *Journal of North African Studies,* 10(2), 201-221.

Jünemann, A. 1999. Europas Mittelmeerpolitik im regionalen und globalen Wandel: Interessen und Zielkonflikte. In *Die Mittelmeerpolitik der EU,* edited by W. Zippel. Baden-Baden: Nomos, 29-64.

Jünemann, A. 2010. Externe Demokratieförderung im südlichen Mittelmeerraum. Ein rollentheoretischer Erklärungsansatz für die Kluft zwischen Anspruch und Wirklichkeit in den EU-Außenbeziehungen. In *Der Nahe Osten im Umbruch. Zwischen Transformation und Autoritarismus* edited by M. Beck et al. Wiesbaden: VS-Verlag, 151-174.

Korso, M. 2011. Algérie-UE: Les négociations pour le report du démantèlement tarifaire à mi parcours. *Maghrebemergent* [Online, 22 March]. Available at:http://www.djazairess.com/fr/-maghrebemergent/2694 [accessed: 13 December 2012].

Lamriben, H. 2011. Alger a 'très mal négocié' le démantèlement tarifaire. *El Watan.* 31 March.

Lavenex, S. and F. Schimmelfennig. 2009. EU rules beyond EU borders: theorizing external governance in European politics. *Journal of European Public Policy,* 16(6), 791-812.

Lowi, M.R. 2009. *Oil wealth and the poverty of politics Algeria compared.* Cambridge: Cambridge University Press.

Luciani, G. 1990. Allocation vs. Production States. In *The Arab state*, edited by G. Luciani. Berkeley/New York: University of California Press, 65-84.

Malik, A. and B. Awadallah. 2011. *The Economics of the Arab Spring.* OxCarre Research Paper No. 79. Oxford: Oxford Centre for the Analysis of Resource Rich Economies.

Manners, I. 2002. Normative Power Europe: A Contradiction in Terms? *Journal of Common Market Studies*, 40(2), 235-258.

Martin, I. 2007. In Search of Development Along the Southern Border: The Economic Models Underlying the Euro-Mediterranean Partnership and the European Neighbourhood Policy'. In *Bridging the Gap: the Role of Trade and FDI in the Mediterranean*, edited by M. Ferragina. Naples, 115-141.

Mattes, H. 2012. *50 Jahre Unabhängigkit Algeriens: Konfliktbeladene Vergangenheit, schwierige Zukunft.* GIGA-Fokus Paper No.7. Hamburg: GIGA-Institute.

Ministère de Finance. 2012. *Statistiques du commerce exterieur de l'Algerie (Période: année 2011)*, Rapport du Ministère des Finances Algérien, Direction Générale des Douanes [Online]. Available at: www.douane.gov.dz/Rapports%20periodiques.html [accessed: 13 August 2012].

Monar, J. 1999. Die interne Dimension der Mittelmeerpolitik der Europäischen Union: Institutionelle und verfahrensmäßige Probleme. In *Die Mittelmeerpolitik der EU*, edited by W. Zippel. Baden-Baden: Nomos, 65-90.

Murphy, E.C. 2011. The Tunisian Uprising and the Precarious Path to Democracy. *Mediterranean Politics*, 16(2), 299-305.

Nancy, G. et al. 2009. *Evaluation de l'état d'exécution de l'Accord d'Association Algérie-UE.* Rapport Final. Algiers.

Ouaissa, R. 2005. *Staatsklasse als Entscheidungsakteur in den Ländern der Dritten Welt.* Münster: Lit-Verlag.

Pace, M. 2007. The Construction of EU Normative Power. *Journal of Common Market Studies*, 45(5), 1041-1064.

Pfeifer, K. 1999. How Tunisia, Morocco, Jordan and even Egypt became IMF 'Success Stories' in the 1990s. *Middle East Report* (210), 23-27.

Pioppi, D. and L.Guazzone. 2009. Interpreting Change in the Arab World. In *The Arab State and the Neo-Liberal Globalization. The Restructuring of State Power in the Middle East*, edited by D. Pioppi and L. Guazzone. Reading: Ithaca Press, 1-18.

Raffinot, M. and Jacquemot, P. 1977. *Le capitalisme d'État algérien.* Paris: Maspero.

Rhein, E. 1998. The New Euro-Mediterranean Partnership. In *Towards Rival Regionalism? US and EU Regional Regulatory Regime Building*, edited by J. van Scherpenberg and E. Thiel. Baden-Baden: Nomos, 164-182.

Schumacher, T. 2005. *Die Europäische Union als internationaler Akteur im südlichen Mittelmeerraum.* Baden-Baden: Nomos.

Smith, K.E. 2005. Beyond the civilian power EU debate. *Politique européenne*, 17(3), 63-82.

Springborg, R. 2011. The Political Economy of the Arab Spring. *Mediterranean Politics*, 16(3), 427–433.

Strange, S. 1988. *States and Markets*. New York: Continuum.

Talahite, F. 2002. Die wirtschaftliche Situation in Algerien. In *Im Herzen Algeriens, das Jahrzehnt des Terrorismus*, edited by M. von Graffenried and S. Hammouche. Bern: Benteli.

Teti, A. 2012. The EU's First Response to the 'Arab Spring': A Critical Discourse Analysis of the Partnership for Democracy and Shared Prosperity. *Mediterranean Politics*, 17(3), 266-284.

Wafi, M. 2011. Accord d'association avec l'UE: Bruxelles refuse la demande algérienne. *Le Quotidien d'Oran*, 20 June.

Weiss, D. 2002. Europa und die arabischen Länder Krisenpotenziale im südlichen Mittelmeerraum. In *Aus Politik und Zeitgeschichte 19-20*, Berlin: Bundeszentrale für politische Bildung.

Werenfels, I. 2007. *Managing instability in Algeria: elites and political change since 1995*. London: Routledge.

Youngs, R. 1999. The Barcelona Process after the UK Presidency. *Mediterranean Politics*, 4(1), 1-21.

Zoubir, Y. 2011. The Arab Spring: Is Algeria the exception? *EuroMeSCo Policy Brief No. 17*.

# PART II
# Persistence and Change in Selected Countries

Chapter 6

# A Revolution in the Logics of Action? Renegotiating the Authoritarian Social Contract in Egypt[1]

Cilja Harders

## Introduction

More than two years after the 'wall of fear' was brought down by unprecedented mass mobilisation in many Arab countries, the optimism of young and old revolutionaries seems to fade. On the one hand, the region has witnessed exceptional mobilisation, politicisation and a myriad of new activisms. The peoples are using newly won freedom, exercising citizenship and claiming unprecedented rights. On the other hand, security apparatuses, new and old, constantly lash out repression and violence. The constant power struggle, which took a decisively violent turn in July 2013, led to deep polarisation and strengthened exclusionary politics. The most heated conflict – the conflict about the role of religion and religious forces in public life – has only partly been channeled into institutionalised arenas of non-violent contestation about the future of state-society relations in the region. Europe and the USA are stuck in their well-known 'stability-democracy' dilemma and tend to compromise on human rights and serious reform efforts.

The impact of the so-called 'Arab spring' on the political systems in the region is context specific, at times contradictory and rapidly changes over time. The following chapter will use the 'authoritarian social contract' as a starting point of an analysis of persistence and change in Egyptian domestic politics. The metaphor of the contract implies that state-society relations are regulated according to certain general rules or 'logics of action' that dominated these before the mass mobilisation of January 2011. Did these logics of action change? And if they did, what is the quality of change and what does this mean for future developments in Egypt?

---

1   This chapter is based partly on earlier German publications (Harders 2002, 2012). This contribution has benefitted from debates and critical comments of numerous Egyptian and German colleagues and friends to whom I am deeply indebted. I owe special thanks to the editors as well as Heba Amr Hussein, Daniel Kumitz, Hania Sobhy und Dina El-Sharnouby for their comments. I thank Daniel Kumitz for his translation of an earlier German version of this text and Hend Labib for helping with editing and formatting.

In order to answer these questions, I will use the Logics of Action (LoA) approach as developed by Horst et al. (in this volume). LoA is based on the assumption that political processes are shaped through the co-determination of agents and structures in a given space and time. The approach combines structuralist and actor-oriented arguments, thus seeks to construct a complex argument rather than search for monocausal explanations of political trajectories. As I argued elsewhere in more detail, the dynamics of mass protest, revolution and its aftermath should be understood in an actor-oriented way. Political transformations are the product of logics of action of contentious agents and the impact their actions had on existing structures and vice versa (Harders 2011 and other papers in *Arbeitsstelle Politik des Vorderen Orients* 2011). In order to assess the quality of change, the approach presented in this volume, LoA, analyses the belief systems of actors. It differentiates between deep core, policy core and secondary beliefs of a given collective or individual actor. Deep core beliefs rarely change, whereas policy core beliefs do change, as actors have a more strategic take on them. If change is restricted to secondary beliefs this will not lead to substantial transformation of a given structure (Horst et al. in this volume). According to the LoA approach, logics of action are time and context specific and need to be assessed against this background. In order to analyse the Egyptian transformation, I delineate five stages.[2] Firstly, a preparatory stage of mass mobilisation, then secondly the revolutionary situation of the 18 days of Tahrir Square, which ended with Mubarak's resignation, and thirdly the more than 16 months of military rule under the Supreme Council of Armed Forces (SCAF). This was followed fourthly by a year of Islamist rule under freely elected President Mohamed Morsi from 30 June 2012 to 3 July 2013. His reign was ended by a mass protest followed by a military coup. The military, then, installed a civil government and proposed a roadmap for constitutional amendments, and elections.

In the following section two, I will first briefly introduce the general background of the ambivalent developments in the region during the last 20 years, which can be dubbed 'transformation without transition'. I will then discuss the major logics of action underlying the authoritarian social contract in section three. In section four I analyse how under the quite repressive conditions in Egypt in 2011 revolutionary mass mobilisation was possible in the first place. In section five, I discuss the dominant new and old actors in the political field, trying to understand

---

2    The following account is based on secondary analysis of available literature and qualitative interviews conducted in Cairo in 2011 and 2012. A note of caution is necessary, though. In order to assess possible changes in deep core beliefs, a different type of research would be necessary. So far, there is not much systematic data available about the perceptions, hopes and assessments of the broader population, ruling and oppositional groups alike. Thus, the realities of the daily formal and informal, individual and collective renegotiations of the Egyptian transformation are part of a much more complex, ambivalent and contradictory picture than this analysis can ever hope to draw.

their logics of action and if and how these are reproduced or challenged throughout the Egyptian transformation.

All in all, it is my assessment that the sheer existence of continuous mass mobilisation in January and February 2011 already represents a major shift in the authoritarian logics of action. Rather than acting according to the well-known patterns of depoliticisation, fear and acquiescence in face of repression, the citizens took to the street in order to fight for 'bread, freedom, dignity and social justice'. This revolutionary experience[3] of reclaiming the political as space of peaceful negotiations of state-society relations has led to a major outcome of the second stage of the revolution: the ongoing politicisation and mobilisation of a previously demobilised population. The people tore down the 'wall of fear' and this represents deep change. In the third and fourth stages of the Egyptian transformation, which are characterised by a continuous power struggle between the military, the Muslim Brotherhood and other oppositional forces, the representatives of the old regime and the politicised populace, the degree of change has been less intense. The current fifth stage, which is dominated by violence, repression and indirect military rule seems to build even more on Mubarak-style logics of action. I assert that the authoritarian social contract has been challenged but – albeit unsurprisingly – not radically altered. The deep core and policy core beliefs of the former regime actors, the military and the security apparatus did not substantially change. At the same time, the ongoing confrontations and the high degree of political mobilisation are an indicator that the core beliefs of some parts of the Egyptian public did, however, indeed change. They struggle for a radical renegotiation of the authoritarian social contract and the logics of action it builds on. These attempts are met by violence and repression on the part of the ruling elites.

## Transformation without Transition

The societies in Maghreb and Mashreq have been undergoing important social, cultural and economic transformations for the last decade and more, which have been initiated by different developments such as demographic change, change in media accessibility, and economic reform. In the young societies of today the economic development cannot keep pace with the demographic change (UNDP 2002, EUCOM 2011). Neoliberal reform and the crisis of older development models have led, on the one hand, to high growth rates and good macroeconomic

---

3    If the Egyptian transformation can still be called a revolution or rather a popular mass movement, which turned into a coup for a second time between 2011 and 2013 is hotly contested inside and outside the country. Following McAdam/Tilly/Tarrow (1996: 165) I hold that Egypt went through different 'revolutionary situations' since 2011 but these processes did so far not create 'revolutionary outcomes'. The whole process is called 'transformation' which means open-ended processes of social and political change.

indicators, but on the other hand also increased inequality and indebtedness (Zorob 2012).

What is more, the new pluralistic media landscapes of digital and satellite networks, which developed over the last years, have greatly contributed to better diffusion of information and initiated a different culture of public debate. This in turn changed the general political culture in the region (Lynch 2007, Radsch 2008, Population Council 2010). Simultaneously with the demographic and media change, the gender and generational relations have changed as well. This becomes evident in the growing challenging of patriarchal structures in the private sphere (Salah 2011, Amar 2011a, UNDP 2006, Jünemann in this volume). Last, not least, the denationalisation of politics has not stopped at the authoritarian regimes of the region either, bringing new transnational actors such as Islamists or human rights networks to the fore (Dessouki and Korany 2008).

These deep cutting social changes have not substantially altered the logics of action of the ruling authoritarian elites. Rather than addressing the antagonisms created by these processes of social transformation, powerholders all over the region relied on a programme of 'authoritarian modernisation' (Heydemann 2007, Schlumberger 2007) within the framework of an authoritarian social contract. This led to a highly contradictory process of social transformation without political transition as I have elaborated elsewhere in greater detail (Harders 2002).

The authoritarian social contract that underlies these processes generates the 'rules of the game' to be followed by both regime elites and their opponents. In a nutshell, its mechanisms can be described as follows: The old Nasserist social contract promised development and wealth in exchange for loyalty that could be controlled and depoliticised through clientelist channels. I hold, in addition, that a new social contract of informality emerged in the 1990s, which kept the depoliticising aspect of the Nasserist relationship between state and society, but in the age of neoliberal economic reform minimised the role of welfare (Harders 2002, Harders 2012, Catusse/Destremau/Verdier 2009). Rights and claims of citizens are replaced by possibilities of informal action and clientelist networks, which are hard to enforce, as I will show later in detail. The major logic of action of the ruling group is centred on sustaining political and economic power at any cost and it is based on core regime beliefs such as a deep mistrust against the populace, fear of 'the street' and any autonomous citizen activity.

Even though the deeply non-democratic and violent nature of the authoritarian social contract was and is well known to the international actors, European and American policies in the region have been shaped by strategies that favour authoritarian stability at the expense of systematic human rights. Thus, international donors have been crucial for providing military, economic and developmental aid as well as legitimacy to authoritarian regimes in the region (Dessouki/Korany 2008). Even though there was growing American pressure for reform after 9/11, these efforts decreased again when Hamas won the 2006 Palestinian elections. The Arab regimes have presented their model of authoritarian modernisation as compatible with and catering to the highly securitised European and US-American interests in the region. At the same time, the EU is normatively bound to democracy and human rights promotion and finds itself caught in a 'security-democracy dilemma' (Jünemann 2009:167). Since the inception of the Barcelona Process, 'Europe' has always opted for security and stability and thus compromised on its own human rights standards hoping that, miraculously, dialogue and upholding pressure on the regimes would lead to change. These international logics of action have so far not been radically challenged (Tocci 2011).


## The Logics of Action of the Authoritarian Social Contract

The authoritarian social contract generated five major regime strategies related to its main logic of action of controlling the population and securing the ruling elites' power. These are: (i) limited political liberalisation, (ii) Islamisation, (iii) repression, (iv) informalisation, and (v) limited economic liberalisation (Harders 2002, 2003). These strategies have provided for decades of regime survival even in the face of massive challenges, on the one hand. On the other hand, they have also developed non-intended effects that have partially turned against the regime. In the following, I will briefly describe the five strategies while 'repression' and 'limited political liberalisation' will be further elaborated later.

*Limited political liberalisation* has already taken place in almost all Arab states in different waves and varying depth since the mid-1970s. This includes elections, multi-party systems, or popular referendums. Still, the boundaries of oppositional engagement have always been defined by the regime. The limited and controlled liberalisation has provided the ruling elites with the possibility to coopt or include both, potential or actual, dissidents and relevant social groups into the system. Cooptation is also part of a 'divide and rule' strategy, which tries to deepen existing splits between e.g. religious and secular or left and (neo)liberal forces and set them against each other. Even though at times, secular and religious forces stood for parliamentary elections on shared lists. Both the politics of divide and rule and the shifting strategic alliances of the opposition itself, weakened the impact of these groups (Makram-Ebeid 1989, Kienle 2001). This situation has caused considerable unease among the representatives of a young generation of activists in Egypt from the left *Tagammu'* party as well as from the Muslim Brotherhood. Thus Egypt's 2011 'revolutionary youth' embraced a politics without the 'old slogans' trying to overcome the well-known ideological divides and hypocrisy of a tamed opposition. This mood was dominant in the second stage of the Egyptian revolution but did not survive the next stages, which were marked by a strong revival of new and old political forces in their ideological diversity.

On the other hand, limited liberalisation has led to a factual pluralisation of the political field and thus to non-intended effects of empowerment and politicisation. For even actors integrated in institutions stripped of their democratic function had developed their own logics of action, which toyed with taking the staged front serious. Thereby the authority of the regime was challenged time and again even before the mass protests of 2011, and even in the most controlled political spaces such as local and national elections. For example in 2010, the extensive exclusion even of the coopted parliamentary opposition and the ruling National Democratic Party (NDP) dissidents at these elections irritated and caused the dissociation of regime followers.

The second major strategy generated by the authoritarian logic of action is *Islamisation*. By this the Egyptian regime reacted to the challenge from radical Islamist forces, which in the 1980s and 1990s fought the regime at times even by violence. Islamisation is the attempt of the ruling elites to fight the cultural hegemony, which religious actors had managed to achieve, by appearing more religious than the Islamists themselves. This translated into severe censorship, recurring scandals about 'blasphemic' literature, show trials against homosexuals and so-called 'Satanists' – or so labelled hard-rock fans – or media campaigns against Western immorality and indecency. The fight against Islamist groups, thus, was fought with violence and repression on the one hand, and by means of cultural policies on the other hand (Ismail 2006, Bayat 2007, Kandil 2011, Büchs 2011). Especially in the second stage of the revolution, religious mobilisation did not play an important role and the Brotherhood was acting along its publicly stated rationale of 'participation not domination'. This changed again in the election campaigns of 2011–12 and the religious discourse grew intensively with a parliament dominated by religious forces and the president being a member of the Muslim Brotherhood. Christian Copts in turn are threatened by Islamists in government and by sectarian violence that has happened in different parts of post-Mubarak Egypt. The violence sadly intensified after the coup of 2013, when Christian Egyptians were again brutally attacked (Tadros 2011 a, b).

*Repression* is a basic pillar of any authoritarian domination. In Egypt it has been legalised by the constitution of 1971, criminal law and the state of emergency which since 1967 has been interrupted only by an 18 month break before Sadat's murder and Mubarak's rise to power. The Egyptian regime has used repression not only against political opponents, but regularly also against ordinary citizens. Merchants on the pavement, students on campus and youths who looked 'suspicious' have been arrested, harassed and beaten up. Torture was (and most probably is again) a daily occurrence (HRW 2012, ai 2011, el-Nadeem 2012) and it came with other types of discursive repression such as media campaigns against opponents and incitement of fear and chaos as I will show in the next section (Sowers/Toensing 2012).

The fourth strategy generated by the authoritarian logic of action is the *informalisation* of state-society relations. It stands for a deeply rooted system of interdependent formal and informal institutions and practices. This includes practices such as informal conflict resolution, prevalence of family and neighbourhood networks as well as clientelism and corruption. The opening of informal spaces of action is meant to replace citizenship rights. It is my argument, that the old Nasserist social contract has been replaced by a 'social contract of informality' (Harders 2002, 2003). In the social contract of informality political exclusion and control are no longer 'paid off' by welfare benefits but only through the opening of informal scopes of action. Thus, for example, the poor inhabitants of Egyptian cities acquire wasteland for affordable construction – leading to enormous informal city quarters. Sewer pipes are laid by people themselves, electricity is diverted and so is water. Asef Bayat (1997) has coined this process 'quiet encroachment', a behaviour that encompasses the quiet, comprehensive, continuous, individual and collective acquisition of resources, mostly to ensure survival. Informal networks based on family, neighbourhood, or common origin are crucial in securing livelihood not only for the poor. In addition, informalisation as corruption that is ubiquitous and relies on '*wasta*' or 'connections' in order to secure service is widespread regardless of social class. Formal institutions like elections are closely linked with informal institutions and practices such as family and spatial networks, saving associations and mechanisms of informal conflict mediation (Singerman 1996, Singerman and Amar 2006). Especially, in the third and fourth stages of the revolution, the withdrawal of security forces and the breakdown of some of the coercive state functions led to a new wave of informal up to illegal activities e.g. in private construction, informal sector trading, and adaptation of public infrastructure to local needs (Harders 2013).

Still, before the revolution, this informal arrangement has increasingly become fragile due to the withdrawal of the state through privatisation and the reduction of subsidies. Given the privatisation of government services it becomes increasingly difficult to acquire public goods such as electricity informally and free of charge. The angry protests around the food crisis in 2008 have shown that people are well aware of the link between economics and politics. It was not just about bread, but also about a critique of corruption. Thus an initially 'apolitical' demand for subsidised foodstuffs was embedded in a broader context of criticising a corrupt and ruthless regime. This reverberated in the Tahrir Square slogans of 'Bread, Freedom and Dignity'.

At the same time, people built on local informal networks in order to set up popular committees or '*legan sha'biyya*' throughout the days of confrontation at Tahrir and beyond. These committees served immediate security needs but were also often, in later stages of the revolution, used in order to organise collective political action or self help activities. Thereby they undermined the regime strategy to purposely cause chaos, destabilisation and incitement of violence by removing regular security forces and using different types of informal groups in order to frighten ordinary citizens in the second and third stage of the revolution. This is closely linked to regime repression through armed gangs of thugs, so-called *baltagiyya* and the public discourse about it. These groups are mostly rooted in the criminal milieu and informally supplement police and state security forces and were regularly deployed during election times under Mubarak. They also rely on informal neighbourhood or family networks and have been integrated in various activities in the grey zone between criminality and informality in poor urban quarters (Harders 2002).

Informalisation is linked to the fifth strategy, *limited economical liberalisation*. Since 2004, Egypt has seen an increased move to privatisation and liberalisation. The main beneficiaries were those economic and political elites who were close to the president's son Gamal Mubarak (Demmelhuber and Roll 2007, Wurzel 2007). They were crucial in preparing and implementing the 'inheritance strategy' followed by his father. Until the protests in January 2011, many of these core elites were members of the cabinet and often in charge of industry-related portfolios. Structural adjustment and liberalisation policies were implemented with the active encouragement of both the US and the EU; as these external actors are the major proponents of trade liberalisation, reduction of state activity and economic reform geared towards globally accessible markets (Zorob 2012). An oligarchic system developed in almost no time whose main actors, unlike the elites of the 1990s, were increasingly willing to roll off the costs of liberalisation and privatisation like inflation, food crises, unemployment, rising land property and real estate prices and reduction of subsidies onto the pauperising majority regardless of long term development considerations. As the economic situation aggravated, even previously little protest-oriented population groups started to consider resistance as the growing labour movement has amply shown (Beinin/Variel 2011, El-Mahdi and Marfleet 2009, Lübben 2012, Baheyya 2008). These strategies of economic liberalisation also impacted on the elites, as they have dealt a serious blow to Egypt's military, which is an important business actor and among other things runs shopping malls and tourist enterprises (Müller-Mellin 2011, Albrecht and Bishara 2011).

Summing up, the authoritarian informal social contract implies five major strategies: limited political liberalisation, limited economic liberalisation, informalisation, repression and Islamisation. The logics of action of the ruling elites are driven by the strong will to hang on to power in the face of outright political and developmental failure. The authoritarian 'deal' – buying acquiescence with welfare state measures – has increasingly come under pressure in the last decade. This in turn creates depoliticisation, frustration and demobilisation as logics of action on the other side, 'the population'. Did these logics of action and the mechanisms of the authoritarian social contract change between 2011 and 2013? In order to answer this question I will first look at repression and violence as major ingredients of coercive power in non-democratic settings. I will then have a closer look at the political field in the different stages of the Egyptian transformation.

## Time and Coercive Power in the Egyptian Revolution

In order to grasp these dynamics, I suggest delineating four major stages of the Egyptian transformation.

The first stage of preparatory mobilisation began in 2000 with solidarity marches for the second Palestinian Intifada. According to activists, Mubarak's resignation was demanded for the first time at Cairo University Campus at a pro-Intifada march.[4] This decade between 2000 and 2011 also saw a re-emerging workers movement and the advent of 'Kifaya – it is enough', as I will explore in greater detail in the next section. During this time, violence mostly originated from regime actors such as regular security forces and the informal *baltagiyya*. Protests were systematically oppressed and demonstrations were small, apart from some Kifaya and Brotherhood rallies in the mid-2000s (El-Mahdi and Marfleet 2009, Kohstall 2006). Only the 'Ultras', football fans of the big clubs, regularly challenged the security forces and took their chances in street battles with the police (Besheer 2011).

Then the second stage of revolutionary mass mobilisation followed from 25 January to 11 February 2011, which ended with Mubarak's resignation. Obviously the main actors were able to form a broad coalition of labour movement, liberal youth and young Muslim Brotherhood activists. Starting from 25 January, this coalition was continuously growing even in the face of brutal repression, which happened at all stages of the Egyptian revolution (El-Ghobashi 2011, Sowers and Toensing 2012, Harders and König forthcoming). At the same time, those who occupied Tahrir Square were increasingly willing to defend the public space, which they conquered physically and symbolically, for days on end with stones and barricades against assaults by police and security forces. This was crucial for the success of the protesters as El-Ghobashy (2011: 2) argues convincingly. The quick spatial spread of protests to other cities in the country between 25 and 28 January helped to overcome the old divides between the major groups and encouraged those political forces, which were reluctant to participate in the first place. As early as 28 January 2011, the police completely withdrew from the scene in the face of growing resistance and burning police stations all over the country. Even though many activists considered this a victory and a greatly empowering experience, it was also part of a counter revolutionary strategy of the old regime. These elites tried to purposely cause chaos, destabilisation and insecurity on the streets and in public perceptions.

After initial hesitation, the military declared its support for the revolutionary demands and announced abstinence from violence thus paving the ground for the third stage, which started after the resignation of Mubarak and lasted until freely elected President Morsi entered office on 30 June 2012. During these more than 16 months of open military rule by the Supreme Council of the Armed Forces (SCAF), Egypt witnessed ongoing violent confrontations including many dead and wounded as I will discuss in further detail in section five. At the same time, steps towards institutional change and renewal, such as parliamentary and presidential elections, were taken. The Muslim Brotherhood and the Military were engaged in a constant tug-of-war between uneasy alliances and outright confrontation (El-Ghobashy 2012). The fourth stage started when President Mohamed Morsi

---

4    As explained by Zyad el-Elaimi, Egyptian MP for the Social Democratic Party Egypt and member of a revolutionary youth group on 8 May 2012 during a presentation at the Free University Berlin.

entered office at the end of June 2012 and ended with the 'tamarrud' (rebellion)-led mass uprising against Islamist rule and the then following military intervention, which deposed Morsi on 3 July 2013. His rule, too, was marked by violent confrontations on the one hand and ongoing mobilisation and politicisation on the other. The extremely weak performance of the government and growing fear of 'brotherhoodisation' or outright state failure let to high degrees of popular mobilisation. This was in turn used by the military to intervene as 'arbiter' in order to prevent further conflict. The coup turned into massive bloodshed in summer 2013, when the civil government, which was put into power by the generals, ordered the eviction of Muslim Brotherhood protest camps in Cairo and put all major Brotherhood leaders including former president Morsi into prison (Baheyya 2013, Shalakany 2013).

Summing up, the logics of action of the authoritarian informal social contract, which heavily built on discursive and material repression, did not substantially change in all stages of the transformation. Rather than encouraging peaceful deliberation on contested issues, ruling secular and religious forces as well as parts of the opposition – are counting on violence and repression in order to control the newly politicised and still massively discontent population.

## Renegotiating the Authoritarian Informal Social Contract

In the following, I will cast a closer look at the actors of change and persistence, trying to gauge the quality of change, which was and still is brought about in the ongoing struggle between those who wish to fundamentally renegotiate state-society relations and those who resist such attempts. Thus I ask whether the old strategy of limited and controlled political liberalisation has been substantially challenged by the revolution? I differentiate two groups – albeit with different participants in the different stages of the transition – consist of the 'regime coalition' and 'opposition' (Schubert/Tetzlaff/Vennewald 1994). Obviously, this present analysis only comprises the collective and organised actors and cannot trace in any detail the changing positions actors took in the different stages of the revolution. This constant political readjustment of collective and individual oppositional actors is one major outcome of a newly liberated political field. But the focus on these groups neglects those parts of the population who would not join a demonstration regardless of their political views – the 'sofa party'. These more or less silent majorities only seem to come into play in times of election or public mass mobilisation.

### Agents of Change

In Egypt a small but growing number of activists have been fundamentally challenging the authoritarian social contract and daring to fight for change during the last decade and since. Some of these groups have articulated general critiques of authoritarian rule; others came to challenge this rule by starting from their practical needs such as neighbourhood activities, food riots or striking workers. The 2011 mass mobilisation built on the experience and emergence of social movements such as the *Kifaya!* ('Enough!'), the women's or the labour movement. *Kifaya!* was very actively campaigning in 2004/2005 against another term for Mubarak, building a broad coalition between secular and religious forces and creating a shared experience on which many activists later relied (Kohstall 2006). At the same time, many local protest activities, such as activism against environmental pollution in the vicinity of Alexandria or food riots in 2007 and 2008, sprang up. Human rights activists started to document police violence on YouTube and Facebook. Women's groups campaigned for rights equality and emancipation (Baheyya 2008, El-Mahdi and Marfleet 2009, Korany and El-Mahdi 2012). Since 2006, strikes have been taking place in the entire country with growing intensity, as many workers have been successful with demands for increasing wages or social protection. In 2007 even the property tax officers went on strike – including sit-ins in front of authorities and government buildings. This in turn strengthened the emerging independent union movement that formed against the massive resistance of the regime unions and that was crucial in 2011 (Beinin 2011, Beinin and Variel 2011, Lübben 2012). Simultaneously, the brutal clampdown on the workers in the textile industry town Mahalla al-Kubra ignited solidarity activities by other activists and thus bridged the old gap between needs-oriented workers, activism and regime critics. This solidarity movement tested new ground by calling for the first time, on 6 April 2008, for a general strike and other forms of civil disobedience afterwards. This was initiated by the very 'April 6 Youth' that should become so important in the second stage of the revolution in Egypt.

Since then, many of these actors, which brought about change, have been excluded from the more institutionalised politics of the third and fourth phase. Their logics of action often build on autonomy, independence and participation. This again is based on an either class oriented, Marxist or liberal, social democratic critique of the old system. Their aim is the 'ongoing revolution' and they struggle to reach real change along the lines of the major calls of the revolution: '*al-sha'ab yurid isqat an-nizam*' – 'the people wants to bring down the system' and '*aish, huriyya, 'adala igtima'iyya*' – 'bread, freedom and social justice'.

In order to achieve this, activists have employed different strategies: building new coalitions among independent activists, joining parties or campaigns and thus entering the institutional realm. Others focus on grass roots work and again others have completely given up on activism. Most of these actors build on public contention, time and again claiming Tahrir and other symbolic and material spaces in order to mobilise against restoration, ongoing violence and politics of exclusion (El-Ghobashi 2012, Schielke 2012).

Next to the new youth and movement opposition organised in networks and oriented towards deliberation, the classical party opposition did play a role in all stages of the revolution, albeit in a limited way. The established opposition parties including the fiercely opposed Muslim Brotherhood were the symbol of a powerless opposition, which more or less voluntarily allowed itself to be coopted in a staged facade democracy under Mubarak. But there are huge differences between generations and individual leaders. For example, the Wafd party, the supporters of Elbaradei and the former presidential candidate Ayman Nour participated in the calls for 25 January, Muslim Brotherhood, the left Tagammu' and the Nasserist party did not (El-Ghobashy 2011). Further, in the second stage individual 'important persons' in economy, politics and science formed different *ad hoc* groups and also initiated new parties after the resignation of Mubarak. Since then, Egypt has witnessed an unprecedented multiplication of organised activism but also a lot of volatility, short-term strategic shifts, construction and deconstruction of coalitions and the re-emergence of old divisions. Thus, even though many of these oppositional actors do share some logics of action and agree on their general challenge of the authoritarian deal, the capacity to build lasting coalitions and to overcome the disturbing effects of decades of an authoritarian political culture is not very strong. This became aptly clear in the third and fourth stage of the transformation.

Over 40 parties nominated more than 6000 candidates for the parliamentary elections in November/December 2011 and January 2012 (Jadaliyya 2012a). In this campaign, the old structural weaknesses of the opposition such as weak local embeddedness, partially over-aged leadership, lack of intra party democracy, lack of programmatic profile backfired, especially on the secular, liberal and newly formed revolutionary forces. They won only about 23 per cent of seats in the new parliament. The Wafd party formed the largest block with 41 seats, followed by the Social Democratic Party and the party of 'Free Egyptians'. The revolutionary youth was almost not represented at all and only 12 women won seats (Jadaliyya 2012a). The rest of the seats went to Islamist parties. The parliament, however, only saw a limited lifespan: it was dissolved in June 2012 by the SCAF based on a ruling of the Supreme Constitutional Court and since then the shura council was used as 'quasi parliament'. In general , the roadmap to transition, which was laid out by SCAF in 2011, was inherently problematic and non-democratic because it timed the drafting of a constitution to occur only after the election of executive and legislative powers. At the same time, these institutional processes were highly significant because they indicated change and continuity in public perceptions. Whereas the parliament was strongly dominated by religious forces in the first round of the presidential elections in 2011, non-religious forces including the representative of the old regime, attracted more than 55 per cent of the electorate with Morsi gaining 25.3 per cent, Shafik 23.74 per cent, Sabbahi 21.60 per cent, Abul-Futuh 17.93 per cent and Moussa 10.97 per cent of the ballot in early summer of 2012. The vote on the constitutional referendum in December 2012 attracted even less citizens and reflects changing voting patterns (Lane 2013). The Egyptian population in 2012 and early 2013 seemed to be split between those who struggle for deep change (the revolutionaries); those who support the current government more or less intensively and those who opt for members of the old elites (Schielke 2012, El-Ghobashi 2012). In the summer of 2013, the old forces seem to be back more or less in full force. Journalist Sharif Kouddous pointedly twittered on 21 August: 'Mubarak out, Morsi in jail, Baradei in Vienna. Hello 2010' (https://twitter.com/sharifkouddous) (Baheyya 2013, Shalakany 2013).

## Agents of Change and Persistence

The Muslim Brotherhood represents one of the main opposition forces in Egypt and their logics of action have substantially changed in the course of their historic development from rather quietist non-involvement to actively claiming a role in Egypt's transformation (Büchs 2011, Lynch 2008, Shehata and Stacher 2012). In the eyes of the independent social movements the Islamists play a highly ambivalent role. On the one hand, they have been subjected to massive repression and therefore have usually avoided direct confrontation with the regime. For instance, the Muslim Brotherhood did not participate in the protest calls for 25 January 2011, and still was immediately accused by the regime of standing behind the insurgency. On the other hand, they are very well organised and capable of mobilising a lot of supporters as the stunning victory of their 'Freedom and Justice Party' at the parliamentary election of 2011/12 has shown. At the same time, since the revolution, major divisions within the Islamist camp became apparent: Already on Tahrir Square it could be observed that the young generation of the Muslim Brotherhood has been pursuing different positions. After the resignation of Mubarak these divisions aggravated into manifest conflicts, for instance, about the participation in mass demonstrations, e.g. against the emergency laws, but also about election issues. The new visibility of the traditionalist and militant Salafiyya movement in Egypt, parts of which were implied in provoking violent clashes between Christians and Muslims after the revolution, represents another challenge for the Brotherhood (Tadros 2011a, b). Besides these tendencies of radicalisation and division in the religious field, Amar stresses that on micro- and meso-level of organisations and institutions such as the Sufi brotherhoods or the al-Azhar establishment, especially in 2011, a new participatory and democratic spirit was strongly felt in 2011 (Amar 2011b). Much of this has turned into hardened and heated confrontation, e.g. in al-Azhar or the constitutional assembly in 2012. Meanwhile, many non-religious actors feel betrayed because the Brotherhood has repeatedly retreated from earlier promises such as not fielding a candidate for the presidential elections or opposing military rule and defending the 'aims of the revolution' (Sallam 2012, El-Ghobashi 2012). In winter 2012, President Morsi provoked a new wave of mass protest and violence with many civilian deaths, when he claimed supra-constitutional powers. His decisions created the highest level of public mobilisation since the second stage of the revolution started in 2011 indicating a high public interest in continuing the transformation and fight for freedom. Human rights activists were strongly critisising the Morsi government for ongoing torture, arbitrary detention and other human rights violations: '(...) the regime did not change, that torture remains systematic, the police continues to enjoy impunity, justice has not been enforced [...] and the revolution continues' (El-Nadeem 2012). At the same time, a strong public discourse on the 'brotherhoodisation' of the state emerged with growing fears that the ruling Islamists would use democratic means only once, in order to reach positions of power. In addition, the public became increasingly critical of a very weak government performance while the president seemed to care more about possible Egyptian involvement in Syria (El-Kouedi 2013).

Summing up, the logics of action and the strategies pursued by the ruling Brotherhood strongly resemble those of the old authoritarian deal: repression rather than deliberation and inclusion in addition to strong contempt towards the poor and the independent opposition. At the same time, they tried to confront and appease the strong claim to ongoing privilege of both the military and the resurgent old security services (El-Ghobashi 2012, Shokr 2012). They failed on both fronts and the military deposed president Morsi in July 2013. Since then, the brotherhood has been labeled as 'terrorists' again and many of its leaders put into jail (LIT).

*Agents of Restoration*

Under Mubarak, a high ranking officer with active military career himself, the military increasingly withdrew from politics and focused on its economic activities (Springborg 1989, Müller-Mellin 2011). This led to a close relationship between military and civilian production and served the privilege of a small group of professional soldiers and the sustaining of military infrastructure (Springborg 1989: 115 ff., Amar 2011a). Since the suppression of the insurgency of the 'Central Security Forces' in February 1986, the army was also able to claim control over these paramilitary units and thus significantly expand its own influence. Even before the mass protests, however, fractures in the formerly close relationship between president and military elite became visible: the military refused the economic policies of the group around Gamal Mubarak; also the idea of office succession by Mubarak's son, who had no military career in his resume. In the further course of 2011, the military appeared neither willing nor capable of assuming actual current government functions, sharing power or performing as guardian of a democratic transformation (Albrecht/Bishara 2011: 15 Marshall 2012). The SCAF instead gambled on repression, cooptation and crisis management behind the scenes. Time and again, the military employed a very risky strategy of trying to subdue revolutionary activism with outright violence, thus massively contributing to even more mobilisation and counter-violence, rather than engaging in a dialogue with its newly empowered citizens. The SCAF assumed supra-constitutional competencies by creating law through 'constitutional declarations' and defining the quite disputable path to new election of the parliament, the Shura Council and the president in 2011 (ICG 2012, Naeem 2012). In June 2012, it dissolved the parliament and sought to secure its own privileges again through constitutional declarations but was at least symbolically curtailed in these efforts by President Morsi. In summer 2013, it deposed Morsi in a coup following mass mobilisation and installed a provisional civil government.

Against social forces, which push for further change in the climate of quite high social mobilisation, the military has opted for targeted repression and a strategy of chaotisation and insecuritisation since Mubarak's resignation. The SCAF accepted violence among civilians or situations in which such violence may occur. The list of incidents is long: destabilisation and escalation of violence by removal of regular police, deployment of sharpshooters, opening of prisons, deployment of thugs, violent attacks against churches and Christians, the events in the football stadium of Port Said in February 2012 (ICG 2012). Furthermore, the emergency laws remained more or less in place throughout most of the transformation despite contrary promises, a law against strikes was rigidly enforced, and sexual violence was specifically targeted against women during protests (Tadros 2011a and b, El-Amrani 2012, Jünemann in this volume). The military is broadly driven by its old logics of action: securing access to economic revenue and control of the highly mobilised population. At the same time, it is not a unified actor; rank and file might be highly divided along political lines – and the generational gap, which has contributed to unrest in Egypt, is also at work in the military institutions itself. Thus, further splits within in the military might happen and this could include both a move towards more civilian control of the military and a deepening of violent confrontations. In summer 2013, though, the ranks seem to be closed and the military seems to be successful in its new and old 'war on terror' against Islamist forces leading to ongoing bloodshed, human rights violations and further polarisation of the political field.

## Conclusion

I set out to analyse the impact of the Egyptian revolutionary mobilisation and ensuing transformation on the logics of action of the authoritarian social contract of informality that has set the rules for both regime and population during the last decades. Confronted with rapid social and economic transformations, which were not accompanied by political transition, the ruling elites relied on five major strategies in order to implement their main logics of action to hang on to power and privilege. These logics of action are embedded in an authoritarian social contract, that traded welfare against political demobilisation but that had increasingly come under pressure. In order to secure power, the Mubarak regime relied on limited political liberalisation, repression, limited economic liberalisation, Islamisation and informalisation. This in turn created fear, division and acquiescence as well as open and hidden resistance as major logics of action on part of 'the' population. Foreign actors like the US or Europe directly or indirectly supported the authoritarian deal by providing aid and legitimacy. How has the revolution influenced and changed this system?

By looking at the strategies generated by both the authoritarian social contract and the major contestations during the past two years, I hold that the logics of action of the military and even the freely elected new rulers of Egypt have not been radically altered. The deep core and policy core beliefs of the former regime actors, the military and the security apparatus did not change substantially: they build on the well-known 'power of repression'. Even though the EU and the US are increasingly weary of the ongoing insecurity and violence in Egypt, they tend to opt for their pre-revolutionary logic of action, i.e. preserving stability rather than pressing for deep transformation. At the same time, immediately after the start of the revolution in 2011, the political field exploded with enthusiasm and Egypt witnessed an unprecedented wave of activism and politicisation. This development and the fact of sustained mass mobilisation do represent a major shift in the logics of action on part of the oppositional forces and the broader population. It challenged the authoritarian social contract and the logics of repression, controlled participation and the ideological focus on religious discourses. Thus, indeed, the revolution has massively impacted political culture and political awareness and brought the old depoliticisation and demobilisation to an end. Still, in 2013 many other Egyptians seem to be tired of so much politics, disappointed by the new islamist rulers and economically deeply distressed. The military instrumentalised this sense of frustration and insecurity and took over again. This move is supported by many in 2013 but it also created even more violence, exclusion and polarisation. This will most probably not help to reach what people stood up for in 2011: Bread, Freedon, and Social Justice. And thus, the revolution and its struggle for a radical renegotiation of the authoritarian social contract will go on.

## Bibliography

Albrecht, H. and D. Bishara. 2011. Back on Horseback: The Military and Political Transformation in Egypt. *Middle East Law and Governance*, 3(1-2), 13-23.

Amar, P. 2011a. Why Egypt's progressives win. *Al Jazeera* [Online: 10 February] Available at: http://www.aljazeera.com/indepth/opinion/2011/02/20112101030726228.html [accessed: 29 April 2012].

Amar, P. 2011b. Egypt after Mubarak. *The Nation* [Online 4 May] Available at: http://www.thenation.com/article/160439/egypt-after-mubarak?page=full [accessed: 29 April 2012].

Amnesty International. 2011. *Amnesty International Annual Report 2011 – Egypt*. [Online] Available at: www.amnesty.org/en/region/egypt/report-2011 [accessed: 29 April 2012].

Arbeitsstelle Politik des Vorderen Orients. 2011. *Proteste, Revolutionen, Transformationen - die Arabische Welt imUmbruch*. [Online: Freie Universität Berlin] Available at: http://www.polsoz.fu-berlin.de/polwiss/forschung/international/vorderer-orient/publikation/WP_serie/WP1_All_FINAL_-web.pdf [accessed: 20 October 2012].

Attalah, L. 2012. The draft constitution. Some controversial stipulations. *Egypt Independent*, [online] available at: www.jadaliyya.com/pages/index/8719/the-draft-constitution/ [accessed: 7 January 2013].

Baheyya 2008. Four Myths about Protest. [Online 16 May]. Available at: http://baheyya.blogspot.de/2008/05/four-myths-about-protest.html [accessed: 29 April 2012].

Baheyya 2013. Fetishizing the State. [Online 8 August]. Available at: http://baheyya.blogspot.de/2013/08/fetishizing-state.html

Bayat, A. 1997. Un-Civil Society: The Politics of the 'Informal People'. *Third World Quarterly*, 18(1), 53-72.

Bayat, A. 2007. *Making Islam Democratic*. Stanford: Stanford University Press.

Beinin, J. 2011. A Workers' Social Movement on the Margin of the Global Neoliberal Order, in *Social Movements, Mobilization, and Contestation in the Middle East and North Africa*, edited by J. Beinin and F. Vairel. Stanford: Stanford University Press, 181-201.

Beinin, J. and F. Vairel. 2011. Social Movements, Mobilization, and Contestation in the Middle East and North Africa. Stanford: Stanford University Press.

Besheer, M.G. 2011. The Ultras Book. The Ultras and the Egyptian Revolution. Cairo: Dar Diwan.

Büchs, A. 2011. *The Egyptian Muslim Brotherhood under Mubarak (1981-2011)*. Hamburg: unpublished dissertation, University of Hamburg.

Catusse, M., B. Destremeau and F. Verdier. 2009. L'Etat face aux 'débordements' du social au Maghreb. Formation, travail et protection sociale. Paris: Karthala.

Cook, S.A. 2012. *The Struggle for Egypt. From Nasser to Tahrir Square*. Oxford: Oxford University Press.

Demmelhuber, T. and S. Roll. 2007. Herrschaftssicherung in Ägypten. *SWP-Studien 2007*, 20. Berlin: Stiftung Wissenschaft und Politik.

El-Amrani, I. 2012. Sightings of the Egyptian Deep State. *Middle East Report Online*. [Online 1 Januar] Available at: http://www.merip.org/mero/mero 010112 [accessed: 29 April 2012].

El-Ghobashy, M. 2011. The Praxis of the Egyptian Revolution. *Middle East Report*, 41 (258). Available at: http://www.merip.org/mer/mer258/praxis-egyptian-revolution [accessed: 29 April 2012].

El-Ghobashy, M. 2012. Egyptian Politics Upended. *Middle East Report Online*. [Online 20 August] Available at:http://www.merip.org/mero/mero082012 [accessed: 7 January 2013].

El-Mahdi, R. and P. Marfleet. 2009. *Egypt: The Moment of Change*. London: Zed Books.

El-Nadeem Centre. 2012. 100 Days of Morsi Rule. 100 days of detentions, torture, violent crash on protests and killing outside the law. Report [Online: El-Nadeem]. Available at: https://alnadeem.org/en/node/421[accessed: 7 January 2013]

European Commission. 2011. EuroMed-2030. Long term challenges for the Mediterranean area. Report of an Expert Group, DG Research and Innovation, Socio-economic Sciences and Humanities (SSH). [Online: EUCOM] Available at: http://ec.europa.eu/research/socialsciences/-reports_ en.html#euromed1[accessed: 29 April 2012].

Harders, C. 2002. Staatsanalyse von unten. Urbane Armut und politische Partizipation in Ägypten. Hamburg: Deutsches Orient-Institut.

Harders, C. 2003. The Informal Social Pact – the State and the Urban Poor in Cairo, in *Politics from Above, Politics from Below: The Middle East in the Age of Economic Reform*, edited by E. Kienle, London: Al-Saqi Publications, 191-213.

Harders, C. 2011. Protest, revolutions and transformations – the Arab World in a Period of Upheaval [Online], *Berlin Working Paper der Arbeitsstelle Politik des Vorderen Orients*, 1, 10-37. Available at: http://www.polsoz.fu-berlin.de/polwiss/forschung/international/vorderer-orient/publikation/-WP_serie/WP1_All_FINAL_web.pdf [accessed: 7 January 2013].

Harders, C. 2012. Neue Proteste, alte Krisen: Zum Ende des autoritären Sozialvertrags, in *Arabische Zeitenwende*, edited by Bundeszentrale für politische Bildung, Bonn: Schriftenreihe (Bd. 1243), 64-75.

Harders, C. 2013. Bringing the Local Back in – Analyzing local governance in an age of transformation in Egypt, in *Local Politics and Contemporary Transformations in the Arab World*, edited by M. Bouziane, C. Harders and A. Hoffmann. Basingstoke: Palgrave MacMillan.

Heydemann, S. 2007. Upgrading Authoritarianism in the Arab World [Online]. *SabanCenter Analysis Paper*, 13. Available at: http://www.brookings.edu/papers/2007/10arabworld.aspx [accessed: 29 April 2012].

Human Rights Watch. 2012. Egypt, in *World Report*, 545-55 [Online: Human Rights Watch]. Available at: http://www.hrw.org/sites/default/files/reports/wr2012.pdf [accessed: 29 April 2012].

ICG. 2012. Lost in Transition: The World according to Egypt's SCAF, International Crisis Group, *Middle East and North Africa Report*, 121.

Ismail, S. 2006. Rethinking Islamist Politics: Culture, the State and Islamism. London: I.B. Tauris.

Jadaliyya. 2012a. Egypts Elections Watch. *Jadaliyya* [Online]. Available at: http://www.jadaliyya.com/pages/index/Egypt%20Elections%20Watch [accessed: 29 April 2012].

Jadaliyya 2012b. Jadaliyya Page on Egypt's Constitutional Referendum, *Jadaliyya* [Online]. Available at http://www.jadaliyya.com/pages/index/9194/jadaliyya-page-on-egypts-constitutional-referendum [accessed: 7 January 2013].

Jünemann, A. 2009. Zwei Schritte vor, einer zurück: Die Entwicklung der europäischen Mittelmeerpolitik von den ersten Assoziierungsabkommen bis zur Gründung einer 'Union für das Mittelmeer'. In *Der Mittelmeerraum als Region*, Europäisches Zentrum für Föderalismus-Forschung Tübingen, Occasional Papers [Online] (35), 26-59.

Kandil, H. 2011: Islamizing Egypt? Testing the Limits of Gramscian counterhegemonic Strategies. *Theory and Society*, 40. 37-62

Kienle, E. 2001. A Grand Delusion: Democracy and Economic Reform in Egypt. London: IB Tauris.

Kohstall, F. 2006. *L'Égypte dans l'année 2005*. Cairo: CEDEJ.

Korany, B. and A. Dessouki. 2008. The Foreign Policies of Arab States. The Challenge of Globalization. Cairo/New York: AUC Press.

Korany, B. and R. El-Mahdi. 2012. *Arab Spring in Egypt. Revolution and Beyond.* Cairo/New York: AUC Press.

Lane, K. 2012. Referendum voting patterns reveal changing political map, dwindling faith in process, *Egypt Independent* [Online 3 January]. Available at http://www.egyptindependent.com/news/-referendum-voting-patterns-reveal-changing-political-map-dwindling-faith-process.[accessed: 10 January 2013].

Lübben, I. 2012. Die ägyptische Arbeiterklasse: Das Rückgrat der Revolution. *INAMO*, 18(69), 23-26.

Lynch, M. 2007. Young Brothers in Cyberspace. *Middle East Report* [Online], 37(245). Available at: http://www.merip.org/mer/mer245/young-brothers-cyberspace [accessed: 29 April 2012].

Makram-Ebeid, M. 1989. Political Opposition in Egypt. Democratic Myth or Reality? *Middle East Journal*, 43(3), 423-436.

Müller-Mellin, M. 2011. Militärbourgeoisie und Militärisch-industrieller Komplex in Ägypten. Kiel: Verlag Graubereich.

Naeem, N. 2012. Vom Abgang des Staatspräsidenten bis zur Verkündung der verfassungsrechtlichen Erklärung für die Übergangszeit. *Jahrbuch des Öffentlichen Rechts der Gegenwart*, 60, edited by P. Häberle. Tübingen: Mohr Siebeck, 643-660.

Population Council. 2010. *Survey of Young People in Egypt.* Cairo: Population Council West Asia and North Africa.

Radsch, C. 2008. Core to Commonplace: The Evolution of Egypt's blogosphere. *Arab Media and Society* [Online], Available at: http://www.arabmediasociety.com/articles/downloads/-20080929140127_AMS6_Courtney_Radsch.pdf [accessed: 29 April 2012].

Salah, H. 2011. Revolution gegen Autoritarismus, Patriarchalismus und Tradition in Ägypten. In *Revolutionen, Transformationen – die Arabische Welt im Umbruch.* [Online] Edited by Arbeitsstelle Politik des Vorderen Orients Proteste, 110-129. Available at: http://www.polsoz.fu-berlin.de/polwiss/forschung/international/vorderer-orient/publikation/Working_Paper_Series/-index.html [accessed: 20 October 2012].

Schlumberger, O. 2007. Debating Arab Authoritarianism. Dynamics and Durability in Nondemocratic Regimes. Stanford: Stanford University Press.

Schubert, G., R. Tetzlaff and W. Vennewald. 1994. Demokratisierung und politischer Wandel. Theorie und Anwendung des Konzeptes der strategischen und konfliktfähigen Gruppen (SKOG). Münster/Hamburg: LIT Verlag.

Shalakany, A. 2013. Pretty Names and ugly Things: Getting to Know the Law of Egypt's Second Transitional Period. [Online] Available at: http://www.jadaliyya.com/pages/index/13292/pretty-names-and-ugly-things_getting-to-know-the-law-of-egypts-second-transitional-period.html [accessed: 20 August 2013].

Shokr, A. 2012. Reflections on Two Revolutions. MERIP 265. [Online] Available at: http://www.merip.org/mer/mer265/reflections-two-revolutions [accessed: 20 August 2013].

Singerman, D. 1996. Avenues of Participation. Family, Politics, and Networks in Urban Quarters of Cairo. Princeton: Princeton University Press.

Singerman, D. and P. Amar. 2006. Cairo Cosmopolitan: Politics, Culture, and Urban Space in the New Globalized Middle East. Cairo: AUC Press.

Sowers, J. and C. Toensing. 2012. The Journey to Tahrir: Revolution, Protest and Social Change in Egypt 1999-2011. London: Verso.

Springborg, R. 1989. Mubarak's Egypt. Fragmentation of the Political Order. Boulder/London: Westview Press.

Tadros, M. 2011a. Sectarianism and Its Discontents in Post-Mubarak Egypt. *Middle East Report* [Online], 41(259). Available at: http://www.merip.org/mer/mer259/sectarianism-its-discontents-post-mubarak-egypt [accessed: 24 April 2012].

Tadros, M. 2011b. Egypt's Bloody Sunday. *Middle East Report* [Online]. Available at: http://www.merip.org/mero/mero101311 [accessed: 29 April 2012].

Tocci, N. 2011. State (un)Sustainability in the Southern Mediterranean and Scenarios to 2030: The EU's Response. *EU Neighbourhood Policy. MEDPRO Policy Papers*. [Online] Available at: www.medpro-foresight.eu [accessed: 29 April 2012].

UNDP. 2006. Towards the rise of Arab Women. *Arab Human Development Report 2005*. [Online] 3. New York. Available at: http://www.arab-hdr.org/contents/index.aspx?rid=5 [accessed: 29 April 2012].

UNDP. 2002. Creating Opportunities for Future Generations. *Arab Human Development Report*. Available at: http://www.arab-hdr.org/publications/other/ahdr/ahdr2002e.pdf [accessed: 5 July 2011].

Wurzel, U. 2007. Limits to Economic Reform in an Authoritarian State. Egypt since the 1990s. Berlin: Klaus Schwarz Verlag.

Zorob, A. 2013. Der Zusammenbruch des autoritären Gesellschaftsvertrags, in *Arabellions. Zur Vielfalt von Protest und Revolte im Nahen Osten und Nordafrika*, edited by A. Jünemann and A. Zorob, Wiesbaden: VS/Springer, 229-256.

Chapter 7

# Blocked Middle Classes as an Engine of Change in the Arab World?

Rachid Ouaissa

## Introduction

The wave of protests across large parts of the Arab world caught both political analysts and experts by surprise. The so-called 'Arab Spring' has triggered a great deal of debate in political and media circles. It is often forgotten that revolts of different forms and intensity, against the ruling class, have been part of everyday life in Middle Eastern societies since the beginning of the nineteenth century (Kazemi and Waterbury 1991, Zubaida 2008, Gran 1999). Following the incorporation of the Ottoman Empire into the world economy, the Tanzimat reforms and the restructuring of the agrarian economy, these riots were an expression of the struggle among different social groups and classes over their position in and the reconfiguration of the system of production (Burke et al. 1988, Burke 1991: 24-27, Thompson 2000: 91-111).

Furthermore, the recent revolts and uprisings in the Arab world can be seen as an expression of a struggle of certain social classes of society in order to stabilise or improve their position. These classes are identified here as 'middle classes' that are blocked with regard to their ambitions for upward mobility. Although in Tahrir Square in Cairo and around the other Arab capitals there were people from all walks of life involved in the demonstrations, it is considered an undisputed fact that the driving forces in these revolts were the middle classes (Maher 2011).

This chapter examines the reasons for the riots in 2011 with a view to analysing the rising middle classes. Using the Logics of Action approach as a reference, the thesis put forward here is that today's uprisings in the Arab world is not a new political phenomenon. They are, rather, cyclical riots which erupt repeatedly because of intense friction between the Middle East's rigid and persistent rentier economies on the one hand and the global economy on the other.

Following the lines of the Logics of Action approach (Horst et al. in this volume) it is my aim to identify the factors and parameters that explain the co-determination of actors (middle class) and structures (rentier structures and global economy) in the MENA region. I assume that the logic of political action of the middle classes can be explained by a combination of various parameters and factors that will be specified in greater detail in this chapter.

## The Co-Determination of Structures and Agents Over Time

The friction between the global economic structures and the rentier structures led to an economic reorientation of the affected region which in turn resulted in revolt-like reactions by the middle classes against the power holders. While the middle classes used – and continue to use – different forms of protest, depending on the specific political context in their respective country, they all remained ineffective against the persistent social and power structures of the rentier system. In a rentier system labour cannot be mobilised as an element of protest, so that the middle classes need to resort to discourses on identity. Thus, it's a combination of the factors' identity and power that have shaped the logics of action of the middle classes in the various revolts in the recent history of the MENA region. These revolts 'only' testify the persistence of the prevailing structures.

Of primary relevance for the following analysis is more than anything else the factor of time. Three cycles in political economy can be identified: The first cycle stretches from the first half of the nineteenth century to the 1930s. This period was labelled by Hourani as the 'The Liberal Age' and occurred, according to Wallerstein, due to the consequences of the inclusion of the Ottoman Empire into the world economy. Commerce was dominant in this period and was, following the introduction of the Tanzimat reforms, based on export-oriented agriculture. The second cycle begins with the Great Depression of the 1930s and the failure of the implementation of the capitalist structures in the Arab world and lasts until the late 1970s and early 1980s. This cycle was dominated by pan-Arabic rhetoric on a planned socialist economy and was based on the income from oil exports. The third cycle was initiated by the Islamic revolution in Iran and continued until the 2000s. This period can be identified with the gradual increase of Islamist power within society, often supported by the West (as happened in Afghanistan). Economically, this phase was characterised by the crisis of the 'development state' and the failure of development models such as the implementation of structural adjustment programmes (SAP). This period is also referred to as the period of neoliberalism. With the revolts in the Arab world in 2011, a new cycle begins. This new cycle is characterised by an ideological fatigue and the attempt by non-organised movements to achieve individual utopias against the social orders enforced from above. This background explains a new logic of pragmatism of today's actors.

Accordingly, I understand today's revolts in the Arab world as a rebellion by a consumer-oriented middle class whose aspirations for (upward) mobility have been blocked. Despite the intensity of the riots and the successful overthrow of the dictatorships, the existing power structures have not been radically changed. In contrast to the European middle classes of the nineteenth century, whose consumption had strengthened the power of labour, mass consumption in the Arab world merely intensifies imports without any impact on the bargaining power of labour.

*The Concept of Middle Classes as (Non-)Change Agents*

The discussion about classes in relation to states and societies in the Middle East is an old one which extends back to the pre-colonial period (Beinin and Lockmann 1987, Lockman 1994, Beinin 2001) and the theoretical debates which dominated in the post-colonial phase in the context of development debates (Vatin 1974, Leca and Vatin 1979, Lazreg 1976, Turner 1984, Amin 1976, Batatu 1978). In summary, one can identify three strands of debate. A first group of authors sees class analysis as unfruitful with regard to MENA societies due to the lack of capitalist structures, failed industrialisation and the dominance of ethnic, religious and tribal mechanisms of mobilisation (Turner 1984: 1-66). For the second group, the application of Marxist-Weberian class analysis is deemed a given (Turner 1984). Samir Amin speaks of classes in pre-capitalist conditions. Although classes develop only under conditions of industrialisation, Amin is nonetheless of the opinion that through imperialist moves by Europe, embryonic classes had emerged (Amin 1976). The third group combines both analytical frameworks and stresses the overlapping of class character and tribal and cultural structures (Halpern 1963). The representatives of this group acknowledge that the interconnection between the specific economic structure of the region and the global economy led to the emergence of class-like structures. Nevertheless they perceive ethnicity, faith, and family as main channels of mobilisation and not the belonging to a class. The recourse to familial and tribal kinship solidarity in response to local and global economic change seems to be necessary because class-consciousness is not present. This explains very clearly why primordial identities are a significant factor in the logic of action of many actors in the middle classes. The interlocking nature of tribal-family-religious structures with class structures has been described by Batatu in the case of Iraq and Syria (Batatu 1978, Batatu 1999).

The term 'middle strata' or 'middle class' is not easy to grasp empirically (Gay 2002, Burris 1999, Savage et al. 1992). In the literature, a distinction is made between 'old' and 'new' middle class (Liaghat 1980). While the old definition of middle class referred to urban traders and self-employed, a new definition would combine technical jobs, employees in bureaucracy, education and the services sector under middle strata or 'professional middle class' (Robinson 1993). In Marxist terminology, the terms 'petit bourgeoisie', 'coordinating class' as well as 'managerial class' and 'professional class' are used (Savage et al 1992: 194). In Europe, this class emerged during the course of industrialisation beginning in 1760 (Hobsbawm 1995, Wahrman 1995). The expansion of capital during the industrial revolution enabled the emergence of new professional groups (engineers, soldiers, engineers, scientists, etc). This stratum became ever wider and called for economic and political participation. As such, 'the' middle class is difficult to detect. There are upper opportunistic segments, which tend to form alliances with the bourgeoisie. Their political ambitions differ quite a lot from the objectives of 'anxious' lower segments that fear nothing more than social decline. Indeed, the lack of collective identity is reflected in the lack of a common strategy, a lack of fighting spirit and therefore a lack of common political goals (James 2006). Against this background, one cannot speak of a common logic of action in the middle class but must differentiate between different context-related rationales for action.

Politically, it is often stressed that processes of democratic transformation are of great importance for the middle classes (Pickel 2012: 138). However, the middle classes are not inherently democratic, *per se*, because they can also function as a medium for extremist and fascist movements. In his essay 'Panik im Mittelstand' Theodor Geiger has shown how economic uncertainties led to extremist patterns of behaviour among the middle class in Germany (Geiger 1930). During the 1930s the middle classes that had been in crises bestowed electoral success on the Nazis. Lipset has referred to the middle class as 'Extremismus der Mitte' (Lipset 1959). The fact that democratisation is not always the main goal of the middle classes can be observed for example in Asia. For the rising middle class in Asia, the development of democracy is not the primary goal but rather the state-led development of a capitalist economy (Schwinn 2006: 213). As long as decent income and prestige are assured, middle classes are willing to accommodate with authoritarian regimes. This background confirms the argument that the logics of action in the middle classes are predominantly shaped by the desire to move up, and the fear to fall down respectively.

In the context of these theoretical considerations, the 'potential' of the middle class as carrier of democratic transition in Arab countries is essentially related to two factors: the question in which economic system they are embedded and which social alliances they are able to forge (Moore 1969).

*The Concept of Power in Rentier Economies*

Typical of the Arab middle classes is their rootedness in the rentier economy. This raises the question whether the revolts produced by the middle class can automatically be classified as a call for radical systemic change and democratic participatory rights.

Rents are a result of restricted competition, either because of natural monopolies or of politically generated market restrictions. Rents influence political structures and thus influence the strategies of actors. Because of the competition in the marked system profits, unlike rents, must be reinvested. Otherwise even the most powerful capitalists risk innovation gaps and might even disappear from the market. Investments are made because entrepreneurs expect higher consumer demand. Innovation resulting from investment leads not only to technical superiority but also to rising real wages. In the Keynesian dynamic, rising real wages lead to increased demand and thus to the valorisation of labour as a bargaining power (Elsenhans 2009). The empowerment of labour not only prevents the superiority by the powerful, but also provides the basis of any bourgeois revolution and is thus a prerequisite for the emergence and maintenance of democratic structures and civil rights. According to this logic, both the state acting as a facilitator between employees and employers (because every unemployed person carries with them a cost) as well as the entrepreneurs who need mass markets in order to increase their profits, have an interest in full employment. Entrepreneurs need qualified workers to enter into the competition of innovation. The government invests in education and structural requirements. Large segments of society benefit from market expansion and this leads to what Hobsbawm has called, following the industrialisation of Europe, the 'self-disempowerment of the aristocracy' (Hobsbawm 1987).

Capitalist structures determine not only the political behaviour of the elite, but also the cultural behaviour of the employees. In capitalism, the mobilisation of labour as a negotiating power becomes the preferred instrument to enforce interests and not traditional mechanisms like ethnic, religious or clan solidarity. It is this development that Toennies describes as transition from community (Gemeinschaft) to society (Gesellschaft) (Tönnies 2012). Even class alliances as an instrument to enforce democratic rights, in the view of Barrington Moore, work only under these particular capitalist conditions (Moore 1969). In other words and in line with the Logics of Action approach, the political goals of the middle classes and the strategies they adopt to achieve these goals are highly determined by the given economic structures.

In economies dominated by rents, surplus capital does not get invested productively. In this type of economic structure work is not tied to productivity but to patronage. Despite exceptions in some sectors in a few Arab countries, these economic structures are dominated by what Hartmut Elsenhans termed 'Marginalität'. A marginal worker is one who costs more than what he can produce and he is thus operating as part of a pre-capitalist social contract (Elsenhans 2001: 210-211). Marginal workers cannot enforce their own interests by mobilising their peers. On the contrary, as clients they are bound to their patron and his clan (or denomination) because they are only employed on the basis of owing *Wasta* (Henni 1993). Any form of organised protest can be used to force the *reserve army* to work for less (Kalecki 1943). This in turn strengthens pre-capitalist social structures, patronage systems and the fragmentation of society as well as communities, as Ibn Khaldun already described in the fourteenth century (Ibn Khaldun 1997).

## Arab Middle Classes and the Liberal Age

As has been evident from recent research on the socio-economic developments in the MENA region, the social and political structures have been significantly determined by the rise and fall of the middle class (Watenpaugh 2006). If one looks at the history of the region since the beginning of the nineteenth century, it is characterised by a kind of cyclical development of such protest movements. The middle classes are the main carriers of the revolts. Their rise, decline and stagnation as well as their forms of articulation are crucial for the explanation of social, cultural and political processes in the Middle East. The respective logics of the middle class are in turn influenced by changes in political and economic structure.

Such was the outcome of the Tanzimat reforms (1839-1876) in the Ottoman Empire, which led at the beginning of the nineteenth century to the rise of a new urban middle class. In the Middle East it was called 'Effendiya', an Ottoman term that derived from the word 'Effendi', which means 'Lord' but is analogous to the terms 'gentleman' or 'Gentilhomme' in European history. However, the rise of this middle class was not, as in the history of Europe, the result of an intensification of industrialisation and a consequent intensification of investment. Rather it was the result of a rent-oriented restructuring of the agrarian economy and the integration of the Ottoman Empire into the world economy. Exemplary for this development was the modernisation and restructuring of the agrarian economy into an export oriented agricultural sector under Mohamed Ali and the consequent establishment of capitalism based on rent (Hafez 2009, Ergil 1975, Kanzancigil 1973, Gran 1998).

As Watenpaugh has shown for the city of Aleppo (Watenpaugh, 2006), the rise of this new cosmopolitan, urban and consumerist middle class articulated the rise of new cultural forms of life (Hanna 2003). Distinctive clothing, consumption and lifestyle were features of Effendiya. Clubs, coffee, debating and philosophical circles all flourished in the centres of Cairo, Alexandria, Istanbul and Beirut. The discovery of the 'savoir vivre' is demonstrated by the art of cigar smoking and alcoholic luxury goods that Zubaida describes as the art of 'Savoir Boire' (Zubaida, 2011:146). It was not just writers, journalists and artists who consorted with transnational networks such as the Free Masons, but also religious reformers and scholars, most notably Al Afghani (Zubaida 2011: 135ff.). This path of modernisation was intellectually articulated by the reformist Nahda movement.

At the same time, economic specialisation and single export strategies led to an increase in the price of essential agricultural products and a deterioration of the quality of life for large sections of society. This is reflected in revolts and violent uprisings in various regions of the Ottoman Empire (Beinin 2001, Burke et al. 2006, Thompson 2000, Burke et al. 1990, Kazemi and Waterbury 1991). The crisis of Mohamed Ali's model ended in a revolt by the Urabi movement. The crisis of the traditional industries (textile mills in Syria and Tunisia, sugar refineries in Egypt, etc) led to unrest in many parts of the Empire (Tunisia 1864, Syria 1860, etc) (Hourani 2000: 340pp). One can describe the unrest as a precursor to anti-Ottoman sentiment. Under the colonialists, the imperialist domination of Europe increasingly promoted modernisation of the region which discredited the agrarian power elite. Nonetheless, based on the spread of the modern education system a 'new Effendiya' developed under colonial rule (Goldschmidt 2005). This new middle strata emerged after the First World War. They were, finally, with the world capitalist crisis of the 1930s, the main carriers of Arab nationalism (Eppel 2005, Shechter 2005 and 2008, Bernstein 2008, Gershoni and Jankowski, 1995: 7-22). The Army officers in Egypt, Syria and Iraq, as well as the revolutionaries in Tunisia, Algeria and Morocco – most of whom were educated in French schools – are exemplary of this new nationalist middle stratum in the 1950s. The colonial powers failed (intentionally) to implement capitalist structures in the countries of the Arab world. The primary interest of the colonial powers was to redirect production of raw materials and primary products from the region to booming European industries. As the dependency theorists have argued (Prebisch-Singer thesis), the specialisation on raw materials seriously hampered the economic catch-up with industrialised countries.

## Arab Middle Classes and Arab Nationalism

With the end of colonialism the middle class gained power in the Middle East. Based on oil revenues they established rentier economies in many of the MENA countries. The integration of these countries into the world capitalist system in the last 20 years reinforced this structure. Rents need not be deployed in an economically rational way, but are at the free disposal of the ruling elites, usually to buy loyalties. The preferred field for the deployment of rents is the social sector. This behaviour results in a political pact between rulers and the ruled based on the strategic distribution of rents. The socio-political effects of such policies include securing education and the provision of health for broad social segments as well as employment opportunities in the very large public sector. With the help of the oil industry, these countries achieved average annual growth rates of up to 11 per cent of GDP, from 1973 to 1983, fed by revenues from oil exports or through the channels of regional labour migration and financial support services by the major oil exporters to the semi-rentiers among the Arab states. The unemployment rate was about 5 per cent in Egypt and 1.6 per cent in Jordan until the 1980s (Winckler, 2005: 88).

One of the consequences of this redistribution was rapid urbanisation. The proportion of urban population increased from 30 per cent in Egypt in 1950 to 47 per cent in 1990, in Syria from 32 per cent to 51 per cent, in Jordan from 38 per cent to 78 per cent, and even Saudi Arabia from 12 per cent to 86 per cent. The modernisation of agriculture has been neglected and thus food dependency has been extended. Finally, there was a population explosion whereby the population of Egypt grew from 21 million people in 1950 to 55.5 million in 1990, in Jordan from 600,000 to 3.5 million, in Algeria and Morocco 9.5 million to 30 million and in Syria from 3.5 million to 16 million people over the same period. Here one can observe a reduction in the median age of the population, especially for the working-age population whose proportion in all countries of the Middle East accounts for more than 60 per cent of the population (Richards and Waterbury 2008: 71).

By the mid-1970s these policies led to the rise of a new middle class (Richards and Waterbury 1990: 408pp, Shechter 2008), which was also denoted as 'professional middle class' (Longuenesse 2007). Since the post-colonial states had seen the overcoming of underdevelopment as their main political objective, they invested particularly in technical disciplines such as engineering. The build up of a huge public sector resulted in the creation of a broad middle strata tied to the state and hence tied to governmental rents (Longuenesse 2007). Along with the prospering economic situation, the pan-Arab rhetoric served as an ideological framework for this middle strata.

However, no later than the middle of the 1980s these policies were in major crisis due to a sharp decline in international oil prices. Most countries in the region had been forced to implement the conditionalities of structural adjustment programmes under the auspices of the IMF and World Bank. The crisis of the rentier state led to the withdrawal of the state from its social responsibilities and put an end to the distribution strategies that so far had secured loyalty. The proportion of socially marginalised youth was growing and with it demands of the middle classes for greater advancement opportunities. The 'social contract' between the state and society, and thus the 'pax politica', was broken. The stream of university graduates (especially with technical degrees) could no longer be absorbed in the crisis-ridden public sector. It is exactly these graduates that form the middle classes blocked in their upward mobility. Their fear of losing out can be conceptualised as the main logic of mobilisation, for it explains the politicisation of religion among the middle classes. Religion became the new channel of articulation.

## Islamist Movements as a Middle Class Movement

Blocked in their upward mobility, the middle classes became the main clients of the Islamist movements (Losurdo 2002: 8). The literature on Islamic movements discusses a 'coalition of losers', which is composed of segments of the bourgeoisie, proletarianised state employees, engineers, industrial proletariat, underemployed intelligentsia, notables, agrarian capitalists and students (Kramer 1986: 106, Ibrahim 1996, Ayubi 1980, Lübben 2013). The Islamist movements could offer refuge to the politically homeless middle classes because their programme criticised the opening of markets and the waste of resources by interventionist governments. At the same time, however, they conceded that the state should retain an important role, especially in foreign economic relations. The texts of these movements originally derived from a culturally influenced description of the principles of 'moral economy'. Yet, as the election campaigns of the Islamist parties show, they ended up with a pragmatic display of a policy under the conditions of 'globalisation', combining the protection of the national economy from import competition and the promotion of export opportunities (Lübben 2008, Ouaissa 2008).

Kepel explains the success of Islamist movements in their ability to create a synthesis between the lower classes and the rising (pious) middle class (Kepel 2000: 9). Thus the Islamists maintain a radical discourse that mobilises the frustrated underclass and, at the same time, propagates middle class oriented economic programmes to facilitate their upward mobility (Clark 2004). In her investigation into the activities of the Islamist Welfare organisations in Egypt, Jordan and Yemen, Janine Clark (Clark 2004: 945) has come to the conclusion that the moderate Islamist groups bind their followers by means of two different strategies: maintaining horizontal relations towards the middle class and a vertical patronage relationship (patron-client) over the lower classes. The author notes that not only are much larger aid programmes and services made available to the middle class as for the lower classes, she also found that Islamic charities such as hospitals, schools, etc., have been built especially for the middle classes of these countries. The movements offer through their various social organisations a roof for the frustrated lower classes and deliver employment and career opportunities for the marginalised middle classes through the bureaucratic apparatuses in the various areas of operation of the movements (Bayat 2010: 24). For example, for unemployed graduates there are now opportunities to practise their professions in the banking industry and in hospitals. This makes these movements, even in a time of withdrawal of the state from its welfare responsibilities, a parallel rentier system *par excellence* (Müller 2002: 126-129). Although the sources of rents for the state and Islamist charity organisations differ – the latter based mainly on donations and private contributions – the strategies used lead to similar rent-related clientalist mechanisms.

After the failure of strategies for violently seizing power in Algeria and Egypt in the 1990s, the various Islamist movements increasingly metamorphosed into political parties that tried to exploit their chances of participation on all levels (Lübben 2013).

The Algerian experience has shown that the Islamist parties through their transformation from mass political movements into political parties, as well as through taking over the responsibility of government, have lost credibility and reputation. After their arrival in national parliaments a new dynamic was deployed, both internally and with party supporters and voters, which are not controlled by simple populist discourse and dogmatic speeches (Esposito and Muqtedar 2000). Moreover, even loyal voters and supporters of these parties can become critical. As such, a new logic of action can, therefore, be identified as a kind of 'desacralisation' of the Islamist movements as well as their affiliated organisations and hence religion as a political mediator.

Through their [formal] political participation these parties become increasingly pragmatic and thereby lose control over their followers (see Fritzsche and Lübben in this volume). The once proclaimed primary aims, goals, and reform projects are long gone. Even the Islamic social utopia of national justice, based on egalitarian distribution, turned out to be a demagogic discourse of clientelism for certain levels of society (Clark 2004: 944). Their economic programmes turned out to be compatible with the neoliberal programmes of the IMF and the World Bank. So it is that these parties through their cooptation (Harders in this volume) become distanced from the marginalised of society and thus alienating an important group of supporters as well as losing credibility overall. The experience of Islamist parties in Algeria shows, however, that they have become stronger rather than weaker (Kurzman and Naqvi 2009). The longer these parties participate in the political contest, the more oriented towards 'Realpolitik' they become. Meanwhile, the Islamist parties have become embroiled in corruption scandals, just like the ruling elite (Ouali 2010). The thesis defended here seems to be paradoxical given the recent election results in Egypt, Tunisia and Morocco. However, while the Islamists remain in power for them there are only two options available: either an authoritarian system, and thus being no better than the preceding nationalist parties, or a process of normalisation, i.e. a type of 'Christian Democratisation'. Thus, in the previously identified logic of action the relativisation of the religious factors in politics has meant a simultaneous increase in the economic power of the parties.

It is precisely because of their parliamentary majorities that Islamist parties face some major challenges. For one thing, these parties must govern in a coalition with the military apparatus, which could lead to their political trivialisation. For another, the urgent socio-economic problems in the countries of the Middle East must be solved quickly and effectively. Solving these problems requires not only political experience but also close cooperation with western states, as well as with emergent powers such as China, India and Brazil. This could be the crucial test for parties with no experience in [formal] power. Furthermore, the management of the rent-dominated economy and its transformation into a productive economy remain the greatest challenge, one that could all too easily fail.

## The Rise of Global Middle Classes

Parallel to the rise of Islamist movements since the mid-1980s, the pursuit of models of development has had some positive results, despite their failures, namely the increase literacy rates, especially among women, as well as urbanisation. This also explains the sharp decline in fertility rates in almost all countries in the region since the mid-1980s. In some countries such as Lebanon and Tunisia, the fertility rate of about 1.7 children per woman appears to entirely correspond to European standards. The crisis of the rentier system initiated, therefore, a new demographic politics in many Arab states. Combined with this are also structural adjustment programmes and the use of new media. All this led to a restructuring of societies in the region, although the Gulf States remain the exception. Small families with high costs of living and expensive children's education, as well as career opportunities for women have destabilised the patriarchal system, but has also led to a reconfiguration of the relationship between siblings, and between parents and children. In addition, the relationship with the state and the government is being questioned and renegotiated. Emmanuel Todd and Youssef Courbage have described this development as the 'unstoppable revolution' (Courbage and Todd 2008). The combination of global economic factors and the failure of the economic policies pursued have led to other ways of thinking among the middle class.

Economically, the new social strata are both the result of and reaction to the failure of models shaped by rent and Arab nationalism. This does not mean, however, that rent has been abolished, but rather that rents have been globalised (Elsenhans 2001). Thus Elsenhans argues that under the dictates of the Washington institutions – the IMF and the World Bank – countries of the Arab world were forced to remove trade barriers. The much heralded free trade zones turned out to be strategies for the procurement of privileged market access for western investors. This half-hearted opening of the market was organised by both the ruling classes in the Arab world and western investors. The first group enjoys 'mafia-like' monopolisation of certain sectors (such as banking, telecommunications, food industries, etc.), while the second enjoys protection against competitors from other continents (i.e. China). The liberalisation imposed by the World Bank and IMF has seen the development of service sectors, especially in the Arab world. Market-leading phone companies (such as Vodafone in Egypt), banks, tourism entrepreneurs, and western NGOs provide advancement opportunities for those graduates armed with modern skills (and fluency in English). The Infitah Policy led to the demise of the old state-bound middle class (the Nasserists in Egypt) and the rise of a global cosmopolitan middle class dependent on rent (Mitchell 2002). This social reconfiguration can be explained by the fact that the crisis of rent-based models meant that the state withdrew from its social responsibilities which, in turn, caused the decline of the old middle class. The neoliberal alliances among large sections of the ruling elite and international investors has resulted in the emergence of new growth industries and with it a new 'global middle class' (Cohen 2004).

Politically, this new generation of middle class is interest oriented, demands more respect and participation. It is no longer tamed by old, archaic mechanisms and discourses and calls for a new 'social contract'. The cultural and political change in the logic of action of this new urbanised, educated and rent accommodating middle class can be analysed by the new characteristics as consumers.

Since the 1990s it is possible to observe in consumer traits and in various branches of production – under the guise of the dominant cultural, traditional and religious orders – a process of self-organisation and shaping of a future individual without any ideological support among the middle class in the Arab world.

These recent developments are described in the latest approaches to research as a globalisation of Islam and Islamisation of globalisation (Pink 2009, Haenni 2009, Abaza 2006). Here, it is argued that we are experiencing the rise of a new middle class in the MENA region which is fostering new forms of consumption. 'Halal products' such as 'Mecca Cola' or fashionably styled, veiled women point to increasingly 'hybrid' forms of consumption. Thus 'globalisation' is Islamised or, that is, 'glocalised'. There is a kind of economisation and increasing abandonment of the ideology of Islam (Haenni 2005). In this context, the new forms of faith are described as 'Cool Islam' (Boubekeur and Roy 2009). In reference to Pierre Bourdieu, the new consumer behaviour can be understood as an indication of the emergence of a new middle class which is differentiated from the rest of society (Bourdieu 1982). By combining elements of new media and globalisation, new spheres of action develop for the middle classes which in turn influence their logics of action.

In Cairo, Istanbul and Ankara modern and traditional forms of life and consumption exist side by side. Department stores, streets filled with music and the barricaded upmarket neighbourhoods of the new rich, adorn the image of cities in the Middle East. In their study of the new cosmopolitan middle classes in Cairo, Koning follows Saskia Sassen in writing of the emergence of new cosmopolitan spaces in Cairo, which is described as the 'reterritorialisation of the metropolis'. The neighbourhoods of the 'nouveaux riches' are culturally and architecturally demarcated from the poor areas of Cairo by private schools, universities, supermarkets and Starbucks cafes (Koning 2009: 7). Similar developments can be observed in many metropolises of the Middle East.

Global consumerism has also reached large parts of the Middle Eastern middle classes. However, this participation in global consumption is not the result of industrialisation and with it thus the full development of purchasing power. Although these developments are similar to those of Europe in the nineteenth century, they remain fundamentally different. In Europe, industrialisation led to the rise of a new market oriented and value-conservative middle class which became the true hallmark of the Victorian era (Hobsbawm 1989).

However, the problem now is that the middle class in the Arab world is not the result of profound structural changes in the region and/or the integration of broad strata in the processes of industrialisation. Rather, they are the result of an intensification in consumption made possible through rent. Therefore, it would be hazardous to attempt to link the new forms of consumption observed in Saudi Arabia (Shechter 2009) and the Yemen (Stohrer 2009) with a push to modernisation or with a strengthening of autonomy of the civil society. Consumption consists primarily of cheap products from the informal sector and from Asia (Koning 2009: 7).

Empirically, these new consumer impulses, especially among women and young people, are not the result of improved living conditions, employment, or access to the labour market (Touahri 2009). According to the Arab Labour Organisation (ALO) the rate of unemployment increased between 1990 and 2000, from 12.7 per cent to 15 per cent. Furthermore, unemployment among certain social groups (youth and women) and marginalised ethnic/religious groups is more than 40 per cent (Dajani 2012). The 2009 'Arab Human Development Report' estimates the ratio of poor – i.e. those who live on less than two dollars per day – in the Arab world at 20.3 per cent of the total population. In addition, the number of undernourished people increased from 19.8 million in 1990 to 25.5 million people in 2004 (Arab Human Report 2009).

For this reason, it is argued here that the new lifestyle is rather a political 'code' (De Certeau 1988) which requires deciphering. As such, it is more an indication of the articulation of certain individual interests than a sign of representation and distinction. Consequently, aesthetic forms of expression become a hugely important factor in the logics of action.

One can assume that this new 'Islamic consumption and production milieu' is a signal for the increasing atomisation of society and of the end of mass movements, and hence a signal for the increased individualisation of Islamic societies. In addition, we can observe a lack of interest in organised active political participation. In Egypt, to give only one example, according to a study of the

Ahram Centre for Political and Strategic Studies, more than 67 per cent of the youth eligible to vote in the elections were not registered (Shapiro 2009).

Medium sized and small business specialising in Islamic trendy products, the detachment among the youth from existing sexual norms in Islamic countries such as Iran and Egypt (Bayat 2010), the shisha smoking, veiled young female students, the rap groups with Islamic texts, or the Husseyn parties in Iran (Bayat 2010), all these phenomena signal the corrosion of the prevailing rules. Principles of Islam are reinterpreted and transformed into tools for liberation. The modern veil is turned into a 'liberating veil' and conceals the individual interest.

These new middle classes articulate themselves by creating new modes of consumption and consumer spaces. Just because these new groups are not the result of market capitalisation but of rentier economies, and because they are still bound to clientelist relationships (locally and nationally), they develop other forms of self-organisation compared to the middle classes in Europe (Koning 2009). These groups are not hierarchically organised, controlled mass movements, but their actions take the form of new social movements, such as 'non-movements' or 'collective actions of non-collective actors' (Bayat 2010: 19). The most important feature of these new 'non-movements' is that, unlike mass movements, they do not develop a collective identity. Here, the 'I' is at the centre of the action and not the 'we'. What we observe is, in line with Rousseau, the disempowerment of the 'volonté générale' in favour of a 'volonté de tous'. Precisely because these groups operate individually for improving or maintaining their own situation, and not in the name of Umma or the nation, they have no common political agenda and therefore it is not surprising that it was the Islamists who triumphed in the first free elections (Ouaissa 2012a).

The current revolt of the middle classes in the Arab world is the result of the failure of social utopias and the concomitant increased fragmentation of society. The primary objective of the rent-oriented middle classes is the realisation of a just distribution of rents in order to achieve particular and individual lifestyles, as described by Schulze (Schulze 2012). Schulze speaks of the liberation of the individual's life-world from government controls. With the failure of the standard state models of society and the rise of the individual lifestyle utopias, it is possible to find, following Charles Taylor, a post-Durkheimian era which is initiated in the separation between norms and values (Taylor 2010, Schulze 2012: 45-6).

The protesters in Tahrir Square demanded equality, freedom and dignity. However, compared to the European middle classes of the nineteenth century, they have virtually no structural leverage to bring new social models into existence. The logics of their actions are determined by accumulated personal frustrations from which no programmatic and political counter-proposals can be derived.

## Conclusion

As mentioned in the introduction, the political and cultural behaviour of the middle strata is related to the type of surplus they generate. Since the beginning of the nineteenth century, the Arab middle classes have been the product of different strategies to acquire rents. The economic history of Europe and the emergence of the concept of rent prove that rents can occur in any society and in all economic systems. Unlike [capitalist] profit, rents occur through imperfections in markets and where market mechanisms are distorted. Rents therefore require different types of monopolies or political access.

The ruling elite coopt social groups via the creation of work, i.e. marginal work, and subsidise most consumer goods. At the same time, the offer of welfare, free education, medical care, and so on, leads to the emergence of a large middle class. These middle strata migrate to the cities because such amenities are usually available there. In addition, agriculture is neglected in many MENA countries, due to the difficult climatic conditions as well as the import policies of the ruling elites. Subsistence agriculture is not enough to feed the rural population. The overpopulation of cities increasingly underpins the importations of food and other consumer goods. The logics of action of the new, marginally employed middle classes are not market oriented and market driven in the sense of Weber (Weber 1985), but are conditioned by rents. They consume more than they produce and consequently their social status depends on the proportion of the surplus they receive from the ruling classes for consumption. Consumption in the Arab world is financed by different forms of rent. Paradoxically, the intensification of imports promotes the monopolisation of imports among the ruling class. Despite their calls for dignity, freedom and justice, the middle classes have no mechanisms for structural leverage. Accordingly, a new social model will not be enforceable. The consumer behaviour of today's Arab middle class serves only to liberate individual ways of life or as an instrument of distinction against the subaltern (Bourdieu 1998). Although primordial identities will be used for mobilisation, these will not form a structural democratic counterweight to the ruling class. This explains my pessimistic conclusion, that the current revolts in the Arab world will, perhaps, lead to a change of government in some countries and may even lead to the establishment of new political elites, but will not compel the establishment of lasting and stable democracies. The Arab middle classes will come to terms with the next regimes as long as they pursue policies that are amenable to the middle strata.

## Bibliography

Abaza, M. 2006. Changing consumer cultures of modern Egypt. Cairo's urban reshaping. Leiden, Boston: Brill.

Albrecht, H. and K. Köhler (ed.). 1997. Politischer Islam im Vorderen Orient. Zwischen Sozialbewegungen, Opposition und Widerstand. Baden-Baden: Nomos-Verlag.

Amin, S. 1976. La nation arabe. Nationalisme et luttes de classes. Paris: Editions de Minuit.

Ayubi, N.M. 1980. The Political Revival of Islam. The Case of Egypt. *International Journal of Middle East Studies*, 12(4), 481-499.

Batatu, H. 1978. The Old Social Classes and the Revolutionary Movements of Iraq. A Study of Iraq's Old Landed and Commercial Classes and of its Communists, Ba'thists, and Free Officers. London: Oxford University Press.

Batatu, H. 1999. Syria's Peasantry, the Descendants of Its Lesser Rural Notables, and Their Politics. Princeton, New Jersey: Princeton University Press.

Barry, J. 1991. Consumer's Passions: The Middle Class in Eighteenth-Century England. *The Historical Journal*, 34(1), 207-216.

Bayat, A. 2010. *Life as Politics: How Ordinary People Change the Middle East.* Stanford, California: Stanford University Press.

Beinin, J. and Z. Lockman. 1987. Workers on the Nile: Nationalism. Communism, Islam and the Egyptian Working Class, 1882-1954. Princeton: Princeton University Press.

Beinin, J. 2001. *Workers and Peasants in the Modern Middle East.* Cambridge: Cambridge University Press.

Bernstein, D. and B. Hasisi. 2008. Buy and promote the national cause': consumption, class formation and nationalism in Mandate Palestinian society. *Nation and Nationalism*, 14(1), 127-150.

Boubekeur, A. and O. Roy. 2009. Whatever happened to the Islamists? Salafism, Heavy Metal Muslims and the Lure of Consumerist Islam. Columbia, London, New York: Hurst.

Bourdieu, P. 1982. Die feinen Unterschiede. Kritik der gesellschaftlichen Urteilskraft. Frankfurt am Main: Suhrkamp-Verlag.

Bourdieu, P. 1998. *Praktische Vernunft. Zur Theorie des Handelns.* Frankfurt am Main: Suhrkamp-Verlag.

Burke, E. III, I.M. Lapidus, and E. Abrahamian (ed.) 1988: *Islam, Politics, and Social Movements.* Berkeley, Los Angeles: University of California Press.

Burke, E. III 1991. Changing Patterns of Peasant Protest in the Middle East 1750-1950, in *Peasants and Politics in the Modern Middle East*, edited by F. Kazemi and J. Waterbury, Miami: Florida International University Press, 24-37.

Burke, E. III and D. Yaghoubian (ed.). 2006. *Struggle and Survival in the Modern Middle East.* California: University of California Press.

Burris, V. 1999: The Old Middle Class in Newly Industrialized Countries. Historical, Comparative and Theoretical Perspectives, in *The East Asian Middle Classes in Comparative Perspective*, edited by H.-H. Hsiao. Taipei: Academia Sinica Press, 435-454.

Clark, J. 2004. Social Movement Theory and Patron-Clientelism. Islamic Social Institutions and the Middle Class in Egypt, Jordan, Yemen. *Comparative Political Studies*, 37(8), 941-968.

Cohen, S. 2004. Searching for a Different Future. The Rise of a Global Middle Class in Morocco. Durham, London: Duke University Press.

Courbage, Y. and E. Todd. 2008. Die unaufhaltsame Revolution. Wie die Werte der Moderne die islamische Welt verändern. München: Pieper-Verlag.

De Certeau, M. 1988. *Kunst des Handelns*. Berlin: Merve.

Dajani, J. 2012. *The New Danger in the Middle East: Unemployment*. [Online]. Available at: http://www.huffingtonpost.com/jamal-dajani/the-new-danger-in-the-mid_b_166696.html [accessed: 5 June 2012].

Earl, P. 1989. The Making of the English Middle Class. Business, Society and Family Live in London, 1660-1730. Berkeley, Los Angeles, Oxford: University of California Press.

Elsenhans, H. 1994. Decolonisation. From the Failure of the Colonial Export Economies to the Decline of Westernised State Classes. *The Maghreb Review*, 19(1/2), 95-122.

Elsenhans, H. 1995. Du malentendu à l'échec? Guerre d'Algérie et tiersmondisme français entre ajustement et engagement libéro-socialdémocrate. *The Maghreb Review*, 20(1/4), 38-62.

Elsenhans, H. 2001. Das internationale System zwischen Zivilgesellschaft und Rente. Münster: LIT Verlag.

Elsenhans, H. 2009. Kapitalismus kontrovers. Zerklüftung im nicht so sehr kapitalistischen Weltsystem. Potsdam: Welt Trends Papiere 9.

Embong, A. R. 2002. State-Led Modernization and the New Middle Class in Malaysia. Basingstoke: Palgrave Macmillan.

Eppel, M. 1998. The Elite, The Effendiyya, and the Growth of Nationalism and Pan-Arabism in Hashemite Iraq, 1921-1958. *International Journal of Middle East Studies*, 30(2), 227-250.

Ergil, D. and R.I. Rhodes. 1975. Western Capitalism and the Disintegration of the Ottoman Empire. The Impact of the World Capitalist System on Ottoman Society. *Economy and History*, 18(1), 41-60.

Esposito, J.L., M.A. Muqtedar Khan and J. Schwedler. 2003. Religion and Politics in the Middle East, in *Understanding the Contemporary Middle East*, edited by D.J. Gerner and J. Schwedler. Boulder: Lynne Rienner Publishers, 363-386.

Gay, P. 2002. Schnitzler's Century. The Making of Middle-Class Culture 1815-1914. London, New York: Norton & Company.

Geiger, T. 1930: Panik im Mittelstand. *Die Arbeit*, 7(1), 637-654.

Gerner, D.J. (ed.). 2000. *Understanding the contemporary Middle East*. Colorado: Boulder.

Gershoni, I. and J.P. Jankowski. 1995. *Redefining the Egyptian Nation, 1930–1945*. Cambridge: Cambridge University Press.

Goldschmidt, A., A.J. Johnson, and B.A. Salmoni. 2005. *Re-visioning Egypt 1919-1952*. Cairo: The American University in Cairo Press.

Gran, P. 1979. *Islamic Roots of Capitalism. Egypt, 1760-1840.* Austin, Texas, London: University of Texas Press.

Haenni, Patrick. 2005. L'islam de marché. L'autre révolution conservatrice. Paris: Seuil.

Haenni, Patrick. 2009. The Economic Politics of Muslim Consumption, in *Muslim Societies in the Age of Mass Consumption. Politics, Culture and Identity between the Local and the Global.* Tyne, Newcastle: Cambridge Scholars, 328-341.

Hafez, Z. 2009. The Culture of Rent, Factionalism, and Corruption: A Political Economy of Rent in the Arab World. *Contemporary Arab Affairs,* 2(3), 458–480.

Halpern, M. 1963. The Politics of Social Change in the Middle East and North Africa. Princeton: Princeton University Press.

Hanna, N. 2003. In Praise of Books: a Cultural History of Cairo's Middle Class, Sixteenth to the Eighteenth Century. Syracuse, New York: Syracuse University Press.

Henni, A. 1993. Le Cheikh et le Patron. Usages de la modernité dans la réception de la tradition. Alger: Office des publications universitaires.

Hobsbawm, E.J. 1987. *The Age of Empire. 1875-1914.* Pantheon Books.

Hobsbawm, Eric J. 1995. Die englische middle-class 1780-1920, in *Bürgertum im 19. Jahrhundert, Band 1: Einheit und Vielfalt Europas,* edited by J. Kocka. Göttingen: Vandenhoeck & Ruprecht, 85-112.

Hourani, A. 2000. *Die Geschichte der arabischen Völker.* Frankfurt am Main: Fischer Taschenbuch Verlag.

Hsiao, H.-H. (ed.). 1999. *East Asian Middle Classes in Comparative Perspective.* Taiwan: Academia Sinica Taipei.

Ibn Khaldûn, A. 1997. Discours sur l'Histoire universelle, Al-Muquddima, Traduit de l'arabe, présenté et annoté par Vincent Monteil. Paris: Sindbad.

Ibrahim, S.E. 1996. *Egypt, Islam and Democracy. Twelve Critical Essays.* Kairo: The American University in Cairo Press.

James, L. 2006. *The Middle Class: A History.* London: Little, Brown.

Kalecki, M. 1943. Political Aspects of Full Employment. *Political Quarterly,* 14, 322-331.

Kazancigil, A. 1973. La participation et les élites dans un système politique en crise: le cas de la Turquie. *Revue française de science politique,* 23(1) 5-32.

Kazemi, F. and J. Waterbury. (ed.). 1991. *Peasants and Politics in the Modern Middle East.* Miami: Florida International University Press.

Kepel, G. 2000. Jihad Expansion et Déclin de l'Islamisme. Paris: Gallimard.

Kocka, J. (ed.). 1995. Bürgertum im 19. Jahrhundert. Band I. Einheit und Vielfalt Europas. Göttingen: Vandenhoeck und Ruprecht.

Koning, A. de. 2009. *Global Dreams. Class, Gender, and Public Space in Cosmopolitan Cairo.* Cairo, New York: The American University in Cairo Press.

Krämer, G. 1986. Ägypten unter Mubarak. Identität und nationales Interesse. Baden-Baden: Nomos-Verlag.

Kurzman, C. and I. Naqvi. 2009. *Islamic Political Parties and Parliamentary Elections.* United States Institute of Peace Working Paper 15. January 2009.

Lazreg, M. 1976. The Emergence of Classes in Algeria. A Study of Colonialism and Socio-political Change. Boulder, Colo: Westview Press.

Leca, J. et al. (ed.). 1979. *Développements politiques au Maghreb, Aménagements institutionnels et processus électoraux.* Paris : Edition du Centre National de la Recherche Scientifique.

Liaghat, G.A. 1980. Changes in a New Middle Class Through the Analysis of Census Data. The Case of Iran Between 1956-1966. *Middle East Journal,* 34(2), 343-349.

Lipset, S.M. 1959. Democracy and Working Class Authoritarianism. *American Sociological Review,* 24(4), 482-501.

Lockman, Z. 1994. Workers and Working Classes in the Middle East: Struggles, Histories, Historiographies. Albany, New York: State University of New York Press.

Longuenesse, É. 2007. Profession et Société au Proche-Orient. Déclin des élites, crises des classes moyennes. Rennes: Presse universitaire de Rennes.

Losurdo, D. 2002. *Was ist Fundamentalismus?* Marxistische Blätter 7.

Lübben, I. 2013. Welche Rolle für den Islam? Die Herausbildung eines islamischen Parteienspektrums im post-revolutionären Ägypten – Eine Annäherung, in *Zur Vielfalt von Protest und Revolte im Nahen Osten und Nordafrika,* edited by A. Jünemann and A. Zorob. Wiesbaden: VS-Verlag für Sozialwissenschaften, 279-306.

Lübben, I. 2008. Die ägyptische Muslimbruderschaft – Auf dem Weg zur politischen Partei?, in *Politischer Islam im Vorderen Orient – Zwischen Sozialbewegung, Opposition und Widerstand,* edited by H. Albrecht and K. Köhler. Baden-Baden: Nomos-Verlag, 75-97.

Maher, S. 2011. The Political Economy of the Egyptian Uprising. *Monthly Review,* 63(6), 32-45.

Mitchell, T. 2002. *Rule of Experts: Egypt, Techno-Politics, Modernity.* Berkeley: University of California Press.

Moore, B. 1969. Soziale Ursprünge von Diktatur und Demokratie. Die Rolle der Grundbesitzer und Bauern bei der Entstehung der modernen Welt. Frankfurt am Main: Suhrkamp-Verlag.

Müller, H. 2002. Marktwirtschaft und Islam. Ökonomische Entwicklungskonzepte in der islamischen Welt unter besonderer Berücksichtigung Algeriens und Ägyptens. Baden-Baden: Nomos-Verlag.

Ouaissa, R. 2008. Aufstieg und Mäßigung des politischen Islam in Algerien, in *Politischer Islam im Vorderen Orient. Zwischen Sozialbewegungen, Opposition und Widerstand.* Baden-Baden: Nomos-Verlag, edited by H. Albrecht and K. Köhler. Baden-Baden: Nomos-Verlag, 143-164.

Ouaissa, R. 2012a. Arabische Revolution und Rente. *Periplus. Jahrbuch für außereuropäische Geschichte 2012*, 57-77.

Ouaissa, R. 2012b. Die Revolution bleibt aus. In Algerien erkauft sich das Regime politische Ruhe. *Informationszentrum 3. Welt 330*, Mai/Juni 2012, 32-33.

Ouali, H. 2010. La scène politique est secouée par une série de scandales de corruption. *El Watan*, 2 February.

Pickel, S. 2012. Mittelschichten als Antriebskraft politischer Umbrüche? Lehren aus dem Arabischen Frühling, in *Globale Trends 2013. Frieden. Entwicklung. Umwelt*, edited by Stiftung Entwicklung und Frieden. Frankfurt am Main: Fischer Verlag, 137-155.

Pink, J. (ed.). 2009. Muslim Societies in the Age of Mass Consumption. Politics, Culture and Identity between the Local and the Global. Tyne, Newcastle: Cambridge Scholars.

Richards, A. and J. Waterbury. 2008. *A Political Economy of the Middle East. State, Class, and Economic Development.* Boulder, San Francisco, Oxford: Westview Press.

Robinson, G.E. 1993. The Role of the Professional Middle Class in the Mobilization of Palestinian Society: The Medical and Agricultural Committees. *International Journal of Middle East Studies*, 25(2), 301-326.

Ryzova, L. 2004. *L'effendiya ou la modernité contestée.* Le Caire: Cedej Collection 15/20.

Savage, M. et al. 1995. Property, bureaucracy and culture. Middle-class formation in contemporary Britain. London: Routledge.

Shapiro, S.M. 2009. Revolution, Facebook-Style: Can Social Network Turn Young Egyptians into a Force for Democratic Change? *New York Times*, 25 January, 34.

Schulze, R. 2012. Die Passage von politischere Normenordnung zu lebensweltlicher Werteordnung. Erkenntnisse aus dem arabischen Frühling. *Periplus. Jahrbuch für außereuropäische Geschichte 2012*, 32-56.

Schwinn, T. 2006. Konvergenz, Divergenz oder Hybridisierung? Voraussetzungen und Erscheinungsformen von Weltkultur. *Kölner Zeitschrift für Soziologie und Sozialpsychologie*, 58, 201-232.

Shechter, R. 2005. Reading advertisements in a Colonial/Development Context: Cigarette Advertising and Identity Politics in Egypt, c1919-1939. *Journal of Social History*, 39(2), 483-503.

Shechter, R. 2008. The Cultural Economy of Development in Egypt: Economic Nationalism, Hidden Economy and the Emergence of Mass Consumer Society during Sadat's Infitah. *Middle Eastern Studies*, 44(4), 571-583.

Shechter, R. 2009. Consumer's Monarchy. Citizenship, Consumption, and Material Politics in Saudi Arabia since the 1970s, in *Muslim Societies in the Age of Mass Consumption: Politics, Culture and Identity between the Local and the Global*, edited by J. Pink. Newcastle: Cambridge Scholars Publishing, 89-104.

Singerman, D. and P. Amar (Ed.). 2006. *Cairo Cosmopolitan. Politics, Culture, and Urban Space in the New Globalized Middle East.* Cairo: The American University in Cairo Press.

Sluglett, P. (ed.). 1997. *The Urban Social History of the Middle East 1750-1950.* Syracuse: Syracuse University Press.

Stohrer, U. 2009. Consumption in Yemen: Continuity and Change, in *Muslim Societies in the Age of Mass Consumption: Politics, Culture and Identity between the Local and the Global*, edited by J. Pink. Newcastle: Cambridge Scholars Publishing, 129-143.

Tylor, C. 2010. Afterword. Apologia pro libro suo, in *Varieties of Secularism in a Secular Age*, edited by M. Warner, J. v. Antwerpen and C. Calhoun. Cambridge: Harvard University Press, 300-324.

Thompson, E. 2000. *Colonial Citizens: Republican Rights, Paternal Privilege, and Gender in French Syria and Lebanon.* New York: Columbia University Press.

Touahri, S. 2009. La classe moyenne au Coeur des débats au Maroc. *Magharebia*, 14 May.

Tönnies, F. 2012. *Studien zu Gemeinschaft und Gesellschaft*, edited by K. Lichtblau. Wiesbaden: VS-Verlag für Sozialwissenschaften.

Turner, B.S. 1984. Capitalism and Class in the Middle East. Theories of Social Change and Economic Development. London: Heinemann Educational Books.

UNDP (ed.). 2009. Arab Human development Report 2009: Challenges to Human Security in the Arab Countries. New York: Regional Bureau for Arab States (RBAS).

Vatin, J.-C. 1974. *L'Algérie politique, histoire et société.* Paris: Presses de la fondation nationale des sciences politiques.

Wahrman, D. 1995. *Imagining the Middle Class: The Political Representation of Class in Britain, c.1780-1840.* Cambridge: Cambridge University Press.

Watenpaugh, K.D. 2006. Being Modern in the Middle East: Revolution, Nationalism, Colonialism, and the Arab Middle Class. Princeton: Princeton University Press.

Weber, M. 1985. Wirtschaft und Gesellschaft. Grundrisse der verstehenden Soziologie. Tübingen: Mohr.

Winkler, O. 2005. Arab Political Demography. Volume one: Population Growth and Natalist Policies. Brighton, Portland: Sussex Academic Press.

Zubaida, S. 2008. Urban social Movement, 1750-1950, in *The Urban Social History of the Middle East, 1750-1950*, edited by P. Sluglett. Syracause: Syracuse University Press, 224-253.

Zubaida, S. 2011: Beyond Islam. A New Understanding of the Middle East. London, New York: I.B. Tauris.

Chapter 8

# Exploring the Logics of Moderate Islamists' Political Actions in the Light of the 'Arab Spring' – The Cases of Jordan and Morocco

Kerstin Fritzsche and Ivesa Lübben

## Introduction

The role of moderate Islamist parties throughout the Middle East and North Africa in the events spurred by the so-called 'Arab Spring' has received wide attention by researchers and the media. Reactions ranged from concerns over Islamist movements gaining momentum in the course of democratic transition to surprise on how little role the Islamists seemed to have played during the popular uprisings. In particular the focus has been on those countries where the 'Arab Spring' led to a regime change and where Islamist movements became the dominant political forces in the newly elected governments, such as in Tunisia and Egypt. Much less attention has been given to countries where the regimes – so far – remained stable despite popular protests and the fact that there, too, large Islamist movements and other societal groups demand reforms.

To shed light on these cases, this chapter discusses the role and political positions of two moderate Islamist parties that have been less studied within the context of the events of the 'Arab Spring': the Islamic Action Front Party (IAFP), the political branch of the Jordanian Muslim Brotherhood, and the Moroccan Justice and Development Party (JDP). An analytical comparison of both cases is rewarding because despite several similarities between Morocco's and Jordan's political systems, significant differences exist with regard to how these countries have been influenced by the 'Arab Spring' and the role that moderate Islamists played in these developments. Both countries are monarchies with rather young monarchs that large portions of the populations set their hopes in for substantial reforms both economic and social. Over the past years, before the events of the 'Arab Spring', the moderate Islamist parties in Jordan as well as in Morocco have followed a distinct strategy of providing a constructive opposition to the regime striving for integration into the political system. Furthermore, in both countries, the monarchies pursued controlled top-down reforms as a reaction to popular protest and the IAFP as well as the JDP have not called for an eradication of the monarchy in the course of a reform process. Instead, they aimed at transforming the all-encompassing powers of the kings into a constitutional monarchy dedicating more political powers to the national governments and the political parties.

However, despite these common features, the two countries and the respective moderate Islamist parties have taken very different paths over the last two years: In Morocco, the JDP, which had been the largest oppositional group in parliament before the elections of November 2011, acted in favour of the top-down reform process which was launched by the king as a reaction to the countrywide protests that started on 20 February 2011. The party supported the preparation of a new constitution and called its followers to vote positively for it in the constitutional referendum. With the elections of 25 November 2011, the JDP became the strongest political force in parliament, winning 107 out of 395 seats. Four days later, based on the new constitution, which obliged the king to appoint the prime minister from the party that gained the most votes in the election, Abdelillah Benkirane, the party's secretary general, became Morocco's first prime minister from an Islamist party.

In Jordan the situation was quite the contrary. After King Abdallah II took the throne in 1999, the relationship of the regime with the Muslim Brotherhood and the IAFP, its political arm founded in 1992, grew increasingly tense and the party gradually disengaged from the formal political process. It boycotted the election in 2010, declined all offers to participate in a new cabinet that was precipitately formed by the king in February 2011 to counteract beginning unrest and refused to join the National Dialogue Committee at the end of 2011. The IAFP criticised the new constitutional amendments that were proposed by a Royal Commission in August 2011 and boycotted the elections in January 2013 after the king had dissolved parliament in October 2012 – less than two years after its election.

Against this backdrop, the question rises why the IAFP and the JDP have taken such different positions in the reform process of their country – with such different outcomes. This chapter argues that both parties follow distinct logics of action. Logics are defined as 'mechanisms shaping social action' (see Horst et al. in this volume). Working with a set of different logics provides a multilevel approach to identify specific factors that affect the creation of the IAFP's and the JDP's political behaviour. The objective is to provide a holistic understanding of the framework conditions in which the decision process of both parties is made. We argue along the concept of Logics of Action that decisive influencing factors are among others the political processes the parties take part in, the actors and structures they provide and encounter, the political, societal and structural context they operate in, interdependencies they might be entangled with as well as the specific historic context of these parties.[1] These factors can be understood

---

1    Different from the other chapters in this book, the Euro-Mediterranean dimension plays a less significant role in the cases presented here. This is particularly due to the fact, that – despite regional and geopolitical factors influencing the dynamics triggered by the 'Arab Spring' – the positions and actions of the parties discussed in this specific context were predominately driven by domestic factors and considerations. However, as Islamist

as logics relating to the dimensions of power structures, identity, space and time which provide the backdrop of the political behaviour of the IAFP and the JDP. Political behaviour is understood as the sum of processes and actions undertaken by the party internally as well as in different public spheres addressing varying stakeholders such as members, followers, sympathisers, political competitors and allies. Based on this approach, political behaviour includes a wide range of elements, such as the interaction with other actors within certain institutions and in the public, reactions to specific events – be it orally, in written or through concrete action, the launch of political activities and the formulation of political positions. Political behaviour is something that could – at least hypothetically – be observed from the outside.

It is assumed that the political behaviour of the IAFP and the JDP is the result of a pragmatic and rational decision-making process based on key logics of action in order to achieve preferred outcomes. Both parties are considered as actors that are capable and willing to analyse the framework conditions of their political behaviour and to learn from this analysis. Based on available information and their experiences gathered in the past, the parties make choices with regard to the formulation of their political positions and their actions that seem most likely to support the parties' objectives and preferences. The chapter's purpose is to explore the logics of action guiding the political behaviour of the IAFP and the JDP in times of potential change. The time period dealt with in this chapter ranges from January 2011, when following the revolution in Tunisia popular discontent became more outspoken in both Jordan and Morocco, to the end of 2011. By providing this analysis, the chapter wants to contribute to a better understanding of moderate Islamist movements' political beliefs and behaviour. The section on each party will first briefly outline how the 'Arab Spring' manifested in the respective country. Then, the key logics of actions of the party will be explored in the four dimensions of power structures, identity, space and time and finally, their interplay and outcomes will be discussed.

## Limiting the Power of the King – the Context of Changing Logics of Action of the IAFP and the Jordanian Muslim Brotherhood

Jordan has not witnessed a revolution like Egypt and Tunisia, but here, too, several spontaneous protest movements by teachers, day labourers and military veterans started even before 2011. Their reasons for protest were very similar to those in other Arab countries: the bad state of the economy, corruption, high youth unemployment and the rise of prices for basic goods (Vogt 2011: 63). The regime reacted promptly: it increased food and fuel subsidies and wages of public

parties gained significant political relevance since the start of the uprisings in the Middle East and North Africa, understanding their logics of action will be decisive for the future of Euro-Mediterranean relations.

employees including the pensions of military veterans. On 1 February it sacked the unpopular Prime Minister Samir Rifai who was criticised by the protestors because of his neoliberal policies. Still, the regime could not stop the new impetus of the protest wave. In particular in the provinces, the traditional strongholds of the king, demonstrations occurred on a regular basis. However, like in the other countries of the 'Arab Spring', it was not the Islamist forces that initiated the protests, but young people and marginalised workers. At the beginning, the Islamic Movement – the Muslim Brotherhood and the IAFP[2] – which constitutes by far the largest opposition force in Jordan, was reluctant to join the new movements that had developed outside the platform of the traditional opposition parties, although the youth organisations of IAFP and the Muslim Brotherhood had joined the new youth alliances. But despite its initial sceptics, the leadership of the Islamic Movement recognised that the impetus of the new grass root movements could be instrumental in forwarding its own reform agenda; this had first been formulated in November 2005 when the IAFP and the Muslim Brotherhood had jointly presented a reform programme which endorsed principles of a democratic state of law based on political pluralism, free elections and the independence of justice. Since the beginning of the movement, the Islamists regularly called for demonstrations and in May 2011 formed together with leftists and national parties the National Front for Reform.

Despite the Islamic Movement's harsh critique of the regime – the Muslim Brotherhood holds the Royal Cabinet responsible for the widespread corruption, the sell out of the country's assets, and the unpopular political and economic normalisation with Israel – it never questioned the legitimacy of the monarchy. The slogan 'The people wants the fall of the regime' that was heard on the streets of Cairo, Tunisia and Damascus was rejected. 'We are looking for a constitutional monarchy as in democratic European states like Britain, Sweden or Denmark, where the role of the queen or the king is exclusively representative', declared Nimr Assaf, the Deputy General Secretary of the IAFP (Interview with N. Assaf 14 September 2011).[3]

In order to understand these self-imposed red lines on the one hand and the growing defiance by the Islamists towards the king on the other hand, one has to explore the spatial and identity-related parameters as well as power structures that deeply impact Jordanian politics – be it on the side of the regime or the opposition.

---

2    Both perceive themselves an organic political union and often act together under the name 'Islamic Movement'. The General Secretary of the IAFP is selected by the Shoura ('Consultative') Council of the Muslim Brothers. Key documents like the reform platform of 2006 are jointly prepared and released. Recently, both organisations formed a Higher Reform Council in order to define a common ground for reacting towards the new protest movement and the reforms initiated by the king.

3    It is interesting to notice that Assaf refers to European political models while the autocratic Jordanian monarchy enjoys support of the EU out of regional considerations although it fails to meet European democratic standards.

They provide the key to understanding the logics of action of the Jordanian Muslim Brotherhood and the IAFP. The first central parameter space is relevant in two ways: The position of Jordan in a crisis-ridden region and the geographical demarcation of what Jordan is and has been. These two dimensions represent one key basis for the Jordanian identity or rather identities and help to explain the specificities of the fragile structure of power relations within the Jordanian state and society.

Jordan is first of all a small and vulnerable country in the epicentre of different chronic crises: civil war-torn Iraq in the East, Palestine and Israel in the West, Syria and Lebanon in the North. All regional crises have immediate economic as well as demographic and security effects on the country. Still, the Jordanian regime largely managed to keep the country out of regional turmoil and prevented this turmoil affecting its internal stability.[4] Stability is a basic feature of Jordanian identity. Its loss is perceived as a danger for the very existence of the state, according to secretary of the IAFP Hamza Manzour: 'Jordan's stability is, to us, a heavenly duty [...]. Stability [...] is a necessity to encounter imperialist and hostile designs which are aimed at weakening both Islamic societies and Islam itself' (Kazem 1997: 14).

Secondly, Jordan as a country is itself an artificial colonial product. It was created by the British in order to create a substitute country for Palestinians after they granted the Jewish Agency the right to found a national home in Palestine. Before the foundation of the Trans-Jordanian Emirate, there was no common Jordanian identity between the tribes in the area, and the urban population saw themselves as being part of a Greater Syria. Although the ruling Hashemites who came originally from the Hejaz had been installed by the British, they became over time the political and symbolic institution which facilitated the integration of the Trans-Jordanian tribes and the small urban middle class that mainly originated from Syria, Lebanon and Palestine into one country. For this historical reason, the Hashemites, who claim to be descendants of the Prophet Mohammed – are central to Jordanian identity. It is not so much the religious legitimacy of the king as it is the case in Morocco, but this integrative and stabilising function of the Hashemite throne which is the reason why the Jordanian Muslim Brotherhood and the IAFP do not question the monarchy as such despite their demand to restrict its authority.

Yet, this common denominator of Jordanian identity is in fact challenged by two main circles of identity that deeply split the Jordanian society and between whom deep distrust exists: the Trans-Jordanian tribes and the Jordanians of Palestinian origin which to some observers form today the majority of the population. This divide is not ethnical. The two different identities are constructed around different narratives and historical as well as social experiences of Palestinians

---

4　An exception is the 1967 war when Israel occupied the West Bank, that had been annexed by Jordan in 1948, as well as the clashes that erupted between the Palestine Liberation Organization (PLO) and the Jordanian regime and ended with Black September in 1970.

and Jordanians in the context of the Israeli/Palestinian conflict: the Palestinians' identity was based on a narrative revolving around the notions of exile, suffering from and resistance against Jewish migration to Palestine. This narrative today forms the basis of an identity by which Palestinians distinguish themselves from other Arab peoples. This is even upheld among Palestinians that are born in Jordan and have Jordanian nationality. On the other hand, Trans-Jordanians constantly feel an inherent threat that their country could become a permanent settle ground for Palestinians, which would even further marginalise them.

This vertical schism within the Jordanian society is used by the regime as a central power instrument adding to the horizontal divides between the regime and opposition forces. The electoral law was one of the instruments to keep up this schism. The districts were drawn in a way that for example, there was one Member of Parliament (MP) for every 20,000 inhabitants in Karak with a nearly exclusively Trans-Jordanian population, while in Zarqa which has a high percentage of Jordanians with Palestinian background there was one MP for 90,000 inhabitants. With this electoral law, the king guaranteed parliamentary majority of apolitical and loyal tribal representatives in the parliament.

Furthermore, the schism within the Jordanian society informs dynamics within the opposition in general as well as within the Jordanian Islamic movement in particular providing one of its key logics of action related to identity. Until the 1980s, the main support base of the Muslim Brotherhood was the traditional Trans-Jordanian society. This changed in the 1990s with the growing influence of HAMAS within the Palestinian national movement and the disappointment of the Palestinian refugees with the PLO that ignored the refugees' right to return in negotiations with Israel and more and more turned away from the people in Jordanian refugee camps. The vacuum was filled by the Islamic Movement that opened youth clubs and welfare centres in the camps. Today, the majority of its members are of Palestinian origin. Many of them have a dual loyalty towards the Jordanian Islamic Movement and HAMAS (Hamarneh 2002). Through the 'Palestinisation', the political agenda of the IAFP became more and more influenced by an external Palestinian agenda at the expense of social concerns for the Trans-Jordanian society not without causing internal opposition. In 2009, three members withdrew from the Executive Office of the Muslim Brotherhood accusing the leadership of 'impeding the Brotherhood's reform projects by [...] insisting on transforming the organization into a mere support group for another organization [an allusion to HAMAS]; [...] and undervaluing [...] the importance of social issues and the lack of seriousness in adopting the causes and concerns of the people' (Abu Rumman 2009: 171f).

Another relevant parameter for the logics of action of the Jordanian Islamic Movement are its historically grown power relations with the regime. Over time, these structures were altered and significantly influenced the context in which the IAFP is acting. This had also profound repercussions on main ideological concepts and priorities of the IAFP. During most of his life, King Hussein had, despite political controversies and tensions on more than one occasion,[5] kept a balanced relationship with the Muslim Brotherhood which he used to counterweigh leftist and nationalist opponents. In contrast to Muslim Brotherhood organisations in other Arab states the Jordanian branch was legal since its foundation in 1944.[6] Muslim Brothers could freely spread their interpretation Islamic message. Members of the organisation were coopted into the ministry of Religious endowments and education where they had influence on religious school curricula (Moaddel: 35). This was honoured by the Islamists by the acceptance of the legitimacy of the throne even after the conclusion of the peace treaty with Israel although the liberation of Palestine is a core aspect of their ideological conviction.

After King Hussein (re-)introduced parliamentary elections[7] in 1989, Islamists – Muslim Brothers and independents – obtained nearly half the seats in parliament. The consequence was not only the politicisation of the parliament, but also that of the Islamists who became more aware of social and foreign politics. They also became more critical to official politics especially after Jordan concluded the peace treaty with Israel and started to engage in economic normalisation. Since then, all state-induced political reform projects – specially the different electoral laws – aimed at limiting the parliamentary representation of the Muslim Brotherhood, respectively the IAFP by strengthening tribal loyalities.[8] After King Abdallah II took the throne, he not only tried to limit the political space of the IAFP, he also started to dry up the social networks of the Muslim Brotherhood by taking over the Islamic Centre, the powerful welfare organisation of the Muslim Brotherhood which runs several hospitals, schools, kindergartens and a private high school in Zarqa. The narrowing of the movement's political space caused by the young king finally caused the disengagement of the IAFP from the formal political process and led to a boycott of the 2010 elections by the IAFP.

Over time, the increase in political experience played a major role for the Islamic Movement's logics of action. Since its foundation, the Muslim Brotherhood in Jordan has been subject to a considerable learning process. Originally, it saw itself as a conservative missionary ('da`wa') movement whose aim was a revitalisation

---

5   In the 1950s Hussein came under heavy criticism because of its positive stance towards the Bagdad pact. The Muslim Brotherhood criticised also that Jordan gave up any claims on the West Bank in the late 1980s and condemned the peace treaty with Israel.

6   For Islamisation as an attempt of the ruling elites to fight the cultural hegemony of religious groupings see also Harders in this volume.

7   Since 1964 there were no parliamentary elections although the parliament formally continued to exist but was diminished by the death of a big portion of its members.

8   Due to the election law from 1989 every voter could cast as much votes as there were representatives from his district. In 1993 this law was replaced by the one-man-one vote-law that allowed only one vote for one candidate. In this case most voters preferred a tribal or clan representative. In 2010 the regime voting districts were divided into so-called virtual districts that had nothing to do with geographical borders like certain neighbourhoods. During the registration the candidates did not know in which district they were registered and against whom they had to run.

of Islamic values. The demand for the application of Sharia that they understood as purist social morals and social responsibility was the core belief that guided their social practice. It lies at the centre of their logic of action. Some factions within the Muslim Brotherhood even objected in the context of the revitalising of parliament 1989 to the participation in the elections, because they saw democracy as incompatible with the Islamic principle of consultation ('shoura'). But a majority within the movement thought that participation in elections could support the demand for social reform on Islamic terms through legislative measures from above.

Since then a new generation of Islamists evolved that has been politicised in the professional unions, which had been the main opposition platform before the legalisation of political parties. Their first success in elections and their integration into the political process had enforced a new political logic onto the Muslim Brotherhood. What had twenty years ago been perceived as a tool to achieve 'Islamic' gains has over time become a value in itself. Today, democratic principles such as people's sovereignty, free elections, and the independence of justice have become core policy beliefs that have been integrated into their Islamic identity and value system. This explains why traditional mechanisms of the Jordanian state of coopting the Islamists by making concessions in 'Islamic matters' have lost momentum.

In the light of the 'Arab Spring' and the Islamic Movement's political behaviour related to the events it triggered, the key parameters influencing the movement's logics of actions can be clearly recognised: space and identity-related factors, the alteration of power relations with the regime and going along with this the changes in core beliefs of the movement as well as the learning process it experienced over time. First of all, the concentration on Palestinian issues was one of the reasons why the Muslim Brotherhood was as surprised as the regime itself by the new social movements that developed in the provinces.

While earlier movements in the 1980s and '90s were organised by the urban middle classes of mainly Palestinian origin, this time it was the neglected provincial towns, the traditional power base of the Hashemites, that rebelled. These new movements were just the surface of a deep change of social relations between the two main segments of the Jordanian society that had been triggered by the neoliberal reforms introduced by King Abdallah II since his regency and which changed the context to which the IAFP had to adopt its strategies. The king had initiated the privatisation of most state-owned companies which were mainly taken over by foreign capital. Since then, he has managed the country like a private company (interview with H. Bustani 20 September 2011). The king tried to limit the economic influence of the state to the disadvantage of the Trans-Jordanian tribal areas that were more and more neglected by the decrease of social services and job opportunities in the local administration, while the mainly Palestinian business community profited from the new economic policies. The local leaders in the tribal areas felt that they no longer were able to deliver to their local clientele.

This is the reason why the Jordanian 'Arab Spring' started in the provincial Trans-Jordanian *hinterland* and not in the capital.

But instead of addressing the economic policies of the regime, Trans-Jordanian Protesters bore the responsibility on the Palestinians whom they perceived as winners of economic reforms – a development that was indirectly fuelled by the state apparatus and parts of the intellectual elite. Since then partial identities (Palestinian versus Trans-Jordanian; tribe versus tribe) have been strengthened at the expense of a common Jordanian identity. The new Movement of the South ('harak al-janubi') was an indicator that the traditional power mechanism did not work any more and that the politics of Devide et Impera by splitting the society along identity lines are threatening social peace and stability and could even backfire onto the regime itself. So the king had to rethink his strategies. In order to consolidate his social base, to split the protest movement, and to appease a part of the opposition without losing the monopoly of power, the Jordanian regime adopted a new electoral law in January 2012, which reserved 18 per cent of the now 150 seats for party lists. This was a clear attempt to convince the IAFP – being the only political force with substantial mass support in both segments of the population – to give up his boycott and to participate in the next elections which are supposed to be held in 2013. The IAFP has demanded that 50 per cent of the mandates should be reserved to party lists in order to give up its boycott.[9] This would allow them to become an influential force within the legislative, ready to press for a more socially biased development strategy, to control corruption and to restrict the economic normalisation process with Israel – one of the core demands of their Palestinian clientele.

To some observers it may seem that the 'Arab Spring' has passed over Jordan. But the country is in a process of political transformation, even if this transformation might be gradual. The Islamist Movement, too, is in a process of adapting its logic of action to the new circumstances. Although it has reiterated its objection to return to the ballot box, it seems pretty aware that there are new chances to reintegrate into the political process. However, this time not as a coopted junior partner, but as a political actor with influence on the political decision-making process. The continued boycott has to be seen as an attempt to bargain with the regime about more substantial political concessions and not only on cosmetic reforms. They are aware that the king needs them as a stabilising factor: 'We are the only organisation in which all groups, Jordanians and Palestinians, all Jordanian tribes are represented on the bases of a joint programme. We don't consider ethnic differences. We consider citizenship as the bases of the community' (interview with N. Assaf 14 September 2011).

Still, there are forces within the so-called moderate, mainly Trans-Jordanian wing of the movement that fear that this strategy of refusal could lose momentum. Ruhail al-Ghuraiba, one of the three members who had resigned from Executive

---

9    Another demand is that the one-man-one-vote is replaced by the former multiple-vote principle.

Office in 2009, recently announced that he had founded a Front for Reform, which is open to Islamists and others. He accused the leadership of the movement and the party of not having a clear reform project, nor a reform strategy. He announced that the front aims at translating the power of the youth movement into political gains not only on the national level, but also within its local context.

### Keeping the Balance – The Logics of Action of the JDP in Morocco's Reform Process

In Morocco, the dynamics triggered by the 'Arab Spring' neither led to a profound change in the political structures nor to a significant replacement of the political and economic elite. Rather, a controlled top-down reform process was initiated by King Mohammed VI. From 20 February 2011 on, Morocco witnessed a series of largely peaceful demonstrations with several tens of thousand participants[10] calling for political, social and economic change in almost 60 cities and towns. The demonstrations were initially encouraged by the 20 February Movement, a youth dominated group that inspired by the events in Tunisia and Egypt called for country-wide protests on 20 February (Desrues 2012: 31).[11] As a reaction to the protests and in order to keep them from escalating, the king increased subsidies for basic goods, improved employment opportunities in public administration and addressed his people on 9 March to announce constitutional reforms. Just one day afterwards, he established a commission of hand-picked experts tasked with drafting the new constitution. The members of the commission were appointed by the king and headed by one of his advisors, while a consultative body established to liaise between the commission and civil society and political stakeholder groups offered only limited room for a substantial engagement of these actors in the drafting process (Ottaway 2011). The new constitution formally increased the powers of the legislative and the independence of the judiciary. However, it reaffirmed the king's all-encompassing power despite some formal limits to his competencies such as the obligation to appoint the prime minister from the ranks of the party that gained the largest number of votes in the parliamentary elections. The lack of substantial change in the political system and the exclusive

---

10    Numbers of how many people took the street vary: the interior minister spoke of approximately 37,000 demonstrators (MAP, 21 February 2011) while the organisers of the protests claimed that 300,000 people participated in the demonstrations (Desrues 2012: 33).

11    In Desrues (2012), the movement is described as a group dominated by young people, which in the beginning was 'structured as a horizontal network, formed out of day-to-day improvisation. It does not have a gravitational centre, but is decentralized and spread across the country, with a predominance in large and medium-sized towns' (Desrues 2012: 33). Later, as Desrues explains, the movement integrated 'activists and political and social organizations that want to join the movement, some – though not all – of whose demands they share' (Desrues 2012: 33).

process of writing the new constitution received a lot of criticism. As a result, the 20 February Movement and the Justice and Charity movement (al-Adl wal-Ihsan)[12] called for a boycott of the referendum to approve the new constitution. The JDP, on the other hand, welcomed the new constitution, declared its intent to support it in the referendum and called its followers to vote in favour of it. For an oppositional party which had been persistently calling for more democracy in the political game over more than a decade, the quick and comprehensive consent with the regime's approach to appease the protests might be surprising. Indeed, it provides proof of the logics of action inherent and constitutive to the party's political positions and behaviour. Four key, yet not exclusive, logics of action will be explored in more detail in the following paragraphs: the adherence of the party to incontestable principles of the Moroccan political system including the avoidance of fundamentally challenging the regime (relating to the dimension of power structures), its strong self-perception as a constructive, pro-democratic political party (identity), the strong orientation towards the urban middle classes (space) and finally, the window of opportunity offered by the events of the 'Arab Spring' (time).

For exploring the relevance of power structures for the logics of action of the JDP, a brief lesson in its history is necessary: the development of the JDP is marked by a complex balancing act between attracting and mobilising its support base and securing its very existence by avoiding harsh confrontation with the regime (Wegner 2011).[13] The JDP is one of two major Islamist movements in Morocco. While the Justice and Charity movement founded by Sheikh Abdessalam Yassine[14] is formally banned due to its fundamental opposition towards the regime, but in practice tolerated by the officials given its significant number of followers, the JDP is a political party created with the blessing of the palace. The party came into being during a period of gradual political opening in Morocco, when in 1996 several members of the Islamist charity organisation Movement of Unity and Reform (MUR), joined a marginal political party, and were elected to its general secretariat (Wegner and Pellicer 2009). Two years later, the party assumed a new name: Justice and Development Party. The party's mother organisation MUR was created by former segments of the Islamic Youth, 'probably [...] the most radical of the Moroccan Islamist organizations' (Wegner 2011: 22) which was dissolved by the authorities in 1976. However, before the creation of the MUR, those segments had undergone a process of moderation and took more pragmatic

---

12    The Justice and Charity movement – often called the largest Islamist movement in Morocco – participated in the 20 February Movement. It ended its support to the movement in December 2011 because – as it explains on its website – some individuals within the movement were pushing it in a direction opposed to the Muslim identity of the Moroccan people (Justice and Charity 2011).

13    Eva Wegner (2011) provides the most recent and comprehensive analysis of the party's development and its strategies to play the political power game in Morocco.

14    Sheikh Yassine died on 13 December 2012 at the age of 84.

stances. The Islamic Group, one offspring of the banned Islamic Youth, which later formed the MUR together with another association, explicitly recognised the legitimacy of Morocco's monarchy in 1990 (Wegner 2011: 23). It deliberately chose a new name, Reform and Renewal, in 1992 to avoid the impression of any claim of exclusively representing Islam (Wegner 2011: 23).[15] Leading figures of the group were three men who later became members of parliament (MP) and members of the general secretariat of the JDP: Mohamed Yatim, Abdallah Baha and Abdelillah Benkirane (Wegner 2011: 23)[16] – who on 29 November 2011 became the first Moroccan prime minister under the new constitution.

The party's adherence to the incontestable principles of the Moroccan monarchy and the religious leadership of the king, affirmed during the 1997 party congress, were essential for the creation of a political branch of the MUR being tolerated by the regime. Knowing how fragile this tolerance could be, the avoidance of any fundamental confrontation with the palace was already laid in the JDP's cradle and provides a central logic for its political strategies conceding to the power relations in Morocco. One example for this logic is the party's behaviour after the terrorist attacks in Casablanca in May 2003. Partially due to pressure from the regime, but also to show that the party does not wish to be linked to terrorism, the JDP had decided to run in less than one fifth of the electoral districts for the 2003 local elections (Boubekeur 2009) and tried to distance itself more from its mother organisation MUR (Wegner and Pellicer 2009: 166). This should be considered against the fact that the JDP had increased its number of seats in parliament from 14 in 1997 to 42 in 2002. The party was aware that becoming too strong might provoke harsh countermeasures from the regime. Indeed, in the 2007 parliamentary elections, a new electoral law and gerrymandering confined the party's electoral success (Wegner 2009: 168-9). Moreover, the creation of the Party of Authenticity and Modernity (PAM) by Fouad Ali El Himma, a man close to the king, in 2009 – which achieved a sweeping victory in the municipal elections – was widely perceived as an attempt to establish a counterweight to the JDP. Despite the party's strong disapproval of the regime's containment strategy, it never disengaged from the formal political process.

In the light of the very recognition of the fundamental power structures in Morocco and subsequently the adoption of pragmatic approaches towards the regime, the party developed a strong self-image as a loyal and constructive opposition. This formed a key element of its identity and an important narrative for attracting electoral support. Closely linked to this and also central to the JDP's political behaviour is the party's dedication to formal democratic structures

---

15    Wegner draws on the newspaper al-Raya from 2 February 1992 as quoted in Shahin (1998).

16    Wegner (2011) added an important footnote to this information which shall be repeated here for a better contextualisation: 'All three were born in the mid-1950s. They were thus in their late teens when the Islamic Youth Association was active and in their later twenties when they founded the new association.'

within the party.[17] Its well-organised internal processes and participative structural elements allow the party to stand out from political competitors and serves as an argument for the party to gain credibility with regard to its political reform agenda.

This dimension of identity is closely related to the societal space the party covers: Due to the fact that the party's roots lie in organisations that recruited heavily among university students and trade unions (Wegner 2011: 25), the JDP is predominately based on the middle classes of large urban centres such as Rabat and its neighbouring town Salé, Casablanca, Tangier and Fes, but also smaller and medium-sized towns. This specific constituency is reflected in the party's political programme and the political positions it brought forward, stressing the need for economic reforms and liberalisation without being at the expense of social justice and security, calling for the elimination of corruption, and the improvement of education and employment opportunities as well as for reforms of the political system. Recently, there are signs that the party is also increasingly opening up for wealthier businessmen (Masbah 2012).

These three logics – conceding to fundamental power structures, having a strong identity as a constructive, loyal and credible opposition and orientation towards the urban middle classes – were, albeit not exclusively, decisive mechanisms that shaped the JDP's political behaviour throughout the year 2011. In addition, the 'Arab Spring' revealed another important dimension relevant for the political behaviour of the JDP: time – or better – timing matters as will be outlined in the following sections.

As everyone in the region and beyond, the 'Arab Spring' took the JDP by surprise. Whoever talked to the party's leaders and members in the first months of the year 2011 certainly sensed the euphoria about the sudden and fierce call for change, enthusiasm that this change could be achieved and insecurity about how the path towards more democracy and improved economic and social conditions would be walked. Yet, it was clear for the JDP that Morocco would embark on the process of change peacefully and without challenging the basic principles the party had dedicated itself to.[18] Moreover, the party felt confirmed in its demands for a more democratic order in the kingdom and the need for economic and social reforms. When the protests reached Morocco, the JDP, however, kept a rather low profile and refrained from officially calling its adherents to join the protests. Indeed, at the behest of the party's general secretariat, the youth organisation of the JDP, the Youth of Justice and Development pulled back from its announcement to demonstrate side by side with the 20 February Movement which even led to harsh criticism of the secretary general's position from inside the party (Badrane

---

17    This aspect was repeatedly pointed out during numerous interviews the author held with party officials and JDP members of parliament during several visits to the country between October 2010 and December 2011.

18    Interviews with JDP officials and members of parliament in February and March 2011.

2011). Nonetheless, members from all ranks of the party joined the demonstrations on the streets.

The unease the party showed with regard to an official involvement in and maybe even encouragement of the protest movement clearly marked its logic of action of conceding to the existing power structures and proved its lessons learned from the past: as mentioned above, the Moroccan regime had proved an efficient manager of the JDP's political rise and curtailed its ambitions when it became too powerful. Following this logic, the JDP did not draw on the actual power of mobilisation it could have played off, but stressed its self-image of a loyal and – actually the only – credible oppositional force. For more than a decade, topics such as the strengthening of the parliament's legislative power have been on the political agenda of the JDP. While other parties that have been engaged in the government before the protests faced troubles regarding their credibility, the 'Arab Spring' had opened a window of opportunity for the JDP to voice its demands in an environment where actual change seemed possible. The party used this to present itself not only as a constructive supporter of the Moroccan reform process, but even more as its defender: after the constitutional referendum on 1 July 2011, the parliamentary elections originally scheduled for 2012 were proposed to take place in October. The JDP as well as the other parties generally welcomed this suggestion arguing that this would allow the country to quickly move forward with its reform process. However, they called for a later date ensuring enough time for a thorough preparation of the election to facilitate its fair and transparent course. Besides, the JDP called for the supervision of the elections by an independent commission and a revision of the register of voters, arguing that approximately five million voters were not included in the list. Moreover, in the discussion of the new electoral law issued before the election, the JDP demanded a restructuring of the electoral districts and to increase them in size for the sake of reducing the risk of electoral fraud.

When the interior ministry presented the new electoral law in August 2011, the JDP as well as the other parties voiced harsh criticism. Over the course of the summer, the dispute between the JDP and the interior ministry grew increasingly tense with the JDP voicing its concern that the parliamentary elections would not be conducted transparently and showing its general disappointment with how the provisions of the new constitution were put into practice. The party argued that the regime deliberately tried to contain the party's electoral potential as it did on previous occasions. This confrontation with the regime brought the JDP a lot of media attention in an overall quite calm election campaign – with the side effect that it pictured itself as defender of the reform process aiming at its potential electorate. Still, the party did not cross a red line with its criticism e.g. by questioning the position and actions of the king. By doing so, it offered the regime the opportunity to accept the electoral victory of the JDP, also as a counterweight to the opposition from the ranks of the 20 February Movement and the Justice and Charity movement.

Furthermore, taking a constructive approach towards the king's reform process reflected the JDP's orientation towards the Moroccan middle class.[19] King Mohammed VI enjoys high popularity among the Moroccan people. Not he, but rather central government officials and the Makhzen, the politically and economically influential entourage of the palace, were held responsible for the country's economic and social grievances. The king's reform agenda which also included a 'moral cleansing of the state administration and increased accountability for public office holders' (Desrues 2012: 35) therefore received broad appreciation from the population. This holds particularly true for the urban middle classes which were for long expecting an improvement of their economic situation, but had no interest in experiencing the same political and economic chaos that Tunisia and Egypt suffers from as one outcome of their revolutions. With its constructive approach, the JDP made clear that it, too, wanted substantial reforms, yet without creating turbulences threatening the country's achievements and explicitly stressing that the Moroccan businessmen would not have anything to fear from an electoral victory for the JDP (Mrabi 2011).

Aside from the logics of actions discussed above – adherence to incontestable principles of the Moroccan political system, strong identity as constructive opposition, taking advantage of the window of opportunity the 'Arab Spring' offered and orientation towards the urban middle classes – another element needs to be taken into account to understand the JDP's behaviour and actions: the party had matured with its political engagement in the national parliament and as a representative in and often leader of local governments throughout the country. Already after the elections of 2007 when the party gained 46 seats in parliament out of 324 and became the largest oppositional group, members within the JDP suggested that they should accept a position in the government if it was offered to the party. However, the leadership of the party rejected this claim arguing that the current political system was undemocratic and the government had no real powers which is why the JDP did not want to join it.[20] The party feared being associated with a bad performance by the government even if it was only a junior partner in the ruling coalition and that becoming part of the government would be interpreted as a disruption of some of the party's fundamental principles. However, the JDP having a sophisticated and well-organised structure containing many participatory elements for engaging its members – compared to other Moroccan parties – has long been ready to take larger responsibility in the country's affairs and to prove its competencies not only on local, but also at national level. The Moroccan reform process triggered by the 'Arab Spring' and in particular the constitutional changes increasing the parliamentary powers have opened the opportunity for the JDP to gain larger political power without losing face and presenting itself as a reform actor and driver of change while at the same time being a warrantor for political stability.

---

19    For the ambivalent role of the middle classes as change agents see Ouaissa in this volume.

20    Author's interview with party cadres in February 2011.

This is a fundamental condition for further economic development in Morocco, also in the light of its strong economic ties with Europe and the importance of foreign investment for the country. Without neglecting achievements with regard to a more democratic way of governance made during the reform process, the JDP, following its inherent logics of action has contributed significantly to preserving the *status quo* of the Moroccan political system. This shows how deeply rooted the JDP is in these structures – despite its background as an oppositional party – and how much it follows the concerns of its key constituency, the urban middle classes, which despite their call for political and socio-economic improvements have never been willing to achieve profound change as the price of security and stability.


## Conclusion

The comparison of the IAFP, respectively the Islamic Movement in Jordan, and the Moroccan JDP revealed the key logics of actions in the dimensions of power structures, space, identity and time which provide the parameters of the parties' political behaviour and influenced how the parties reacted to the events triggered by the 'Arab Spring'. Both parties face power structures that aim at restricting their actions and political leverage. However, while the IAFP as a consequence gradually disengaged from the formal political process, the JDP strengthened its role as a loyal oppositional party. In contrast to the IAFP, by far the largest political movement in Jordan, the JDP faces a variety of political competitors. This explains why the IAFP can be much more demanding *vis-à-vis* the regime than the JDP which is very well aware that it would easily put its political position at stake if it seriously challenges the palace.

Space was explored in different ways for both parties: for the JDP with regard to the societal sphere it is based on and operates in – the urban middle classes – and for the IAFP in the light of the geographical location of Jordan in the crisis-ridden heart of the Middle East. For both parties, this results in a strong desire for stability and majorly influences their identity and the logics of actions attached to it. In the case of the IAFP, the schism between Trans-Jordanians and Palestinians in the Jordanian society serves as a key logic of action of the IAFP. In Morocco – as heterogeneous as its population is – a similar situation cannot be observed. Over time, both parties passed through a major learning process and became professional political actors.

The events of the 'Arab Spring' challenge both parties though in very different ways: The IAFP has worked to increase its influence within the movement and to overcome at the same time the ethnic split in favour of a social and economic reform agenda. It is aware that it is the only political force in Jordan at the time being that could enforce substantial change and uses its influence as a bargaining power towards the monarchy. In the case of the JDP, the party's political rise over the year 2011 suggests that it plays the political game for its own benefit quite well. The main challenge for the JDP will be to meet the expectations of its constituency, put its electoral programme into practice and remain credible despite the constraints and challenges its new responsibilities in government bring. The tasks and difficulties this implies could likely lead the JDP to lose its balance between the courtesy of the palace and the approval of its followers – and might alienate one or the other side.

## Bibliography

Abu Rumman, M. 2011. *Jordanian Policy and the Hamas Challenge: Exploring Grey Areas and Bridging the Gap in Mutual Interests*. Amman: Friedrich Ebert Foundation.

Al-Hamarneh, A. 2002. The Social and Political Effects of Transformation Process in Palestinian Refugee Camps in the Amman Metropolitan Area (1989-1999), in *Jordan in Transition 1990-2000*, edited by G. Joffé. London: Palgrave Macmillan, 172-190.

Badrane, M. 2011. *Le parti de la lampe ébranlé* [online]. Available at: http://www.maghress.com/fr/lematin/147237 [accessed: 15 December 2012].

Boubekeur, A. 2009. *Morocco: The Emergence of a New Palace Part* [online]. Available at: http://carnegieendowment.org/2009/07/28/morocco-emergence-of-new-palace-party/4abt [accessed: 15 December 2012].

Desrues, T. 2012. Moroccan Youth and the Forming of a New Generation: Social Change, Collective Action and Political Activism. *Mediterranean Politics*, 17(1), 23-40.

Hizb jabhat al-amal al-islami (IAFP) 2011. *al-Harakat al-islamiya tu`lin ru'yatiha min al-ta`dilat al-dusturiya* [*The Islamic Movement Announces its Position towards the Constitutional Amendments*]. Amman. Statement from 15 August 2011.

Justice and Charity 2011. *Al Adl Wal Ihsane décide la suspension de sa participation au mouvement 20 février* [online]. Available at: http://www.aljamaa.net/fr/document/4134.shtml [accessed: 15 December 2012].

Kazem, A. 1997. *The Historic Background of the Muslim Brotherhood and its Ideological Origins*, in *Islamic Movements in Jordan*, edited by H. Hourani. Amman: Sindbad Publishing House.

MAP 2011. *'20 février': Déclaration du ministre de l'Intérieur. Cinq corps calcinés à l'intérieur de l'une des agences bancaires incendiées à Al Hoceim* [online]. Available at: http://www.aufaitmaroc.com/-actualites/maroc/2011/2/21/20-fevrier-declaration-du-ministre-de-linterieur-cinq-corps-calcines-a-linterieur-de-lune-des-agences-bancaires-incendiees-a-al-hoceima [accessed: 15 December 2012].

Masbah, M. 2012. *The Party Just In (and Developing)* [online]. Available at: http://carnegieendowment.org/-sada/index.cfm?fa=show&article=48743&solr_hilite=Morocco [accessed: 15 December 2012].

Max Planck Institute for Comparative Public Law and International Law. 2012. *Jordan* [online]. Updated 9 November 2012. Available at: http://www.mpil.de/ww/en/pub/research/details/know_transfer/-constitutional_reform_in_arab_/jordanien.cfm [Accessed: 10 December 2012].

Moaddel, M. 2002. *Jordanian Exceptionalism – A Comparative Analysis of State-Religion Relationships in Egypt, Iran, Jordan, and Syria.* New York: Palgrave.

Mrabi, M.A. 02 November 2011. *Benkirane au Club de L'Economiste Pourquoi le JDP est devenu fréquentable* [...]. Available at: http://www.leconomiste.com/node/888391 [accessed: 15 December 2012].

Ottaway, M. 2011. *The New Moroccan Constitution: Real Change or More of the Same?* [online]. Available at: http://www.carnegieendowment.org/2011/06/20/new-moroccan-constitution-real-change-or-more-of-same/6g [accessed: 15 December 2012].

Shahin, E.E. 1998. *Political Ascent: Contemporary Islamic Movements in North Africa.* Boulder, CO: Westview Press.

Vogt, A. 2011. Jordan`s Eternal Promise of Reform. *Internationale Politik und Gesellschaft,* (4), 61-76.

Wegner, E. 2011. *Islamist Opposition in Authoritarian Regimes. The Party of Justice and Development in Morocco.* Syracuse, New York: Syracuse University Press.

Wegner, E. and M. Pellicer 2009. Islamist moderation without democratization. The coming of age of the Moroccan Party of Justice and Development? *Democratization,* 16(1), 157–175.

Chapter 9

# On the Logics of the Egyptian Transformation Process: Continuity and Change

Ingrid El Masry

## Introduction

The overthrow of the Mubarak regime in Egypt 2011 was quickly identified as a revolution. More specifically, it has been designated as a spontaneous 'Facebook' or a 'youth revolution' whereby the Arab and international media have focused on specific means and agents of action. Given its reductionist message, such a characterisation can be called into question as it ignores a long and established culture of protest, the real rather than virtual organisational interrelations and cross-generational structures. Furthermore, it dismisses the question of the content as well as the quality of change. Based on these perceptions a more substantial and broader analyses of the ongoing changes in Egypt – as well as their roots – must be undertaken. To begin such a process is the aim of this chapter – to the degree that such an analysis is possible given the relatively short period since the overthrow of the Mubarak regime and the fact that ongoing events in the country remain in flux.[1]

While there exists some common ground for understanding revolution as 'a forcible, irregular, popularly supported change in the governing regime' (van Inwegen 2011: 4), we nonetheless lack 'a systematic, historically grounded analysis of revolutionary processes that connects them firmly to our accumulating knowledge of state formation' (Tilly 1995: 5). This implies that our understanding of a specific revolutionary process is tied to more than just our understanding of a specific state formation and its surrounding system of states. Rather, we have to embed our understanding of a specific revolutionary process in the broader framework of socio-economic and human development, as well as the international environment, i.e. contexts and constraining structures. It is in this wider context where structures meet agents and agents meet structures. There are profound differences regarding the contexts of revolutionary processes: in classical European settings (i.e. bourgeois or social revolutions) or revolutionary processes in peripheral countries (i.e. Developing World or Global South), marked by a

---

1 This chapter has been finished before the overthrow of the Morsi regime.

path of historical development characterised by foreign domination and resulting in structural heterogeneity or dependency. Within these different structural contexts one finds different social agents characterised by very heterogeneous manifestations of human development. This is where the structure of agency in revolutionary processes becomes relevant, as the theory of human development has shown. Conceptualised in terms of enlarging human freedom (Sen 2003: 13, UNDP/ RBAS 2002: 15ff) there is a historical logic of human development following a path of interests from material to political to self fulfilment (Welzel 2002: 53ff). This development is shaped by the social environment but at the same time also impacts on the structure.

This chapter argues that the revolutionary process in Egypt represents a subversive movement which began long before the overthrow of the Mubarak Regime. It is based on a complex combination of heterogeneous human interests, rooted in the extreme structural heterogeneity of Egyptian society and in the broad mixture of social problems which have accumulated over previous past decades. In addition, it is argued that the bulk of heterogeneous revolutionary agents in Egypt acted on the basis of highly pragmatic personal interests: first, to settle the score with their own rulers, i.e. primarily with Mubarak and his cronies and only then with the 'West'. In a sense this also marks an end to post colonialism (see Dabashi 2012: 9-10). This entire process is, nevertheless, embedded in the structural context of the globalisation of capitalism, a process without definite ends concerning the development of indigenous structures and agents' interests.

These arguments are developed through a diachronic sociological analysis of changes in the relationship between structure and agency in recent decades of Egyptian social development. The empirical analysis is guided by the Logics of Action approach, which is grounded in structuration theory (Giddens 1992). The Logics of Action framework is developed with a focus on specific logics of change and persistence in order to identify the challenges for and opportunities of the revolutionary process. The question in any revolutionary process is whether the power structure has changed qualitatively. As such, the research questions pursued in this chapter focus on four logics of action which are viewed as central elements in the development of post-colonial Egyptian power relations:

- The logics of civil-military relations
- The logics of labour-capital relations
- The logics of secular-religious relations
- The logics of gender relations

As it is structure that delivers the context in which human interests and actions are formed, the empirical analysis starts by asking how a change in the ideational and structural logic of the post-colonial Egyptian model of development – from patrimonial socialism to authoritarian liberalism – prepared the context for a kind of liberal Islamism. Focusing on the above-mentioned spheres of power relations I analyse these changes as driven primarily by the elite or top-down politics up until the overthrow of Mubarak in 2011 which marks a turning point in structures of action, now characterised as bottom-up and revolutionary. However, the turbulent and ongoing power struggle during the last two years of post-overthrow development does not allow for significant insights into possible future development and, as outlined in the closing section, the conclusion drawn is that (so-called) democratic revolutions mark the beginning of revolutionary processes, and not their end.

## Logics of Action – Studying the Egyptian Transformation Process

The Logics of Action framework is an analytical approach which is suited to overcoming the classical dualism between structure and agency in social science theory. The basic assumption is: there are no structures without agents and no agents without structures, and both categories are intertwined according to a notion of human interests. On this basis, the Logics of Action approach allows for the development of a heuristic concept of how social change takes place: why, under which conditions, and how far social structures are perpetuated or changed in revolutionary processes, beginning with individual human interests.

In order to transfer this general theoretical concept into a concrete analytical framework to understand the Egyptian transformation process, a set of preliminary hypotheses have been developed. First, the logic of social change has its roots in the development of human interests. Second, the articulation of human interests by revolutionary social movements is mediated by respective challenges, choices, and opportunities. Third, changes in social structures are the logical outcomes of changing social relations, i.e. power relations in different spheres of society.

### *The Developmental Logic of Human Interests*

The ultimate vanishing point of human interests is, according to Amartya Sen, freedom; freedom in the sense of enlarging human choices within the constraining context of human society (Sen 2003: 13). Realising free self-fulfilment is, according to Sen, related to a set of intertwined instrumental freedoms, the most important being personal and political freedoms, disposal over economic resources and social chances, e.g. education, health and social security (Sen 2003: 52). Additionally, as Welzel has pointed out in his empirically grounded theory of human development (Welzel 2002: chapter A. III), we may embrace a contextual logic in the development of human interests: given that the disposal over economic resources influences human freedom – most basically and directly – economic interests build the basis of contextually determined interests. These are followed by the constraints of restrictive ethics, i.e. informal norms, values and identities, which limit claims for emancipation, and the interest of overthrowing them. Last but not least, there exists a set of interests based on formally institutionalised freedom rights. Whereas the different sets of interests mark a broader general logic of society's social developments, they shall not be viewed as rigid stages. On the contrary, they overlap. Most interesting for our analysis are Welzel's conclusions about the effects of adaptation: On the one hand, social interests adapt to disposable resources as the latter lay the groundwork for those interests which are articulated. On the other hand, concessions by political elites adapt to articulations of interests, or political institutions come under revolutionary pressure as and when they no longer adequately meet articulations of social interest (Welzel 2002: 53-4). Furthermore, the rather abstract concept of logics of human interest development is complicated by the fact that progress may be different in different social spaces, i.e. social strata or classes of a given society, which potentially give rise to heterogeneous social struggles when different sets of interests are simultaneously challenged.

*Revolutionary Social Movements as Logics of Challenges, Choices, and Opportunities*

The argument outlined thus far leads us to the question of why revolutionary social movements form and how they achieve success. Whereas these questions imply a necessarily complex analysis, given the constraints of this contribution I will elaborate only the most basic arguments relevant to the research interests.

First, it is argued that a combination of theories of structure and action are required to answer the multitude of questions and categories of interests and preferences in order to bridge both. Whereas structural theories often describe constraints to which people react, agency theories usually attempt to explain why people engage.

Concerning structural theories, one basic conclusion which may be drawn is, as implied above, that challenges of existential interests arise from problems in the disposal of economic (material basics of life) and social goods (education, health etc), restrictions on changing value or identity structures, and last but not least, a violent repression of interests related to political goals. I argue with Huntington (1968), that a comprehensive and aggregated challenge, such as those outlined, often poses a problem for rapidly modernising patrimonial authoritarian regimes when they reach the limits of material, ideational and organisational capacities to fulfil the growing heterogeneity of individual interests and aspirations and at the same time remain in control of society (see also Goodwin 2001). Nevertheless, as Theda Skocpol has highlighted in relation to revolutions as functions of structural conditions (Skopcol 1979: 17-18), structural theory alone cannot deliver logics of revolution as structures are only able to indicate probabilities. Structures themselves do not act – only people do.

Why then do people engage in revolutionary movements? Though social science research has produced a broad body of literature on social movements over the last decades (see Della Porta and Diani 2006: chapter 1, Beinin and Vairel 2011: Introduction), it has been primarily psychology which delivered the most important insights into the missing links of revolutionary practice: why do people engage, and/or why do they fail to engage, despite finding their interests challenged? One possible answer is that people become active to the extent that their interests are constrained.

Such a conclusion, however, is convincing only at the first glance as deprivation theory shows us. Drawing on the distinction between relative and absolute deprivation this approach suggests that a situation of absolute deprivation (extreme poverty and marginalisation or segregation) diminishes the probability of social action, as absolutely deprived people simply lack the intellectual means and the power to address the roots of their situation. Hence, a great deal more attention has been given to the dimension of relative deprivation which may be defined – according to Gurr's well-known question 'Why do men rebel?' (Gurr 1970: 13) – as 'perceived discrepancy between men's value expectations and value capabilities', which itself is framed by previous debates.[2] It appears that it is a feeling of social injustice (Runciman 1972, Moore 1982), simultaneously combining despair and hope, which makes revolutionary engagement 'necessary' as well as 'purposive' and 'visionary' (Kimmel 1990: 12).

The bulk of explanations for why people engage in dangerous action have made reference to psychology and economics and focused on rational choice theories (Walt 1999: 10-11). A challenge which remained for these approaches is the so-called free rider problem, i.e. answering the question why people engage in dangerous action for collective goods like democracy if they could also benefit from such an indivisible good by simply letting others conduct the struggle (Olson 1965: 16, 60-61).

Both problems seem well treated by strategically orientated explanations addressing logics of the psychology of large groups and mass behaviour. So-called contracts and convention theories and tipping models focus on strategic assumptions in the logics of human group behaviour. Whereas the former refers to the approach of an 'all-or-none proposition', i.e. not one person contributes unless everyone who would be needed to provide the good contributes (Moore 1995: 436ff), the latter offers help explaining how small individual actions may initiate widespread upheaval by reducing other people's action threshold, i.e. sparking revolutionary bandwagoning (see Kuran 1991).

---

2　Such as the following lively commentary by Marx: 'A house may be large or small; as long as the neighbouring houses are likewise small, it satisfies all social requirements for a residence. But let there arise next to the little house a palace, and the little house shrinks to a hut. The little house now makes it clear that its inmate has no social position at all to maintain, or but a very insignificant one; and however high it may shoot up in the course of civilization, if the neighbouring palace rises in equal or even in greater measure, the occupant of the relatively little house will always find himself more uncomfortable, more dissatisfied, more cramped within his four walls. [...] Our wants and pleasures have their origin in society; we therefore measure them in relation to society; we do not measure them in relation to the objects which serve for their gratification. Since they are of a social nature, they are of a relative nature' (Marx 1975: 411f).

Both approaches are potentially of interest for the case of the Egyptian upheaval (as well as events in Tunisia). They both highlight aspects of the national political cultures, characterised by group and status and they identify broad accumulation of social discontent as one of the root causes of revolutionary upheavals. Moreover, they fit with the well-known narratives of Tunisia's Mohamed Bouazizi and Egypt's Khaled Said as triggers of social upheaval, highlighting that everybody may be the next victim and there is nothing to lose. In this sense, moments of the unexpected become windows of opportunities.

In summary, a research hypothesis that takes into account structural challenges, strategic action and windows of opportunities may well be suitable for exploring the question of why revolutionary movements develop and how they become successful in overthrowing authoritarian regimes.

*Social Structures, Social Action and Structuration*

In classical social science literature, which takes structure as nothing more than social relations (see, for e.g., Weber 1920: 252, Engels 1973: 206, Simmel 1908: 10, Marx 1974: 176, Marx 1980: 548), one of the biggest problems has been to develop an understanding of how structures are formed by human action and, at the same time, how human action is constrained by structures. One way to address this problem is by taking up a historical-functional perspective, that is to ask: why do particular structures exist in a given historical phase and why are they challenged and overthrown in a second historical phase, and to what end.

Drawing on Anthony Giddens' structuration theory, I assume a duality of social structures as the result, and at the same time, a constraining context of human action (Giddens 1992: 77). I use his differentiation between a 'realm of structures' and a 'realm of interaction' to make sense of the structure of dominance, referring to the political and economic institutions executing power over people. Giddens' theory of the interplay between structures and agents (his so-called modalities, see Giddens 1992: 81) has been taken up by Barley and Tolbert (1997) that turned Gidden's thoughts into a methodological framework. They argue that institutions 'vary in their normative power and their effect on behaviour' where this variation depends 'in part, on how long an institution has been in place and on how widely and deeply it is accepted by members of a collective' (Barley and Tolbert 1997: 96). It should be noted, however, that institutions do not only exercise normative power but also violence, as it is often the case in authoritarian regimes in crisis.

Moreover, Barley and Tolbert transform Giddens' rather abstract category of 'modalities' into the term 'scripts', defining them as 'observable, recurrent activities and patterns of interaction characteristic of a particular setting', encoding the social logics of interaction (Barley and Tolbert 1997: 98). Lastly, they made clear that structuration processes can only be studied through a diachronic method of empirical analysis based on longitudinal data. The core question which remains is: what are the triggers causing agents to replicate or revise scripts? This recommits us to the developmental logics of human interests as well as to the strategic choice approaches explored above.

*Operationalising the Agent-Structure Problem for the Study of the Egyptian Transformation Process*

Inquiring after the character (content and quality) of changes induced by the Egyptian transformation process requires understanding the social roots, continuities and changes of the existing social and power structures. In the case of Egypt the most central of these structures are the civil-military, labour-capital, civil-religious, and gender relations. The set of theoretical hypotheses preliminary outlined above can now be transformed into the following set of research theses and questions:

1. If a society's development of human interests contradicts its chances of realisation, we must sooner or later arrive at a situation of revising scripts, i.e. a power struggle or revolution. In order to identify the social roots of the Egyptian revolutionary process the empirical analysis, thus, has to study the central power structures and the genesis of conflicting human interests.
2. This general hypothesis is complicated by the assumption that societies characterised by structural heterogeneity – e.g. the functional coexistence of modern, subsistence and informal sectors in economy and society – may be confronted with the development of different manifestations of human interests in these contexts. The concluding hypothesis is: only if there exists a cross-social contradiction to the existing power structures – i.e. the existence of some kind of broad counter hegemony – are the conditions for the overthrow of existing power structures given. As such, the empirical analysis has to identify whether there exist different sets of interests pursued by different groups of social agents and to what degree they conform.
3. Finally, the cross-social counter hegemony may split in the process of institutionalising new power relations, offering the chances of either establishing a cross-social unity power structure, a new special interests power structure, or hindering the construction of any new power structure for an undetermined period of time. As sustainable regime change in the context of heterogeneous interest constellations depends on the maintenance of a broad social consensus in the process of institutionalising new political and social structures, the empirical analysis has to identify the character of the evolving new power structure as an indicator of whether and how far revolutionary change has taken place.

## Change and Persistence: Logics of Action in the Egyptian Revolutionary Context

Muhammad Ali may not have been the ultimate founder of modern Egypt (Marsot 1984: 1), but since his reign social development in Egypt has been state-centred, military backed and secular (excluding the period of British-imposed colonial-liberal interplay in the late nineteenth and early twentieth century). Whereas his initially successful project laid the foundations for the cleavages of modernisation discussed in this contribution, it has at the same time been inspired and counteracted by western influences – a complicated process to be reproduced by the experiences of the Nasserite regime of the 1950s and 1960s, and with different political omen by the later Sadat and Mubarak regimes.

All in all, the structuration of Egyptian development until the 2011 overthrow has been elite led and heavily influenced from outside. Western Europe promoted secular modernisation (late nineteenth century French influences) only to bring it to a halt (British colonialism). Eastern Europe promoted state-centred secular modernisation and at the same time drove Egypt into an authoritarian impasse (1950s and 1960s). In the early 1970s, the US supported political Islam in Egypt as a counterforce to combat leftist state-centred development, reinforced by an oil sponsored new Arab Social Order, the Arab role in the Cold war and Saudi regional hegemony. Lastly, Western Europe complicated Egyptian political culture by simultaneously promoting secular-pluralistic, welfare focused modernisation and economic deregulation and collaboration with authoritarian regimes in the context of the Barcelona Process. The ultimate result is an Egyptian political culture which is deeply split and is searching for identity following its first 'bottom-up' development beginning with the 2011 overthrow.

### The Logics of Civil-Military Relations

The relevance of civil-military relations for the structuration of state power in Egypt has its roots in the role of the military as the formative founder of the modern Egyptian state. While it was Muhammad Ali who in the first half of the nineteenth century undertook comprehensive attempts to push Egypt into a modern nation state, it was Gamal Abd An-Nasir and his colleagues who overthrew the monarchy in a military coup in 1952 which has been widely acknowledged as the start of a political and economical revolution under the auspices of the military. In the following decades the army came to be identified as a force of national, and to a certain extent, Arab liberation and independence, largely through fighting wars in 1948, 1956, 1967 and 1973. Though all later Egyptian presidents or heads of State until 2012 have been army officers – i.e. Anwar as-Sadat following Abd An-Nasir in 1970, and Husni Mubarak succeeding the latter in 1981 – there have been progressive processes of civilian institutionalisation over time. Starting in the 1950s with a strongly centralised one party system based on the president's personal charismatic power, as well as on the overwhelming presence of military representatives, the 1970s saw the formal introduction of a multi-party system, albeit without any real alternative to the dominant National Democratic Party (NDP) established by Sadat and later controlled by Mubarak. While the number of military officers chosen to be members of parliament decreased significantly at this time, to be replaced by new business elites, constitutional attempts to bring the military under civilian control (Art. 143, 150 and 182 of the 1971 constitution – see Egypt State Information Service: 1971) remained initiatives on paper only. Having seen his predecessor executed by military officers in 1981, President Mubarak's strategy to bridge the widening gap and growing distrust between governing and military elites was to control promotions to senior officer grades through executive decree. He exerted influence by increasingly favouring the Republican Guard (charged with protecting the President himself) for the highest level appointments and by 'the presidential power to determine the composition of the officer corps and select the cabinet, including the minister of defence and the minister of military production' (Springborg 2013: 97f). Nevertheless, the most effective as well as most obvious strategy to counterbalance the military was the politics of favouring the interior ministry, the police force and the intelligence service, not only in terms of building up secret political files, but especially by promoting them financially: whereas 'the police budget was multiplied by a factor of more than six over the last decade' projected to reach 2.2 billion pounds (3.7 billion US Dollar) in 2011/12], 'the military's barely doubled' (International Crisis Group 2012: 10).

The rivalry for power and influence between the military and the apparatus of internal security is undeniably an old one in Egypt, but it reached an unprecedented level during the last two administrations of Mubarak. This resulted from the combination of favouring the interior ministry along with the newly emergent class of private business entrepreneurs. An accelerated implementation of neoliberal structural adjustment and privatisation programmes, coupled with accelerating corruption of state elites, began in particular under the Nazif government in 2004, parallel to the president's younger son, Gamal Mubarak, rising to become a political mastermind in the NDP. This change of elite's interests introduced new intra-elite power structures which should be institutionalised by controlling the presidential succession. Moreover, these structures were cemented through the campaign to build up the president's son, Gamal Mubarak, as a future leader, although he is not rooted in the army but in the business elite which emerged in the 1970s.

This evolving structuration of civil-military relations in Egypt affected the anti-monarchical, republican identity of the army as well as its economic interests as a big power in the public sector. In sum, it called 'into question the pillars of the Nasserite socio-political system established in the early 1950s, which relied on military control over key aspects of the economy and state bureaucracy' (International Crisis Group 2012: 10), having originally committed itself to independent national and welfare development.

Thus, the logics of civil-military relations in Egypt are strongly tied to the logics of labour-capital relations.

However, what emerged as an intra elite power struggle over the past decade, leaving civil society out of the game, ultimately developed into a revolutionary civil society action after the early 2011 takeover of the Supreme Council of the Armed Forces (SCAF). Discussing the political or economical role of the army had been one of the three political taboos[3] as well as a kind of a 'social non-theme' in public Egyptian political culture. This was because the military generally showed no interest in intervening in daily politics, and because it did not function as a force of internal suppression. The Egyptian military ruled but did not govern (see Cook 2007), and in general has been regarded as eminently respectable by the people based on its historic roles.

The political script changed, however, when the SCAF decided not only to rule but also to govern in early February 2011. The concrete circumstances for this development remain unclear up to date: were they driven to power or did they grasp power, outmanoeuvring a president and a political class unwilling to resign? However, governing also meant confronting the daily challenges of politics, and it did not take long before the civil society realised that the early revolutionary slogan 'The people and the army are one' had been a naive illusion. It quickly became clear that there was little overlap between the interests of the military and those gathered at Tahrir Square. Whereas the protesters at Tahrir Square demanded the overthrow of authoritarian, alienated structures based on heterogeneous identities and interests – symbolised in the slogans of bread, freedom, social justice, and human dignity (Tahrir documents 2011) – the military had its own perception of the revolution, reducing it to a protest against 'the slide towards hereditary government; the excesses of neoliberal politics, ostentatious corruption by networks associated with the president's family' (ICG 2012: i). The generals saw no reason to disband the military dominated political system or the military dominated state-centred economy. This may be due in part to a strong nationalist conviction, in the positive sense, that this is the best way to rapid modernisation of an underdeveloped country. However, as is shown below, the military profited a lot from this structure since the 1980's. Thus, this entire empire was at risk with the possibility of a freely elected president not rooted in the military. From this perspective, what appeared as a poorly designed transition process during the year and a half of SCAF government[4] for large parts of the Egyptian and the international public, can be regarded as a well conceived strategy to split the civil opposition and test the chances of a public acceptance of military governance, or at least to gain time to further entrench prevailing interests (El Masry 2012: 78ff). Events began to go wrong for the SCAF with its Constitutional Declaration of 30 March 2011 (Egypt State Information Service 2011), providing the military with absolute governmental power during a transition period which was only

---

3    These taboos being politics, sex and religion. E.g. shouting 'b-tatakallam bi siyasa' (you talk about politics?) was suitable to stop any further discussion about politics.

4    Consider the repeated changing of time frames and sequences of main institutional steps: elections of parliament, shura council and president, constitution building.

vaguely defined. The declaration of supra constitutional principles (the so-called El-Selmy Document) on the 1. November 2011, granting the military a veto power in the constitutional process and therefore preventing political control over military budget spending, then marked a turning point in the public perception of the SCAF (Fathi 2011). These approaches to secure some kind of special social role for the military, as well as the latter's repeated violent suppression of the ongoing public protests during the first two post-Mubarak years qualitatively changed the traditional political script of civil-military relations. The 'Down with Mubarak slogans' were rapidly transformed into 'Down with the SCAF/military slogans' under united mass protests. This development opened a very small door to the possibility of restructuring the modern post-colonial Egyptian power regime. Nevertheless, the new constitution adopted in December 2012 with a majority of 63.8 per cent and with just 32.9 per cent voter participation, does not restrict the political and economic power of the military (see ACUS 2012).

Thus, all that remains which could potentially disrupt 'the once fixed constellation of linkages between government and armed forces' (Welch 1993: 87) are the implementation of specific policies and furthermore effective democratisation.

## The Logics of Labour-Capital Relations

In the 1950s and 1960s the primary model of post-colonial Egyptian development rested upon a kind of patrimonial state socialism, adapting the national situation to the world political constellations of the day. This refers to: non-alignment, self reliance, state-centredness, import substituting industrialisation and modernisation, welfare politics and social partnership combined with political disenfranchisement, that is to say: offering bread for freedom, or establishing a democracy of bread (*dimuqratiayyat al-khubz*). Despite remarkable successes with development, the model fell into crisis at the end of the 1960s and thereafter followed the typical path of economic liberalisation and privatisation since the early 1970s (see El Masry 2011: 132-3). Despite high growth rates, the new economic structure generated a version of crony capitalism, corrupting the state economic sector as well as new emerging and old private capital (see Zaalouk 1989). All together, the Egyptian economy failed on the road to sustainable development, a problem which has only deepened and at the same time been delayed by the country becoming a semi rentier state based on oil, tourism, Suez-Canal charges and labour migration remittances, since the 1970s.

At the end of the 1980s, the Egyptian government was dependent on external loans and forced to open structural adjustment negotiations with the International Monetary Fund which lasted until 1996 (see El Masry 2011: 134). While the government was honoured as 'World's Top Reformer', especially after substantially intensifying privatisation and liberalisation in 2004, it more or less ignored the resulting growth in social inequality and political tension in the country, the consequences of which had long since begun to marginalise the middle classes (see El Masry 2011: 135-6. For the weak role of the middle classes as political change agents see Ouaissa in this volume)).

Nevertheless, a considerable number of the traditional state-owned enterprises, including broad segments of the military-industrial complex, resisted the privatisation process. The military as a central figure managing the traditional public sector since the 1950s gained considerably higher economic relevance after the 1979 US-mediated Camp David Peace Treaty between Egypt and Israel. It has been compensated for sticking to a peace treaty, which was perceived as unjust and humiliating, and for keeping out of politics externally as well as internally. From that period on, up to and including the present day, Egypt could rely not only on 1.3 billion US Dollar annual military aid, but also on becoming heavily privileged within the domestic economy (Müller-Mellin 2011: 98-9). The outcome was that the Egyptian military succeeded in building an economic empire, which not only comprised the classical sectors of arms production, but also included the transport sectors, energy (oil, gas and renewable energy), real estate (land, housing and tourism), major consumer goods as wells as foodstuffs, and much more. In addition, the role of the military was not confined to the state economic sector but reached far into the private sector. The military ventured beyond the bounds of the domestic private sector and risked undertaking joint ventures and other forms of international cooperation (see in detail: Müller-Mellin 2011: chapter 4, Marshall and Stacher 2012: 13). One conclusion that we might draw is that the military's interests were not principally conflicting the agenda of neoliberal restructuring which also explains why it banned all labour strikes during its governing time.

Labour resistance to neoliberal politics grew substantially with the intensification of liberalisation and privatisation after 2004, as growing unemployment, sinking wages and the gagging of state unions did not produce a way out of growing mass pauperisation – the share of people living under the poverty line was between 20 and 40 per cent from the mid 2000s on (El Masry 2011: 135-4, Solidarity Center 2010). Whereas labour and union movements and their actions have been basic pillars of the 2011 overthrow, a fundamental change of labour-capital relations has become improbable since the elected Islamist parliament and president have not previously been opposed to the neoliberal policies of the Mubarak state, with the exception of its corruption. Existing structures and scripts of labour-capital relations are likely to remain in place in the near future.

*The Logics of Secular-Religious Relations*

Secularism and Islamism, the latter representing the regional expression of conservatism, have been competing ideologies under Egyptian development since the nineteenth century, as indicated above. In this broader context, the post-colonial Egyptian development model experienced a profound change from state-centred welfare politics to political authoritarianism and economic liberalism from the 1970s. Simultaneously it experienced a shift in its basic structures of identity from moderate secularism to different forms of Islamism, albeit with considerable external influence and the form of Islam varying from militant to moderate articulations. It has never been the case, however, that the development of the modern Egyptian state – state centred, military backed and secularly oriented – followed a laicistic script. Rather, it subordinated Islamic identity to the programme of modernisation. At the same time, this programme of modernisation has never been pluralist-secularist, meaning that alternative secular political forces were also weakened. This is because there are limits to the suppression of Islamic political voices in Egypt, as these are able to build on scripts of traditional indigenous identity and simultaneously construct this traditional identity as a solution to contemporary development crises. In particular, they could point to the fact that many of the nation's crises since the late 1960s resulted from secular led development, equalling the latter to an exogenous, imported development project.

New Islamic models for action have been implemented on different levels since the 1970s, making their position quite clear (e.g. Farah 2009: 97): first, they articulated themselves through popular social bases, undertaking social tasks which the state had failed to deliver under neoliberalism and was not able to fulfil under conditions of foreign pressure and structural adjustment. This allowed Islamic groups to present themselves as people centred and well organised political forces. Second, they combined basic social work with propagating traditional Islamic ideology as a general solution to social problems, challenging an authoritarian and deregulating state as well as a secular opposition described as alienated. Third, despite formal suppression on the organisational level, they undertook the arduous march through the institutions, that is the small gates of political participation open to individuals, winning significant official votes e.g. in Egypt's parliamentary elections 2005.

Since the early 1970s, the hegemonic framework characterised by the dominant narratives of declining secularist ideology and rising Islamic ideology, according to recent studies, has been supplemented by the formation of cross-ideological *rapprochements* and the simultaneous widening of gaps between the secular and Islamic (Browers 2009: 16, Shehata 2010: 145). Whereas the former discourse arises by positioning the authoritarian regime as a common political enemy, the latter is owed to persisting ideological and political contradictions between secularists and Islamists concerning basic questions of organising social life. Each of these contradictions turned up decades before the 2011 overthrow in Egypt. What is new, however, is that the programme of collective action, uniting the Islamist and secular opposition against the old regime as their common enemy, has been superseded by conflicting programmes concerning the future structure of the country's collective identity at the very moment when the representatives of the old regime had been removed from power. The uprising itself can be characterised as pragmatic and non-ideological, particularly claiming social justice and political freedom as overlapping human interests. In the initial post-overthrow phase, from January 2011 until June 2012, there was a clear articulation of the common interests between secularists and Islamists concerning an end to military governance. Nonetheless, as early as spring 2011 articulations pointing to conflicting interests began to emerge centring on the question of how to design the transition process being tasked with writing a new constitution and managing parliamentary as well as presidential elections. This question cannot be viewed as a mere technical one, as it was assumed that early elections would favour the deep rooted and organised Islamic movements, linking their election campaign to some kind of basic religious identity among the people. The secularists, fearing that such a religious bias would distort the protracted political process of writing a new constitution, wanted to first build a constituent assembly representative of the heterogeneous Egyptian society, then adopt the new constitution, and finally undertake further elections. The Islamists, however, found common ground with the military in order to proceed with events in a reverse chronological order, starting with parliamentary elections and having a constituent assembly elected out of parliament. As a result, Egyptians undertook four elections in the period after January 2011, beginning with a referendum on Constitutional Amendments and a Constitutional Declaration designing the transition process in March 2011, the People's Assembly elections in November-December 2011, Shura Council elections in January-February 2012 and Presidential Elections in May-June 2012 (see for details El Masry 2012: 79). As a result of overwhelming electoral victories for candidates of the Islamic parties, and a representative majority in the constituent assembly, by December of 2012 the country has become deeply divided. Once again Egypt experiences brutal, polarised street battles as people were forced to vote on a new constitution that was not consent-based but labelled as Islamist. To a large extent this is due to the fact that the constitution creates an exclusive Islamist 'guiding culture', threatening the goal of freedom in the revolutionary process. Furthermore the new constitution raises the spectre of the Iranian revolution. Whereas the front lines do not appear to be mobilised along a strongly secularist-Islamist divide, it remains an open question why the constitution was actually accepted, albeit by a narrow majority and with low voter turnout. This appears puzzling, as many people – while identifying with Islam in general – nonetheless do not want an Islamist constitution. All in all, barely two years after the overthrow, secular-religious relations are openly debated, and may well, in the years to come, constitute a focal point of political conflict in Egypt.

*The Logics of Gender Relations*

Gender relations can be seen as an important element of power in the Egyptian regime as its dominant patriarchal character is supposed to have reinforced the patrimonial-authoritarian nature of previous political regimes, and *vice versa* (Sharabi 1992: 7). In this general context, what lies at the heart of societal gender relations is a concept of the family, which is informed by structures of patriarchy, as domestic gender relations not only mirror societal gender relations but also reproduce them. In other words, the family is the place where 'the areas of politics, economics, religion, and social life interact' (Botman 1999: x).

Discussing domestic gender relations in Egypt is, and has been, a question comprehensively ruled out as a social taboo, and the overwhelmingly conservative majority of society simply does not recognise such a discussion as legitimate and rejects any dissenting opinion as unnatural. It should be noted, however, that this problem does not refer generally to women's rights on education or wage work outside the home, as these claims have previously been legitimised – and instrumentalised – by long-standing arguments that educated women are better qualified to educate their children and that women earning a wage are clearly able to contribute to household income. The issue, which is at the core of gender relations in Egypt, is the sanctity of women's primary responsibility in caring for their home, their husband and their children. This concept, however, keeps opportunities for women's education, waged work and public engagement within narrow limits and dismisses any alternative conceptions of how women may live.

The sanctity of domestic gender relations as well as the personal status laws codifying women's legal status is demonstrated by the fact that, despite the comprehensive efforts to modernisation since Muhammad Ali's times, not one political regime has dared to address this question in principle (Farah 2009: 135). Though there have been some changes in the judicial sphere, these remained contradictory. The 1971 constitution made gender relations dependent on the interpretation of Islamic law – speaking of gender equity rather than gender equality in contemporary terms. The most sweeping improvements for women's legal status have been reached by the so-called 'Jihan Laws' of 1979, advancing women's rights concerning polygamy, divorce and alimentation (see Botman 1999: 83-4), to travel abroad without male permission and to confer their nationality to their children regardless of their husband's nationality since 2000 (see Farah 2009: 140-1).

Nevertheless, gender relations in Egypt cannot be reduced to questions of legal status as the former are heavily influenced by prevailing socio-economic structures. These were favourable for women during the 1950s and 1960s, with socialist-oriented state-led development granting free education, job guarantees and social services to everybody, including women. This was considerably enlarging the feminine labour force in the state economic, education and administrative sectors (see Farah 2009: 144-5, Botman 1999: 57). Working conditions for women have qualitatively deteriorated since economic restructuring began in the early 1970s with the general abolition of job guarantees and growing unemployment, as the competition for jobs between males and females started the worldwide well-known script of returning to conservative ideologies, sending women back to the stove (see for detailed data Farah 2009: 147ff).

Women of every identity and age began to rewrite the dominant conceptions of gender, previously formed along traditional lines, perhaps never more intensively than when they actively participated in the 25 January uprising. Amongst others they broke with significant taboos such as camping with their male counterparts at Tahrir Square. Nevertheless, they subordinated gender specific demands to the general aims of the revolution, and at the same time became victims of repeated cynical insults, sexual harassment and physical abuse by agents of the regime (Sholkamy 2011, Jünemann in this volume). While it is a huge success that the decades-long and rampant sexual harassment of women has finally entered the public consciousness, that this discussion has been freed from social taboos, and that many counter-initiatives have been undertaken, it remains the case that gender-democracy has a very long way to go in Egypt.

## Conclusion: Perspectives of Changes in Power Structures and Action Frames

The overthrow of the Mubarak regime was initiated by social and democratic concerns, mirroring the interests of modernised social classes in political freedoms and emancipation from restrictive ethics. In addition, there are also the prevailing social interests of the increasingly marginalised lower and middle income classes and last but not least the crisscrossing interests of the Egyptian military. This confirms the preliminary remarks on structurally heterogeneous societies and their manifold structures of overlapping interests and articulations, which makes transition processes in such countries difficult and unpredictable, although they are not without logics of action.

Therefore, answers to the basic research questions regarding the character of change at the end of the first institutionalisation phase in December 2012 – dominated by elections of political and referenda on constitutional institutions – must remain preliminary.

It is to be assumed that neoliberal policies of adjustment and dependent development will continue to characterise the field of labour-capital relations, perhaps changing only in terms of a more effective tax regime. In the field of gender relations it has also to be assumed that traditional concepts will prevail over the short term, as women's participation in the revolutionary process has not been adequately reflected in subsequent election processes, and a traditional division of labour is defined in the new constitution of December 2012. Nevertheless, gender relations have begun to change, for example sexual harassment against women has turned from a social taboo into a public issue. Civil-military relations can be regarded as remaining in an open status, as the military has lost its direct grip on the presidency for the present but, at the same time, has not been subordinated to civil institutions. Also its economic empire remains untouched, for now. An obvious and qualitative change has marked the field of civil-religious relations: relatively free elections for the first time in modern Egyptian history changed the programme of post-colonial development from secular to Islamist, although with elusive effects for the political and popular culture of the country. Perhaps the most important element of qualitative change in revolutionary Egypt is the mere existence and continuity of public political contest, symbolising a new political culture and an emerging political democracy. Already the uprising in itself points to a revolution in political awareness among the people about their human rights.

Whereas this hints at the partial revision of scripts, its outcome remains an open question, as changes of basic power structures in the country are less obvious.

As it stands at the end of 2012, the analysis of the transition process allows characterising the overthrow as a civil or democratic revolution, the social and gender contents of which are absent for now. The element of political freedom is framed by diffuse religious concepts. The logical conclusion, supported by Thompson's work on democratic revolutions, is that such preliminary outcomes are characteristic of democratic revolutions, that they mark the beginning of democratic transition and not their end, indicating that their outcomes are not defined (Thompson 2006: 120). Moreover, it may be concluded that democratic revolutions refer to a much broader time frame than two years, referring not only to institutionalisation but also to the processes of implementation and consolidation. This is to reject using the popular slogan 'after the revolution' to mark Egypt's social structures at the end of the year 2012 as it is often done in the media.

However, questions of gender-democracy and of workers' political and economic rights need to be brought into line with evolving socio-economic agendas which, furthermore, are in need of radical change, not only in order to realise the emancipatory interests of women but also to match the fundamental labour-capital dimension of the uprising. Given the extraordinary economic dependence of the country, it is up to international institutions to help the country find a way out of the vicious circle of economic crisis-producing policies and freedom-threatening ideologies and politics. Of particular importance here is the European Union which has an agreement with Egypt in the frame of the Euro-Mediterranean Partnership, calling for freedom, welfare and justice. The original aims of the revolution have not yet been realised, rather the revolution in Egypt has just begun.

## Bibliography

ACUS. 2012. Final Draft of Constitution [Online Arabic]. Available at: https://www.dropbox.com/-s/w6c5jebknvjkcl7/Egypt%20Constitution%20Final%20236.pdf. [accessed: 4 January 2013]

Barley, S.R. and P.S. Tolbert. 1997. Institutionalisation and Structuration: Studying the Links between Action and Institution, *Organization Studies*, 18(1), 93-117.

Beinin, J. and F. Vairel. (ed.). 2011. *Social Movements, Mobilization, and Contestation in the Middle East and North Africa*, Stanford: Stanford UP.

Botman, S. 1999. *Engendering Citizenship in Egypt*, New York: CUP.

Browers, M.L. 2009. *Political ideology in the Arab world: accommodation and transformation*. Cambridge: CUP.

Cook, S.A. 2007. *Ruling But Not Governing: The Military and Political Development in Egypt, Algeria, and Turkey*. Baltimore: Johns Hopkins UP.

Della Porta, D. and M. Diani. 2006. *Social Movements. An Introduction*. Malden-Oxford-Victoria: Blackwell Publishing.

Egypt State Information Service. 1971. *Constitution of the Arab Republic of Egypt 1971*. [Online]. Available at: http://www.sis.gov.eg/En/Story.aspx?sid=355 [accessed: 16.12.2012].

Egypt State Information Service. 2011. *Constitutional Declaration: A New Stage in the History of the Great Egyptian People*. [Online]. Available at: http://www.sis.gov.eg/En/LastPage.aspx?-Category_ID=1155 [accessed: 16.12.2012].

El Masry, I. (2011a). Zu den soziökonomischen Hintergründen des Umsturzes in Ägypten. *Kurswechsel*, 17 (2), 131-136.

El Masry, I. 2012. Der 'Arabische Frühling' – eine transformationstheoretisch orientierte Zwischenbilanz der Fälle Ägypten und Tunesien. *Forschungsjournal Soziale Bewegungen*, 25 (3) 70-82.

Engels, F. 1973. Engels an W. Borgius, *Marx-Engels-Werke*. Bd. 39, Berlin: Dietz Verlag, 205-207.

Farah, N. R. 2009. *Egypt's Political Economy*. Cairo/New York: The American University in Cairo Press.

Fathi, Y. 2011. *Egypt's political forces throw down gauntlet over 'supra-constitutional principles'* [Online]. Available at: http://english.ahram.org.eg/News/26468.aspx [accessed: 16.12.2012].

Giddens, A. 1992. *Die Konstitution der Gesellschaft*. Frankfurt/New York: Campus.

Goodwin, J. 2001. *No other way out: States and revolutionary movements, 1945-1991*. Cambridge: CUP.

Gurr, T. R. 1974. *Why Men Rebel*. Princeton, N.J.: PUP.

Huntington, S. 1968. *Political Order in Changing Societies*. New Haven: Yale UP.

International Crisis Group. 2012. Lost in transition: The World according to Egypt's SCAF, *Middle East Report* 121 [Online]. Available at: www.crisisgroup.org/~/media/Files/Middle%20East%-20North%20Africa/North%20Africa/Egypt/121-lost-in-transition-the-world-according-to-egypts-scaf.pdf [accessed: 16.12.2012]

Kimmel, M.S. 1990. *Revolution: A Sociological Interpretation*. Philadelphia P.A.: Temple UP.

Kuran, T. 1991. Now out or never. The Element of Surprise in the East European Revolution of 1989, *World Politics*, 44(1), 7-48.

March, J.G. and J.P. Olsen. 1989. *Rediscovering Institutions*. London: Macmillan.

Marshall, S. and J. Stacher. 2012. Egypt's Generals and Transnational Capital. *Middle East Report*, 262 (spring), 12-18.

Marsot, A.L. 1984. *Egypt in the reign of Muhammad Ali*. Cambridge: CUP.

Marx, K. 1974. *Grundrisse der Kritik der Politischen Ökonomie*. Berlin: Dietz Verlag.

Marx, K. 1975. Lohnarbeit und Kapital, *Marx-Engels-Werke*, 6, Berlin: Dietz Verlag, 397–423.

Marx, K. 1980. Brief von Karl Marx and P.W. Annenkow, *Marx-Engels-Werke*, 4, Berlin: Dietz Verlag, 547-557.

Moore, B. 1982. *Injustice. The Social Basis of Obedience and Revolt.* New York: M.E. Sharp.

Moore, W.H. 1995. Field Essay: Rational rebels: Overcoming the Free-Rider Problem. *Political Research Quarterly*, 48(2), 417-454.

Müller-Mellin, M. 2011. *Militärbourgeoisie und Militärisch-Industrieller Komplex in Ägypten.* Kiel: Graubereich.

Olson, M. Jr. 1965. *The Logic of Collective Action. Public Goods and the Theory of Groups.* Cambridge, Mass.: HUP.

Runciman, W.G. 1972. *Relative deprivation and social justice: a study of attitudes to social inequality in twentieth-century England.* London: Penguin.

Sen, A. 2003. *Ökonomie für den Menschen. Wege zu Gerechtigkeit und Solidarität in der Marktwirtschaft.* München: DTV.

Sharabi, H. 1992. *Neopatriarchy. A Theory of Distorted Change in Arab Society.* Oxford: OUP.

Shehata, D. 2010. *Islamists and Secularists in Egypt: Opposition, conflict, and cooperation.* New York: Routledge.

Sholkamy, H. 2011. *From Tahrir square to my kitchen.* [Online]. Available at: http://www.opendemocracy.net/print/58502 [accessed: 16.12.2012]

Simmel, G. 1908. *Soziologie. Untersuchungen über die Formen der Vergesellschaftung.* Leipzig: Duncker & Humblot.

Skocpol, T. 1979. *States and Social Revolutions: A Comparative Analysis of France, Russia, and China.* Cambridge: CUP.

Solidarity Center. 2010. *Justice for all. The struggle for workers rights in Egypt.* A Report. Washington.

Springborg, R. 2013. Learning from failure: Egypt, in *The Routledge Handbook of Civil-Military Relations,* edited by T.C. Bruneau and F.C. Matei, London/ New York: Routledge, 93-109.

Tahrir documents. 2011. *Freedom ... Social Justice ... Human Dignity.* [Online]. Available at: http://www.tahrirdocuments.org/2011/12/freedom-social-justice-human-dignity-revolutionary-egypt-volume-8/ [accessed: 16.12.2012].

Thompson, M.K. 2006. *Democratic Revolutions: Asia and Eastern Europe.* London-New York: Routledge.

Tilly, C. 1995. *European Revolutions, 1492-1992.* Cambridge: Blackwell Publishers.

UNDP/AFESD. 2002. *Arab Human Development Report 2002. Creating Opportunities for Future Generations.* New York: UNDP.

van Inwegen, P. 2011. *Understanding Revolution.* London: Lynne Rienner.

Walt, S.M. 1999. Rigor or Rigor Mortis? Rational Choice and Security Studies, *International Security*, 23(4), 5-44.

Weber, M. 1920. *Gesammelte Aufsätze zur Religionssoziologie I.* Tübingen: Mohr Siebeck.

Welch, C.A. 1993. Changing Civil-Military Relations, in *Global transformation and the Third World,* edited by R.A. Slater, B.M. Schutz and S.R. Dorr. Boulder: Lynne Rienner, 71-90.

Welzel, C. 2002. *Fluchtpunkt Humanentwicklung. Über die Grundlagen der Demokratie und die Ursachen ihrer Ausbreitung.* Wiesbaden: Westdeutscher Verlag.

Zaalouk, M. 1989. *Power, Class and Foreign Capital in Egypt. The Rise of the New Bourgeoisie.* London: ZED.

# PART III
# Transnational Actors and their Logics of Action

# Chapter 10

# Welcome to the Desert: Regional Integration and Identity Change through an EU-MENA Energy Partnership?

Delf Rothe

## Introduction

The vision of the Desertec concept reads ambitious: the large-scale installation of concentrated solar power (CSP) plants in the deserts of the MENA (Middle East and North Africa) region,[1] it is hoped, will provide clean energy for Europe and the producing host countries.[2] Moreover, Desertec, it is believed, will provide solutions for the challenges of food and water scarcity, global climate change and overcrowding. This political vision, since 2009 represented by the Desertec label, has received broad political support from the EU. For example, the Union for the Mediterranean (UfM), which was founded in 2008, integrated the idea of a renewable energy partnership as one of its priority projects. And also European Energy Commissioner Günther Oettinger repeatedly promoted the concept (Oettinger 2010).[3]

This growing political interest in the Desertec concept since 2009 is puzzling given the fact that the idea behind the project exists since the early 1970s. Yet, it never attracted major attention beyond a smaller circle of solar businesses and specialised scientists. My first aim in this chapter is thus to explain how and why in the late 2000s the old discourse of a EU-Mena renewable energy partnership could be transformed into a political project, with such strong resonance in the UfM and

---

1   Neither the MENA nor the Mediterranean naturally or genuinely constitute a region. Rather, both are contingent political spaces which can change over time (see Horst et al. in this volume). For matters of simplicity, however, I will stick to the established terminology in this chapter.

2   In 2012, the Desertec Industrial Initiative argued that CSP and wind power would be able to satisfy the total energy demand of MENA countries by 2050. Through the establishment of a super-grid of high voltage direct currents renewable energy could be transported to Europe. By 2050, it is suggested, Europe could satisfy 20 per cent of its electricity needs from imported solar power (Dii 2012a).

3   The UfM explicitly made the promotion of renewable energies in the region one of its major goals. For this it adopted a Mediterranean Solar Plan, which for the first time ever translated the Desertec idea into a concrete policy framework (Brauch 2010: 26).

other EU bodies.[4] In the second part of the chapter I then turn to the implications of the 'Arabellions' for the project and the question of how the revolutions have been treated or interpreted within the Desertec discourse. I outline how the Desertec label successfully united a whole series of different political actors in a transnational discourse coalition (Hajer 1995). This establishment of a discourse coalition, as I show in this chapter, went hand in hand with a discursive reframing of the project as a 'weapon' in the fight against different global crises, such as climate change, development and energy. This transformation, the vision promises, could take place without any fundamental change in the socio-economic and power structure in the region. This logic is so dominant in the Desertec discourse that it was not even challenged or altered by the politicising events of the 'Arab Spring'. The discourse about the Desertec concept hence represents a paradigmatic example of persistence in times of change.

For this purpose, in the first part of the chapter I introduce the main arguments of the Logics of Action (LoA) approach and discuss how these can be used to study the political effects of discursive change. In the second part of the article I start with outlining the relevant context conditions of the Desertec project, i.e. the existing material and discursive structures in the fields of European Mediterranean and energy policy. Based on this description of main context factors, I study the evolution of the Desertec project as a discourse coalition and investigate the dominant beliefs and storylines in the Desertec discourse. In the following section, I shift the focus to the public discourses in Europe and MENA countries, to search for possible counter-coalitions and study possible differences in the discourses between North and South. The last section is used to reflect on the implications of the 'Arab Spring' on the dominant logic of action in the Desertec discourse in early 2011.

Methodically the contribution combines a discourse-analytical approach inspired by Maarten Hajer's argumentative discourse analysis (Hajer 1995) with techniques of the Grounded Theory (Strauss and Corbin 1990). Using in-vivo-coding the dominant subject positions, ideas and narratives are identified in the empirical material. The empirical data consists of a) Desertec flagship publications; b) reports and speeches by proponents of the project and c) 90 newspaper articles from both European as well as MENA countries.[5] To raise analytical rigour, I

---

4    Since 2009 the Desertec project has been promoted by two institutional bodies: the Desertec Industrial Initiative (Dii) and the Desertec Foundation. The Desertec Foundation is a civil society organisation that seeks to spread the Desertec idea (see Desertec Foundation 2010). The Dii is an international industrial consortium comprising 19 shareholders and 36 associated business partners – among them major European energy corporations, insurance companies, banks and also businesses from MENA countries (Dii 2012b). Due to internal differences the two bodies stopped their cooperation in Juli 2013 but continued their promotion of the project independently.

5    I am aware of the fact that studying media articles from MENA countries does not allow grasping the whole complexity of discourses in these countries. However, for

differentiate between the official Desertec discourse (flagship publications and speeches), the European public discourse and the public discourse in MENA countries (media articles).

## Logics of Action and the Study of Interaction in the Euro-Mediterranean

The LoA approach is not a comprehensive theoretical framework, but rather provides a holistic research perspective on political interaction in the Mediterranean. To analytically account for this complexity the LoA approach formulates a set of interdependent hypotheses. First, there is no such thing as a genuine Mediterranean region – rather the region is considered to be a historically specific political construct. Second and related, political and cultural identities are not fixed but are themselves the product of processes of political interaction and 'othering'. Third, power relations in the region cannot be reduced to the domination of the southern Mediterranean by the EU. The LoA framework rather highlights the heteronomous character of power, characterised through fluidity and fragmentation. Fourth, the approach stresses the role of time, process and change: power relations, discourses, economic structures etc are historically contingent and change over time. In the following I try to show that these hypotheses perfectly match with the basic assumption of a discourse theoretical approach[6] in IR.

## The Discursive Construction of Identity and Space

The LoA approach takes up a social constructivist view on the related concepts of space and identity.[7] The Euro-Mediterranean political space is thus regarded as a contingent product of discourses shaped in specific historical, political, and social contexts. The particular discourse on a Euro-Mediterranean region is shaped by mechanisms of inclusion and exclusion that relate to identity and strategy (Horst et al. in this volume). Furthermore, the contingent and constructed character of dichotomic identities – like 'north' and 'south' – is stressed. Here, the approach explicitly refers to the notion of 'othering', i.e. the formation of collective identities on the basis of some excluded other. Processes of 'othering' are usually based on incompatible categories like modern and traditional, civilised and uncivilised,

---

the present case this is not a major problem as the article does not demand studying the southern discourse in detail but to sketch out its differences to European public discourses, which become apparent from the studied 'elite-oriented' print-media.

    6   With discourse theory I refer to the assumptions of (mainly French) poststructuralist thinkers such as Michel Foucault, Jacques Derrida or Ernesto Laclau and Chantal Mouffe.

    7   The concept of a political space as it is formulated by the LoA approach includes the issues of both space and identity, as a particular political space is always constructed through reference to a respective collective identity, like the people, a community, etc.

good and bad. Such a perspective perfectly coincides with the assumptions of discourse theory, which stresses that all meaning and hence identity is necessarily contingent. The meaning of a certain object, of a social identity or a certain region, is only temporarily fixed.

This temporary fixation of identity and meaning works through the two logics of difference and equivalence. For discourses of space this means that the unity (equivalence) of a certain region, e.g. Western Europe, or of a political community like the EU is always dependent on the differentiation from something excluded – like for example its 'dangerous' neighbourhood in the southern Mediterranean. Such identity constructions are contingent and change over time in relation to the broader discursive patterns they are embedded within. To analytically account for these historically contingent identities, I suggest drawing on the concept of subject positions (Hajer 1995; Zizek 1990). The term position here points to two different ideas. On the one hand, every discourse provides a variety of different positions, or 'places of enunciation' (Howarth 2010: 314) that individuals can take up to speak or to act. Examples are the subject positions of climate scientists, radical Muslims or humanitarian aid workers. Each position is endowed with certain behavioural norms, public attributions, authority or a specific habitus. On the other hand, the term refers to the process of 'positioning' and thus to the fact that all these endowments are not naturally linked to a certain individual but are ascribed to them through mutual differentiation.

However, the LoA framework does not understand political processes as being determined by structural developments. On the contrary, it is interested on the practices of political actors that through their very actions shape, reproduce or challenge discourses or power structures. This is exactly the question of discursive agency – of how actors can have an influence and change discourses on identity or space. To be fixed discourses have to be rearticulated by actors from different subject positions. To account for this co-determination of agents and structures (discourses) I suggest drawing on the concept of discourse coalitions (Hajer 1995). Following this concept politics involves an ongoing struggle about meaning (e.g. the struggle about the proper definition of a Mediterranean region). These discursive struggles take place in a specific context (the existing ideational structures) comprising a specialised discursive vocabulary. This discursive vocabulary is structured through repeating generative narratives and storylines.[8] In discursive struggles actors from different subject positions draw upon these storylines for argumentation or to give meaning to a certain phenomenon. This gives weight to the respective narratives – especially if they are taken up by subject positions with a high moral authority. And this weight makes them even more

---

8   Generative narratives are stories that organise discursive knowledge (by relating discursive elements), establish correlations and causalities, generate explanations for empirical phenomena, provide normative judgements etc. Storylines are short versions of such narratives that condense them into single emblematic short cues (see e.g. Somers 1994).

attractive for other subject positions to draw upon for their own argumentations. A group of different subject positions that revolves around a certain set of storylines, then, can be regarded a discourse coalition (Hajer 1995: 95). The influence of a discourse coalition increases, when it manages to include subject positions from very different political angles, e.g. major businesses as well as NGOs; government officials as well as scientists, etc.

## The Heteronomy and Productivity of Power

Like in the LoA approach, power in the perspective of discourse theory goes beyond its conventional conception of repression or coercion. Power is not a resource that can be owned by political actors. It is neither necessarily repressive nor is it restricted to the sovereign. What discourse theory adds to the conception of power in the LoA approach is the close link between power and knowledge (Foucault 1977: 27). As discourses define and constrain what can be reasonably said at any given moment and what accounts as true, they clearly have certain power effects. At the same time, the ability to shape discourses, to bring in new ideas and perceptions or to question established ones, also represents a certain form of power. One possibility to account for such forms of (discursive) power is the concept of hegemony developed by Ernesto Laclau and Mouffe. Hegemony refers to a form of power, which works through the construction of consent between relevant classes of society (Laclau and Mouffe 1985: 93-105). Hegemonic discourses are thus discourses which have become so strongly taken for granted that they define what can be said and thought at a particular moment. This means that they both produce consent between different voices while at the same time excluding or silencing others. Power understood through this lens, thus, is not reducible to the actions of ruling elites. It can be exercised by a variety of societal actors, as far as these have an impact on political discourses.

However, again the LoA approach allows to fill out a certain blind spot, which can be found in discourse theory – and this is the relative ignorance of material (power) structures – first and foremost the political economy.[9] By accounting for the (political) economic context of political processes, the framework allows to explain, for example, the salience of certain logics of action in times where dominant ideas and narratives are questioned – such as in the situation of the 'Arab Spring'.

---

9   I am well aware of the fact that poststructuralist thinking transcends the boundaries between the material and the discursive world – arguing that even the hardest material fact still needs some symbolic representation to make sense for us. And I would agree with that. Yet, this too often leads to the concentration on linguistic phenomena (i.e. speech and text) in empirical investigation. Even if the economy is discursively constituted, its institutionalised manifestations have a huge impact on political processes, actors' logics of action and on discourses in many other fields.

## Learning and Discursive Change

The concept of learning draws our attention to the fact that the adoption of novel ideas is something very common that happens every day. At the same time this does not imply fundamental change because most change happens at the level of secondary beliefs – while deep core beliefs remain untouched. I would argue that discourse theory can benefit from these assumptions. Following the typology of the political learning concept I would suggest three basic mechanisms of ideational change referring to three generic elements of political discourses. At the most fundamental level lie *political rationalities* that basically structure the way we see and deal with political problems and condense the various political rationales and practices of a polity into a coherent whole. Below this general level of political discourse lies a second one which comprises *problematisations*, i.e. narratives, arguments, and so on, that construct certain phenomena as political problems and thereby transform societal grievances into political demands. Lastly, there is the level of political technologies, which refers to the different means and related ideas, images etc. to achieve the articulated political goals.

Change, as assumed by the learning concept, can take different forms or have different qualities. First, at the lowest level, novel political measures might be introduced, or old ones might prove being insufficient. Second, at the intermediate level discourse coalitions can bring in novel issues into the discourse by framing them as political problems. Also the form of certain problematisation can change as a result of discursive struggles – for example an issue that has been framed as a mere humanitarian issue like refugees might eventually be constructed in security terms. This logically affects the higher level of political technologies as a certain framing (e.g. as a security issue) renders some measures (e.g. a military engagement) more adequate than others. Lastly political rationalities and ideas and norms as the most fundamental narratives, in political discourses are seldom altered. In this respect, discourse theory just as the concept of political learning shares much with the notion of path-dependency in historical institutionalism. Once political rationalities have become collectively accepted, they gain a certain taken-for-granted status. Discourses, which themselves become the reference points for what is hold true and right at a given point in time, are hence difficult to overcome and follow a path-dependent development. Change, then, is restricted to novel technologies and problematisations, which are then adopted by and integrated within the dominant paradigm. Yet, this path-dependent evolution can also be disrupted at so called dislocative moments (Laclau and Mouffe 1985: 142). Here, unforeseeable events or crises challenge our established knowledge – which then opens up a window of opportunity for new political rationalities to evolve. Moments of dislocation thus take up a central position in discourse theory, as they represent opportunities for fundamental structural changes.

**Operationalising the LoA Framework for the Study of the Desertec Discourse**

To explain the political success story of the Desertec concept it is helpful to condense the theoretical considerations of the LoA approach into three preliminary theses, referring to the construction of political spaces and identities, the notion of power as well as the possibility of change:

1. The Desertec discourse constructs the 'EUMENA' region as a common political space. This is discursively backed by presenting the various crises (climate, energy, development etc.) as a common threat for the whole region.
2. The power of the Desertec project stems from its ability to construct consent between different socio-political actors (like businesses, environmental and humanitarian NGOs, governments from both shores of the Mediterranean etc).
3. The success of the Desertec discourse stems from the fact that it perfectly fits into the existing logics of action and material structures and promises to make fundamental change unnecessary. However, the 'Arab Spring' represents a dislocative moment for the whole region, which fundamentally challenges the ideational and material structures, which the Desertec project links up to – and hence its dominant logic of action. So the question arises, how the established discourse coalition deals with this dislocative moment.

**Renewable Energy Matters ... So Does Its Context**

In this section I concentrate on those context factors which are either explicitly taken up or challenged by the Desertec project. The latter exactly lies at the intersection between two different but partially overlapping European policy fields. First, the field of European region-building policy that culminated in the establishment of the UfM and second a European energy field.

*The European Mediterranean Policy Field*

A first important context element of the Desertec and MSP projects is the heterogeneity of the Mediterranean region both at the socio-economic level as well as the level of culture and identity. At the level of the (political) economy the spectrum ranges from rich industrialised countries, over rather poor industrialised countries like Greece, oil and gas exporting developing countries to agricultural and or nomadic economic structures. This is echoed at the level of political systems: there are liberal democracies, constitutional monarchies, quasi-authoritarian hybrid systems and neo-patrimonial rentier-states. These different economic and political systems are embedded within and stabilised by regional and international economic structures, i.e. globalised capitalism. With respect to the level of culture since the colonial independence of MENA countries the differences in the region have been translated into a variety of political antagonisms (Buzan and Wæver 2003: 217). Antagonistic identities like Muslim versus Jewish-Christian, Israel versus Arabs, Maghreb versus Mashriq or North versus South have been exploited in various political projects, such as pan-Arabism, and fuelled a variety of conflicts. In the recent past transnational or sub-national forms of violence by radical Islamists like local Al-Qaeda groups in many parts of the region have become more severe, which has shifted antagonisms to different levels, i.e. moderate versus radical Islam (Scholwin 2009).

The major logic behind past European approaches to Mediterranean regional politics was thus to overcome and modify these established structures. From a LoA perspective European politics in the region can be read as attempts to construct a political space and a collective political identity that could overcome the deeply sedimented antagonisms (Pace 2006: 2). From this perspective it its clear that 'there is no primeval Mediterranean unity, neither historical, nor in cultural or ecological terms' (Öktem 2010: 31). Since the beginning of EU Mediterranean policy in the 1970s different competing spatial constructions of 'the Mediterranean', the 'MENA-region', or 'EU-MENA' have been articulated. Who was inside and who was outside the political community of a Mediterranean region varied over time and was subject to the concrete discursive context.

A second characteristic of the EU's logics of action in Mediterranean policy has been the tendency of the EU to reproduce its own success story of liberalisation and integration in other regions (Bicchi 2006). This logic is mainly informed by the prominence of two discourses within the EU, that of economic modernisation (see Horst in this volume) and of democratic peace (Jünemann and Maggi 2010: 116). Both discourses come to similar conclusions. While economic modernisation, in a nutshell, refers to the belief that economic liberalisation and growth would come along with a political and social liberalisation, the democratic peace narrative assumes that the development of democratic political institutions would also raise the capability for the peaceful resolution of conflicts and could thus have a stabilising effect for regional relations.

Until 2008, however, the achievements of the EU in promoting a regional integration or the spread of liberal democracy have been relatively limited. Due to the unresolved Middle East Conflict cooperation in the region was often completely blocked. Cooperation agreements were accepted by authoritarian governments of the MENA countries as long as they were perceived as profitable (Heese 2009: 67). In this respect, the Mediterranean politics neither ever succeeded with their aim of a regional integration nor with attempts to pacify and thus stabilise the region.

*The European Energy Field*

The European energy field is shaped by material context factors: the structure of a globalised political economy based on the exploitation of nature, i.e. fossil fuels (Altvater 2007). It is furthermore strongly characterised by a logic of energy nationalism of the EU member states, i.e. the will to define the means to satisfy the own energy demand. At the EU level this logic of energy nationalism leads to a strong fragmentation of energy policy (see Geden and Fischer 2008: 72). In a nutshell one could argue that the European energy field is characterised by the existence of different, partially contradicting, logics of action of member states. Obviously, the Czech Republic, which is dependent on Russian oil and gas imports, does not follow the same rationales when it comes to a common European energy policy as for example Spain.

Like in the field of Mediterranean policy we have seen several attempts of EU institutions, first and foremost the European Commission, to overcome this situation of fragmentation. The overall logic of action behind past political projects could be described as one of market liberalisation and deregulation (Geden and Fischer 2008: 23). The environmental aspect of energy politics, the transition to a renewable, low-carbon energy system, was partially implemented by the EU in a cooperative manner through the adoption of the EUs climate and energy package in 2007.[10] Yet, two other major demands in energy policy, security of supply and competitiveness, so far have rather been addressed unilaterally by the member states (Werenfels and Westphal 2010: 27). Claims for competiveness and energy security have been used by member states to protect their energy markets from liberalisation. In summary, then, one could argue that until 2008 the logic of action of a national sectionalism has overweighed the logic of integration in the energy policy field.

## Desertec as a Political Project – Or How to Establish a Discourse Coalition

The heart of a transnational Desertec discourse coalition is the storyline of a renewable energy partnership between the MENA region and Europe, which represents a win-win-situation for everyone. This idea came up for the first time already in the 1970s in the context of the Club of Rome known by its publication 'The Limits to Growth' (Meadows et al. 1972). Yet, it did not receive any major attention until the early 1990s when it was taken up by a couple of German scientists, basically Gerhard Knies, Hans Günter Brauch, Franz Trieb and Holger Czisch (see e.g. Brauch 1997, Trieb et al. 1999). Once entered into the public debate the concept soon attracted political support from members of the German Green party but also from employees of the environmental ministry. The government funded German Aerospace Centre in the 1990s started some first pilot projects in Almeria, Spain (German Aerospace Centre 2000). In addition a number

---

10    In this the EU-members obliged themselves to a common goal of a EU-wide emission reduction of 20% compared to the baseline year 1990 as well as to reach a share of 20% for renewables in the overall European energy-mix – the so called '20-20-20 goal' (MSP Experts Group 2010: 1).

of medium-sized solar businesses developed a commercial interest in promoting the idea of a renewable energy partnership with the MENA countries (see e.g. Clute-Simon 1994). During the 1990s the vision also received increasing support from civil societal actors, for example by the German section of the Club of Rome as well as the NGO 'Hamburger Klimaschutzfond'.

An analysis of the media discourse about the project in the 1990s, however, reveals the problems it faced at that time. While the idea was indeed perceived as a 'keen vision', it was nevertheless surrounded by a notion of science-fiction (see e.g. Der Spiegel 1998). Proponents of the concept were sometimes negatively depicted as 'sun worshippers' (see e.g. Clute-Simon 1994). Major environmental NGOs like Greenpeace, which at that time clearly favoured decentralised photovoltaic power generation, remained sceptical (Korff 1997). Proponents of the idea furthermore faced serious economic challenges: the decline of global oil prices in the 1990s made it impossible for the CSP to economically compete against fossil energy (Blum 1999). As such it was clear that it would rely on governmental support in form of subsidies or feed-in-tariffs for quite a long time. Yet, this public support depended on the public popularity and acceptance of the project.

In the 1990s/early 2000s, however, the discourse coalition around the vision was further expanded. Crucial was to win over the support of institutions and elites from MENA countries, such as HRH Prince Hassan bin Talal of Jordan, and national energy research agencies of countries like Morocco, Egypt or Jordan. A critical moment in the establishment of a transnational discourse coalition on the Desertec idea was the establishment of the *Transmediterranean Renewable Energy Cooperation* (TREC) in 2003, which united the various political, scientific and societal actors that lobbied for the idea of Desertec (TREC 2003). Crucial for the establishment of the Desertec Foundation in 2009 was to win over the support of major German and international businesses beyond the field of renewable technologies – above all the German insurance corporation Munich Re and industry giant Siemens. The birth of the Desertec Foundation and the DII in 2009, which evolved out of the TREC, then represented a further expansion of the coalition and can be regarded as the moment when it became hegemonic. This hegemony stems from the fact that the Desertec storylines were now promoted by such diverse actors as businesses from the EU and from single MENA countries (see Desertec Industrial Initiative 2011), political actors from the German government (see e.g. Brüderle 2011), from EU institutions (see e.g. Ferrero-Waldner 2009) and from MENA countries (Desertec Foundation 2009: 45p.), scientific institutions (Desertec Foundation 2010) as well as major NGOs (Schinke and Klawitter 2010, Greenpeace et al. 2009).

## Desertec Discourse and the Construction of a Euro-Med Political Space

This expansion of a Desertec discourse coalition came along with a reframing of the idea of a renewable energy partnership. Not only was Desertec introduced as a label symbolising the different storylines around this partnership, also the content of these storylines shifted considerably (see Table 10.1). Articulations turned away from the purely technological and economic storylines of the 1990s and instead began framing the issue in terms of development, security and crisis. This can be seen as a reaction to changes in the discursive context of the project. On the one hand, in 2007 we have seen a dramatic increase of global attention for the threat of climate change. The 2007 Nobel Peace Prize honoured to Al Gore and the Intergovernmental Panel on Climate Change or the UN Security Council debate on climate change and security in the same year demonstrate this trend (Brzoska 2009: 137). On the other hand, the Russian-Ukrainian gas conflicts in 2006 and 2009, as well the discourse on peak-oil had similar effects in the case of global energy discourses (Kurze 2010: 15). Coached in terms of discourse theory these developments represent dislocative moments that put the basis of our global economic system, energy supplies, lifestyles and many more issues into question.

The discursive shifts in the official Desertec discourse, then, can be understood as a successful exploitation of these dislocatory moments by linking a whole series of different demands affected by those dislocations. These different demands were: the aim to keep climate change at a tolerable level, the demand for a secure and stable energy supply, for economic development as well as for stability and security in the Euro-Mediterranean region (Brauch 2010: 56). In constructing a chain of equivalence between these demands (see Figure 10.1) they were linked to the call for a Euro-Mediterranean energy partnership which was thereby translated into a universal demand. This universal demand was moreover backed by articulations of the Euro-Mediterranean region as a political space with a common political identity. In the official Desertec discourse this is for example expressed by the construction of the Mediterranean region as a 'community of fate' (MSP Experts Group 2010: 1). The construction of a common Euro-Mediterranean identity was also supported by the invention of completely new labels – such as 'EUMENA' (Desertec Foundation 2009: 8).

According to this framing, despite the differences between countries in the Mediterranean it is assumed that they would develop a common political demand for a 'Mediterranean renewable energy partnership' (Desertec Foundation 2009: 53). This common demand is justified by linking discursively the climate, energy and development crises and presenting them as an overall threat or even personified enemy of the whole region. Desertec, then, is constructed by drawing on a win-win-metaphor or as a 'unifying vision that crosses boundaries of religions, cultures and politics' (Desertec Foundation 2009: 52). This win-win-metaphor draws on the discursive reduction of the southern Mediterranean to the availability of desert space (Greenpeace et al. 2009: 69p.). European countries, on the other hand, are equalled with regard to their high energy demand and technological potential (Desertec Foundation 2009: 8). Out of this follows a differentiation between the two regions along the criteria of energy supply/demand, which seemingly offers a win-win situation for all countries in the region.

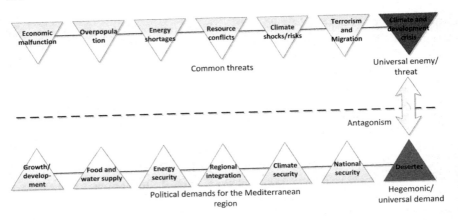

**Figure 10.1    Desertec as a universal demand for the region. Source: author's depiction**

The basic logic of action that inform the official Desertec discourse is a logic of securitisation. The climate and development crises are identified as existential threats for the whole Mediterranean region. This is accompanied by a call for exceptional measures – in form of massive public financial support to make the project profitable or in form of overcoming political antagonisms necessary for the realisation of the project. Through this the project promises to overcome the existing logic of action of nationalist particularism in the fields of Mediterranean and energy policy identified above.

**Table 10.1    Comparison of the Desertec discourse-coalition in the 1990s and today**

| Period | Subject positions | Storylines and plot |
|--------|-------------------|---------------------|
| 1990s | Scientists, Ministerial bureaucrats, Businesses | Exporting solar power from the deserts to Europe is no science-fiction but is technically feasible and economically profitable<br>® Europe as protagonist (technical and economic potential)<br>® MENA countries as passive victims (rescued by Europe) |

| Period | Subject positions | Storylines and plot |
|--------|-------------------|---------------------|
| Late 2000s | Think-Tanks, Businesses, NGOs, EU-bureaucracies Governments/ politicians Elites from the MENA-region | The climate, energy and development crises threaten the region as a whole<br>Desertec leads the 'community of fate' out of crisis<br>® works as an integration measure<br>Desertec is a silver bullet for a whole series of political demands<br>® External enemy of climate change as anti-hero<br>® The region as victim (community of fate)<br>® Desertec as a hero, who prevents the dawning tragedy |

## Political Revolution or Just New Wine in Old Skins?

When one turns to the political implementation of the Desertec project, however, one quickly notices that this follows a different logic of action than the official Desertec discourse would suggest. Here, political action does not follow the call for exceptional measures. Rather, the project is embedded within the already dominant logics of action, which in the Mediterranean field is basically the liberal logic of an economic modernisation. This logic of economic modernisation becomes apparent when it is argued that the installation of CSP-plants in MENA-countries would stipulate the local economy and create jobs (European Union 2010: 11). This would in turn lead to more political stability in the region (Werenfels and Westphal 2010: 9). The decisive feature of Desertec is that it promises to overcome several structural barriers, for example for a transformation of the energy system or for regional cooperation, *and* at the same time keeps the established economic and political structures untouched. For example, the capital intensive and centralised character of CSP plants makes them highly compatible with the existence of private or public energy monopolies. For elites in the MENA countries Desertec could hence provide a possibility to generate economic rents even if fossil fuels sources dry up.

In terms of the framework outlined above the Desertec discourse on the one hand problematises particular features of present political practices: the dependence on fossil fuels, the related energy insecurity and climate challenge as well as the underdevelopment and lack of integration in the MENA region. Yet, this does not lead to a questioning of the general political rationalities or logics that guide European energy and Mediterranean policy. On the contrary, the Desertec project is completely adapted to the dominant governmental logics of action. In the case of the UfM the dominant logic of action equals an advanced liberal government (Dean 1999: 164), referring to policies that restrict themselves to the promotion of technical expertise or try to empower local stakeholders so that these can manage their affairs themselves. Likewise, the MSP does neither include the implementation of renewable energy projects nor their support through subsidies or feed-in-tariffs. Rather, it reduces its role to the development of expertise and best practices that should guide the stakeholders in the MENA region (Union for the Mediterranean 2011: 3p.). The Desertec idea is subsumed under the broader rationale of an energy market liberalisation (Oettinger 2010). The major aim of the MSP is hence to support a regulatory and infrastructural harmonisation as well as to create attractive investment conditions in MENA countries.

### Public Perception, Criticism and Counter-Coalitions

As outlined above, the hegemony of any political discourse, such as the one on Desertec, does not go back to political elites, but also stems from winning over the support of broader parts of society. Considering the public media discourse in Europe this already differs considerably from the official Desertec discourse. On the one hand, we can notice that storylines, which present Desertec in a humanitarian, security or developmental tone, are hardly rearticulated in a broader media discourse. Rather, the most dominant framings present Desertec as an option to supply Europe with energy and to deal with the problem of climate change. Also the idea of an Euro-Mediterranean integration through Desertec is seldom expressed in media articles. On the other hand – and even more important – one can notice the existence of a coalition of critics, which promotes a set of storylines that attacks the assumptions of the Desertec discourse. Table 10.2 sums up the subject positions making up this coalition as well as the promoted storylines. The latter can be found in nearly every article analysed. Above all they put the Desertec issue into an energy security context highlighting the danger of terrorist attacks and political turmoil in the region, as expressed in the following example (see e.g. Zeller 2009).

The critical tone that characterises the European public discourse becomes even stronger when it comes to the public discourse in MENA countries. For example, the inability of Maghreb governments to cooperate in economic or political questions is seen as an obstacle or major challenge to the realisation of the Desertec vision (Trade Arabia 2009a). The promise to earn huge amounts of money with the export of electric energy to Europe could even reinforce rivalries as 'all countries in this region will compete for stakes in the overall Desertec project' (Trade Arabia 2009a). Desertec, it is feared, could even reinforce the territorial conflict between the Saharauis and the Moroccan state instead of fostering regional cooperation (Hamrouche 2010). In the overwhelming majority of representations in MENA media discourse Desertec is framed as a mere (German) industrial or business initiative and reduced to its economic aspects. In this respect, Desertec is often reduced to the export or selling of solar energy and not so much associated with satisfying the own energy demand in the region. Selling solar power to Europe is seen as an enormous business opportunity for the own country (Trade Arabia

2009b). Yet, this business discourse contradicts the humanitarian or environmental narratives in the European Desertec discourse.

**Table 10.2    The discourse coalition of European Desertec critics**

| Subject position | Storylines and plot |
|---|---|
| Lobbyists (Humanitarian) NGOs | 1. Centrally produced solar power from desert regions threatens the 'domestic' solar industry in northern Europe (especially Germany)<br>® Antagonism between foreign/domestic energy<br>® Desertec as a threat; domestic industry as a victim<br>2. The centralised character of Desertec benefits major energy corporations<br>® Antagonism between major and smaller energy producers<br>3. Desertec benefits authoritarian regimes; the dependency on authoritarian regimes in the MENA-region increases; threat of terrorist attacks on power lines = energy security<br>® Antagonism between the north and the insecure and authoritarian south<br>® Securitisation: 2 scenarios: energy security and terrorism. Desertec as a threat, European countries as victims |

**Table 10.3    The discourse coalition of sceptics from the MENA-region**

| Subject Positions | Storylines and plot |
|---|---|
| Political elites (National) energy businesses | 1. Desertec is a future option to make profit with the export of electricity when fossil resources are depleted (or for countries that do not own fossil resources)<br>The project must benefit the MENA-countries in the first place<br>® Trade-metaphor<br>® MENA-countries as producers and sellers (active); Europe as consumers and importers (passive)<br>2. More radical variant: Desertec could take the form of a neo-colonial project<br>® Europe as aggressor (anti-hero), MENA-region as victim |

As a result we can identify a second counter coalition (see Table 10.3), which is a peculiarity of the discourse in MENA. Its main storylines revolve around the argument that MENA countries must come first. In its mildest form such storylines depict the Desertec idea as a business opportunity, combined with the claim that it has to profit the MENA countries in the first place. Yet, some articulations even express reservations *vis-à-vis* European business enterprises that invest in the former colonies: 'We don't want foreign companies exploiting solar energy from our land' (Pfeiffer 2009). Also the foreclosure of the European market for products from the south is criticised (Bouterfa in Bendada 2010, Salami 2010).


## The 'Arabellions' and their Impact on the Desertec Discourse

The political upheavals we have seen in many MENA countries since early 2011 have the potential to induce fundamental change also with regard to the Euro-Mediterranean energy partnership. The current unstable situation that resulted from the upheavals in many MENA countries is furthermore grist to the mills of Desertec's critics which had warned of the political instability in the region. Some statements of Desertec representatives – in retrospect – have the potential to discredit the whole project. For example, Dr Gerhard Knies, chairman of Desertec's supervisory board, asked about the stability of the host countries in 2009 replied that 'when you look at the Mediterranean region, the most unstable country is Italy' (Knies quoted in Zeller 2009). Moreover, the Desertec project not only promised them economic profits or rents, which they could use for buying the compliance of their populations, it also promised positive PR-effects: 'The export of green power will [...] be an outstanding image factor' (Harrison 2009). This European cooperation with authoritarian regimes has been publicly criticised in the course of the 'Arab Spring'. Lastly, the Arab revolutions also meant that a part of the discourse coalition supporting the project in the southern Mediterranean broke away (Hädischke and Werner 2011, Knust 2011).

Against this background the reactions by members of the Desertec discourse coalition are surprising. The most prominent reaction has been: 'now more than ever' (Knies 2011). While the cooperation with authoritarian regimes remained unmentioned, the project is even presented as a part of the solution to the crisis in the MENA countries. This goes back to a framing of the upheavals as a reaction to an environmentally induced food crisis (see Mazo 2011). Climate induced scarcity, this storyline goes, led to societal grievances that turned into political protests. Moreover, it is argued that the Arabian youth rebelled because it lacked employment and prospects (Brüderle 2011). And Desertec promises to exactly overcome these socio-economic grievances by making a major contribution to economic development and mitigation environmentally induced stress. In this context, articulations even exploit a rising fear from immigrants flooding Europe and thus present Desertec as a sort of preventive security policy (Töpfer in Frankfurter Rundschau 2011). Despite the transformative or dislocative character of the recent events, the Desertec discourse coalition holds up the established storylines and arguments that revolve around an economic modernisation discourse. The project is not interested in substantial changes of the European approach in the region, e.g. a shift away from economic cooperation towards democracy promotion.

Articulations of European politicians mirror this argumentative pattern. These in general emphasise the need to promote economic development in the region in order to produce stability. This is paradigmatically expressed by the call for a Mediterranean 'Marshall Plan' (Whittel and Charter 2011). While the predominant rhetoric purports a 'wind of change', the concretely suggested policy measures mirror the already dominant logic of action, namely stabilisation through the promotion of economic modernisation and liberalisation in the first place. The MSP, then, is embedded within this logic and framed as a possibility to the historic opportunity of the 'Arab Spring' to trigger a sustainable economic development that fosters the democratic process in the region (Whittel and Charter 2011). Consequently, the High Representative of the European Union for Foreign Affairs and Security Policy, Catherine Ashton, integrated the concept of an 'EU-MENA Energy Partnership' in her proposal for a renewed North Africa policy of the EU (EurActiv 2011). In sum, the dislocative moment of the 'Arabellions' increases the discursive struggle on the Desertec project – as it supports the arguments of critics but at the same time is taken up into the storylines of the official Desertec discourse. The public perception – and with it the chances for and the concrete form of its realisation of the concept – are more open than ever.

## Conclusion

With this contribution I sought to give an answer to the question of how and why the private sector and civil society based Desertec initiative managed to formulate its interests into a political project with strong repercussions at the European level and how its dominant logic of action have been challenged by the 'Arab Spring'. I drew upon the LoA approach, which was enriched by the concept of discourse coalition and allowed studying agency in a discourse-sensitive way.

By applying this framework to the case of the Desertec project, the latter could be described as the evolution of a transnational discourse coalition from the early 1990s until the late 2000s. The study of the official Desertec discourse could explain its success in the end of the 2000s. At that time, Desertec was discursively reframed from a mere renewable energy issue into a solution in the fight against the energy, climate and development crises in the MENA region. Desertec became framed as a simple but effective technical solution for a variety of political challenges and demands such as development, food and water security for the MENA region as well as energy and even national security for European countries. It thereby promised an easy way to overcome structural barriers in European Mediterranean and energy policy. At the same time, the dominant logics of action in the European Mediterranean and energy policy fields, namely economic modernisation and market liberalisation, remained untouched or unquestioned. This would make fundamental change unnecessary, or so it seems. Yet, the empirical analysis also showed that many storylines of the officials discourse, like the securitisation of climate change, are not taken up in public media discourse. Rather, Desertec is often framed as what it initially was: a business project with the possibility to generate further profit from the export of energy. The current situation in the

MENA region even reinforces this scepticism towards Desertec as it highlights the problematic of cooperating with authoritarian regimes and reinforcing Europe's energy dependence on politically instable regions. However, a brief analysis of Desertec official's reactions also showed that they try to redefine the current crisis as an opportunity or historic chance. The dominant logic of action, presenting a techno-fix for solving regional problems in an apolitical way that stands behind the concept thus remained untouched by the 'Arabellions'. This represents a clear case of persistence in times of radical change.

## Bibliography

Altvater, E. 2007. The social and natural environment of fossil capitalism. *Socialist Register*, 4337-4359.

Bendada, Y. 2010. Le pays doit connaître les détails du projet Désertec avant de s'engager. *La Tribune.* 21 Sepember.

Bicchi, F. 2006. 'Our Size Fits All': Normative Power Europe and the Mediterranean. *Journal of European Public Policy*, 13, 2286-2303.

Blum, W. 1999. Sonnenkraft auf Kreta. *Die Zeit.* 11 February.

Brauch, H.G. 1997. Energieoptionen für eine langfristige Nord-Süd-Energiepartnerschaft im westlichen Mittelmeer, in *Energiepolitik: Technische Entwicklung, politische Strategien, Handlungskonzepte zu erneuerbaren Energien und zur rationalen Energienutzung*, edited by H.G. Brauch, Berlin: Springer, 487-505.

Brauch, H.G. 2010. *Climate Change and Mediterranean Security: International, National, Environmental and Human Security Impacts for the Euro-Mediterranean Region in the 21st Century*. Papers IEMed No. 9. Barcelona: IEMed.

Brüderle, R. 2011. *Desertec – Von der Vision zur Realität*. Speech of the German minister of industry and technology. Berlin. 10 February.

Brzoska, M. 2009. The Securitization of Climate Change and the Power of Conceptions of Security, *Security and Peace, Special Issue on Climate Change and Security*, 27(3), 137-145.

Buzan, B. and O. Wæver 2003. *Regions and powers: the structure of international security.* Cambridge: Cambridge University Press.

Clute-Simon, E. 1994. Wann geht die Sonne auf? *Die Zeit.* 18 November, 77.

Dean, M. 1999. *Governmentality.* London: Sage Publications.

Der Spiegel 1998. Absprung vom Zug. 9 February, 178-180.

Desertec Foundation. 2009. *Clean Power from Deserts – The Desertec Concept for Energy, Water and Climate Security* [online]. Available at: http://www.desertec.org/fileadmin/downloads/-DESERTEC-WhiteBook_en_small.pdf [accessed: 2 February 2013].

Dii, Desertec Industrial Initiative. 2012a. *Desert power 2050: Executive summary* [online]. Available at: http://www.dii-eumena.com/fileadmin/flippingbooks/ dp2050_exec_sum_engl_web/index.html [accessed: 12 February 2013].

Dii, Desertec Industrial Initiative. 2012b. *Shareholders* [online]. available at: http://www.dii-eumena.com/home/shareholders.html [accessed: 30 January 2013].

EurActiv. 2011. *EU-Energiegemeinschaft mit Nordafrika: Chance für Desertec* [online]. Available at: http://www.euractiv.de/energie-und-klimaschutz/artikel/ eu-energiegemeinschaft-mit-nordafrika-chance-fr-desertec-004490 [accessed: 11 February 2013].

European Union. 2010. *Identification Mission for the Mediterranean Solar Plan* [online]. Available at: http://ec.europa.eu/energy/international/international_ cooperation/doc/2010_01_solar_plan_report-.pdf [accessed: 11 February 2013].

Ferrero-Waldner, B. 2009. *The Mediterranean Solar Plan – A Necessity not an Option.* Brussels. Speech at the European Union Sustainable Energy Week, 13 February.

Foucault, M. 1977. *Discipline & punish.* Toronto: Random House of Canada.

Geden, O. and S. Fischer 2008. *Die Energie- und Klimapolitik der Europäischen Union. Bestandsaufnahme und Perspektiven.* Baden-Baden: Nomos.

Knies, G. 2011. '*Jetzt erst recht*' [online]. Available at: http://www.energlobe.de/- index.php?type=100&id=721#721:6:0:0:0 [accessed: 8 February 2013].

German Aerospace Centre. 2000. *Company Profile on Solar Thermal Power – Consulting, Research and Development.* Stuttgart: DLR.

Schinke, B. and J. Klawitter 2010. *DESERTEC – Baustein einer neuen Sicherheitsarchitektur innerhalb des MENA-EU-Raums?* Bonn: Germanwatch.

Greenpeace, European Solar Thermal Electricity Association and IEA SolarPACES. 2009. *Concentrating Solar Power Global Outlook 2009 – Why Solar Energy is Hot.* Amsterdam: Greenpeace International.

Hädischke, G. and K. Werner 2011. Desertec soll Nordafrika stabilisieren. *Financial Times, Germany.* 4 February.

Hajer, M. 1995. *The politics of environmental discourse: ecological modernization and the policy process.* Oxford: Clarendon Press.

Hamrouche, G. 2010 Une ONG l'a demandé hier aux autorités allemandes – Les territoires sahraouis doivent être exclus du projet. *La Tribune.* 15 March.

Harrison, R. 2009. Easy solar energy: Is the writing on the wall for fossil fuel? *Arab News.* 29 August.

Heese, B. 2009. *Die Union für das Mittelmeer – Zwei Schritte vor, einen zurück?* Münster: Lit-Verlag.

Howarth, D. 2010. Power, discourse, and policy: articulating a hegemony approach to critical policy studies. *Critical Policy Studies* 3(3-4), 309–335.

Jünemann, A. and E. Maggi 2010. The End of External Democracy Promotion? The logics of action in building the Union for the Mediterranean. *L'Europe en formation* (356), 9-24.

Knust, C. 2011. Multimilliarden-Solarprojekt Desertec – Kairo antwortet nicht. *Manager Magazin.* 2 February.

Korff, J. 1997. Darf es auch billiger Solarstrom sein? *Die Tageszeitung.* 15 July, 6.

Kurze, C. 2010. *Changing Discourse of Energy Security: A new impetus for energy policy integration in the European Union?* Transatlantic Research Papers in European Studies 3/10. University of Osnabrück..

Laclau, E. and C. Mouffe (1985) *Hegemony and socialist strategy: Towards a radical democratic politics.* London: Verso Books.

Meadows, D.L., D.H. Meadows, J. Randers and W. Behrens 1972. *The limits to growth.* New York: Universe Books.

MSP Experts Group. 2010. *Mediterranean Solar Plan Strategy Paper* [online]. Available at:http://ec.europa.eu/energy/international/international_cooperation /doc/2010_02_10_mediterranean_solar_plan_strategy_paper.pdf (accessed: 12 February 2013).

Oettinger, G. 2010. *Energy in the EU from Northern Africa: a realistic option?* Speech of Commissioner Oettinger at Desertec Industrial Initiative. Barcelona. 26 October.

Öktem, K. 2010. Mediterranean frontiers. Borders, conflict and memory in a transnational world, in *The library of international relations,* edited by D. Bechev and K. Nicolaidis. London: Tauris Academic Studies, 13-34.

Pace, M. 2006. *The Politics of Regional Identity: Meddling with the Mediterranean.* London: Routledge.

Pfeiffer, T. 2009 Plans to power Europe using Saharan sunlight: miracle or just a mirage? *The Daily Star.* 25 August.

Salami, Y. 2010. Les pays du Maghreb et l'UE en réunion ministérielle à Alger – L'Union magrébine dans l'intégration du marché de l'électricité. *La Tribune.* 28 June.

Scholwin, S. 2009 *Desertec: Wirtschaftliche Dynamik und politische Stabilität durch Solarkraft?* GIGA Focus 11/2009. Hamburg: German Institute of Global and Area Studies.

Strauss, A.M. and J. Corbin 1990. *Basics of Qualitative Research: Techniques and Procedures for Developing Grounded Theory.* London a.o.: Sage.

Töpfer. K. 2011. '"Wir müssen Stabilität bieten" Interview with Klaus Töpfer', *Frankfurter Rundschau.* 1 February 2011.

Trade Arabia. 2009a. Mena 'can earn $90bn from green energy project'. 20 July.

Trade Arabia. 2009b. Middle East to become solar boom center in 10 years. 15 December.

TREC. 2003. *Transmediterranean Renewable Energy Cooperation: for development, climate stabilisation and good neighbourhood* [online]. Available at: http://www.desertec.org/fileadmin/-downloads/media/TREC_ Amman_2003.pdf [accessed 13 March 2013].

Trieb, F., G. Czisch and H.G. Brauch 1999. Klimaschutz und Arbeitsplätze durch Solarthermische Kraftwerke: Das Synthesis Programm bis 2010, in

*Regenerativer Strom für Europa durch Fernübertragung elektrischer Energie*, edited by G. Knies, G. Czisch and H.G. Brauch., Mosbach: Afes Press, 69-76.

Union for the Mediterranean. 2011. *Building the MSP Master Plan* [online]. Available at: http://www.ufmsecretariat.org/wp-content/uploads/2011/02/DISCUSSION-PAPER-MSP-Master-Plan.pdf [accessed: 8 February 2013].

Werenfels, I. and K. Westphal 2010. *Solarstrom aus Nordafrika: Rahmenbedingungen und Perspektiven.* SWP-Studie 3/2010. Berlin: Stiftung Wissenschaft und Politik.

Whittel, G. and D. Charter 2011. West urged to seize the chance to boost arab democracy with a huge aid plan. *The Times.* 21 February.

Zeller, T. 2009. Green Inc. – Europe looks to Africa for solar power. *International Herald Tribune.* 22 June, 20.

Chapter 11

# Mediterranean Players *Par Excellence*? Sketching Foreign-Educated Syrians' Logics of Action

Tina Zintl

Since foreign-educated persons spent considerable time abroad and gained extensive knowledge, experiences, and contacts across the globe their logics of action are very complex: Their 'transnationality' opens up new opportunities, not only for them but also for the persons and institutions they interact with. This chapter investigates how foreign-trained Syrians and their surroundings have been using these opportunities – or failing to do so – both before and during the Syrian uprising. It will show that Syrian returnees had good chances of gaining influence in their home country's as well as their destination country's politics but this did not mean they played a decisive role in all political developments: Their in-between-ness comes also with specific uncertainties and drawbacks, which were made visible and reinforced by the unpredictability of the 'Arab Spring'.

The Logics of Action approach is particularly suited to investigate these 'in-betweens' because it stresses the mutually constitutive interaction between agents and structure.[1] Agents have to interpret and react to both material and ideational structures and outcomes often are not solely agents' active and intentional decision. Furthermore, agents' behaviour is shaped by their identity which, in turn, develops in interdependence with power relations and the factors time and space – with the factor 'space' playing a particular role for transnational agents' identities and actions.

This chapter will, first, look at the main characteristic of this group of people, i.e. their 'transnationality'. In order to better classify their intermediate position and incentives for becoming politically active, this will be followed by a brief section drawing on literature by Robinson (1986, 1972), Moon (1985) and Levitsky and Way (2006, 2010). Subsequently, the main section will concentrate on three different perspectives on foreign-educated Syrians: how much they

---

1    Structures constrain agents' course of action while agents leave an impact on malleable or 'soft' parts of the structure, i.e. institutions, interests, and policies which develop due to actors' influence and interaction. In contrast, 'hard' structure comprises e.g. historical events, like the 'Arab Spring', which cannot be altered by agents since the past cannot be changed (only concealed or interpreted).

themselves capitalise on their transnationality and how much their transnationality has been sought after by Western partners and by the Syrian leadership. Each of these accounts will address the positions of these actors both before and during the 'Arab Spring': in the investigated Syrian example[2] a post-'Arab Spring' or post-civil war order is not yet in sight. Finally, conclusions will be drawn from this, qualifying the widespread perception that foreign-educated persons are dominant actors in interregional communication and actions.

## Foreign-Educated Arabs' Unique Selling Proposition: Transnationality

The group of actors investigated here, Arab foreign-educated returnees and expatriates, is by no means homogeneous, e.g. in terms of generation, social background, or professional specialisation. In social science analyses they usually form part of a variety of other groups, e.g. civil society actors, professionals, political elites, bureaucrats, or entrepreneurs. So why should we investigate them as a group at all?

Many of those who studied abroad follow a common logic of action as identities are forged through life-long learning processes and experiences. Hence, foreign-educated individuals share a particular part of their identity generated by living a prolonged time in a foreign country. Those features distinguishing foreign-educated persons from other agents – both from fellow countrymen and from international experts – constitute their 'transnationality' and can be used by returnees to their own advantage. Transnationality thus can be defined as a person's degree of exposure to the store of knowledge, culture, and mentality of one or several countries other than his or her native country. Depending on the depth and nature of their 'learning process' whilst staying abroad, transnationality comprises the following elements[3] to a varying degree:

1.  Specialised knowledge and skills, working experiences, as well as values obtained abroad (*cultural capital*). The assets in this category are very diverse because of different destination countries, different duration of staying abroad, different fields of work and/or studies, different degrees of

---

2    The pre-2011 analysis is mainly based on interviews with foreign-educated Syrians and foreign experts based in Syria. For my fieldwork in Syria, March to May 2010, I gratefully received a Russell Trust Award by the University of St Andrews. 65 interviews, mostly with foreign-educated Syrian returnees, were conducted in 2010, and an additional 12 interviews during a second field stay in spring 2011. Interviews are coded with a date and, where applicable, with a letter indicating the number of the interview conducted on that day.

3    Following Bourdieu's terminology (e.g. Bourdieu 1986), I call these elements 'capitals' as this is most illustrative and widely understood. I will not apply Bourdieu's oeuvre beyond that, as other concepts are more suitable for my purposes.

institutionalisation (e.g. by a certificate), and different depth of learning, i.e. of purely technical nature or also influencing norms and beliefs.

2. Contacts with international colleagues, business partners, and friends (*social capital*). These can be further delineated into different kinds (private, business, scientific, official) and according to intensity (frequency, closeness i.e. influence on persons' thinking and decisions).

3. Money or other material resources acquired abroad (*economic capital*).

4. A high status linked to cosmopolitan lifestyle and/or international higher education, i.e. prestige attained by virtue of one or several of the above-mentioned capitals (*symbolic capital*).

Also non-foreign-educated persons can acquire some of these capitals through shorter touristic and business travels or visits abroad, by learning a foreign language, by using trans-border means of communication like the internet, or simply by displaying a lifestyle which is perceived as 'cosmopolitan'. By doing so, they aspire to increase their career chances and social status but, arguably, their degree of exposure and the associated reputation will always remain lower than that of foreign-educated peers. Likewise, foreign-educated returnees have advantages *vis-à-vis* foreign experts since they are truly transnational and not international, i.e. their transnationality includes local knowledge as well. For instance, this local capital comprises language skills (i.e. fluency in Modern Standard Arabic and one of the Arabic dialects), personal contacts in their native country, as well as the knowledge of how to get things done in a specific cultural environment.

The combination of multiple locally and internationally acquired capitals shows that transnationality is a very special and precious asset, which has been accumulated over several years and is not easily imitable. Foreign-educated persons' transnationality therefore can be described as these persons' 'unique selling proposition'. However, because of its complexity, transnationality is hardly measurable. Since transnationality's effects on political and economic life depend to a large degree on how actors display and perceive, i.e. *use* it, this will be discussed in the following two sections: firstly, accounts from the literature shedding light on the political impact of transnationality will be introduced before, secondly, discussing the involved actors' perspectives based on empirical data from the Syrian case study.

## Foreign-Educated Persons: 'Collaborative Elites' or 'Double Agents'?

Foreign-educated individuals' role in diplomacy and politics has so far drawn surprisingly little scholarly interest. In the following, I will briefly discuss three concepts which, though not concerned with migration or foreign-educated persons *per se*, cast useful light on their intermediary role. Firstly, I will introduce Ronald Robinson's historical account of 'collaborative elites' in the service of imperialist powers and show how its focus on individuals' decisions and actions is still useful in today's world of sovereign states. Then, two similar approaches by Bruce Moon and by Steven Levitsky and Lucan Way underline the importance of ideational factors that is also stressed by the LoA approach: In states' interactions, ideational factors not only supplement but sometimes even overrule material factors.

The first concept by Ronald Robinson seeks to explain the functioning of indirect imperialism – as opposed to direct imperialism by means of force – through local elites that collaborated with the imperialist powers. Robinson argues that, in order to reduce expenses, imperialist powers needed to 'translate [...] European economic and power inputs into multiplied indigenous outputs' (Robinson 1986: 282). Therefore, they looked for 'intermediates who [... were] pliable without being ineffective' (ibid.: 271), persons he calls 'collaborative elites'. While Robinson neither refines the actions involved nor gives a description of the collaborative elites' backgrounds, James Onley (2004), who applies Robinson's theory on nineteenth-century politics in the Gulf, is more explicit about the involved persons' logics of action. Focusing on local collaborators[4] and on imperialist power representatives, he illustrates that both groups used this collaboration to their own advantage, thus gaining important resources. Local collaborators were rewarded with wealth and prestige as well as protection by the foreign rulers while imperialist powers' local representatives received local knowledge and contacts from relatively low-paid, highly flexible labour. Though there were also certain disadvantages for both sides, they were either highly improbable or minor in comparison to the advantages.[5]

Though many of Robinson's and Onley's considerations remain valuable for describing foreign-educated persons' bargaining power in contemporary international cooperation, an important post-imperialist adaptation needs to be made. The local government, which could be largely ignored in historical accounts of imperialist rule, now also tries to win over the support of agents who are familiar with both the local and the foreign way of working – so three different perspectives need to be taken into account. Thus, after their respective native country's independence 'collaborative elites' now can side with different potential partners and turn into 'double agents' with more leeway in their intermediate position.

The second concept by Moon (1985; from an international relations point of view) respectively by Levitsky and Way (2006, 2010; from a comparative politics perspective) offers additional insights into post-independence North-

---

4    Onley stresses that he and Robinson use collaboration not in a pejorative sense but neutrally as 'working together' (2004: 129). Onley applies Robinson's theory to Gulf merchants, trading with British partners, but unfortunately does not mention the possibility of international education or whether some of them had lived abroad.

5    Local collaborators faced a great risk of negative repercussions if foreign powers looked for a scapegoat for misguided imperialist politics. For imperialists' representatives the sole disadvantage was that local collaborators also followed their own agendas, and thus were not always fully reliable (Onley 2004: 130-134).

South relations. Both stress the importance and effectiveness of 'soft power' in comparison with coercion and external pressure: Decision makers in 'southern' (Moon) or 'authoritarian' (Levitsky and Way) states often act voluntarily and deliberately in concordance with Western key players to achieve their economic and political goals, a mechanism Moon calls 'consensus' and Levitsky and Way designate 'linkages'. This, they claim, is often more influential than powerful states' attempts to secure 'compliance' (Moon) or 'leverage' (Levitsky and Way) by direct foreign pressures through withdrawing or promising financial, military, and other resources.[6] Levitsky and Way flesh out useful analytical categories: in addition to economic, intergovernmental, social, informational, as well as geopolitical linkages, they point to 'technocratic' linkages through foreign-educated or otherwise transnationalised elites (2010).

While this chapter draws on these valuable observations on the nature and importance of 'linkages', it does not share the authors' implicit assumption that transnational forces are always democratising forces, i.e. necessarily working against authoritarian regimes. First, transnational elites can decide how – and whether at all – they become active and, second, authoritarian states also have an interest in controlling transnational influences, e.g. through coopting suitable transnational personnel. Thus, transnational 'linkages' and 'consensus' work in both directions and are shaped by interaction, as will now be elaborated by the Syrian example.

## Three Perspectives on Foreign-Educated Syrians' Transnationality

As the preceding section has already implied, the mechanisms and assets of transnationality are advantageous not only for the foreign-educated themselves but also make them ideal cooperation partners for their native country and the country in which they studied: Whether this intermediary position leads to foreign-educated Arabs' privileged access to interregional relations, making them Euro-Mediterranean players *par excellence*, is the leading question of this section, and one that gained additional significance due to the 'Arab Spring'. This is because transnational persons' roles are negotiated by a multitude of different actors who face different incentives and constraints which, in turn, are subject to historical changes such as the 'Arab Spring' (see Figure 11.1 for the interlocking 'transnational' logics of actions of foreign-educated persons, their sending and their receiving countries). All actors follow their own interests and, when confronted with transnationality, promote the role of foreign-educated persons

---

6   Furthermore, the impact of 'leverage' does not solely depend on the actual pressure through economic sanctions, threats to suspend military proliferation, or diplomatic quarrels but to a large extent on the respective authoritarian government's vulnerability to such pressure (Levitsky and Way 2010), a vulnerability which is, to a large extent, shaped by 'linkages'.

in very different ways. Foreign-educated Arabs thereby enjoy an intermediary position while the 'North' has little possibility to influence transnational persons' relations with their Southern native country, just as the 'South' has little possibility to do so with these persons' relations to their Northern host country.

**Figure 11.1    Foreign-educated persons' intermediary position in north-south relations**

*Arab Regimes' Strategy towards Foreign-Educated Citizens – The Syrian Case*

While pre-'Arab Spring' many Arab regimes[7] in need of 'authoritarian upgrading' (Heydemann 2007) tended to view transnational individuals as 'technocratic modernisers', during the 'Arab Spring' the rationale tilted towards demonising them as 'oppositional traitors serving the case of Western imperialism'. Thus, authoritarian regimes' stance towards foreign-educated nationals is torn between cooperation and political exclusion. On the one hand, they bring up-to-date expert knowledge and an untainted, meritocratic look which helps in combating domestic economic crises as well as critique by the international community. On the other hand, it is exactly their transnational experience which, for authoritarian regimes, could provide the seed for new political dynamics and the fall of the regime.

During the 2000s, Arab regimes increasingly recognised that they could no longer turn a blind eye towards transnational dynamics and increasingly tried to reach out to their transnational citizens.[8] Also the Syrian regime's stance towards its transnational citizens changed for the period between 2000 and early 2011,

---

7    I use the term 'regime' here as denoting the executive leadership and ruling elites of a country.

8    Laurie Brand (2006) offers a valuable and detailed account of four Arab regimes' policies towards expatriate citizens: While the Moroccan and the (pre-Jasmine revolution) Tunisian government were reasonably successful in claiming a degree of authority and control over nationals living abroad, the Lebanese and Jordanian authorities were less able to do so. Brand describes how, in the Lebanese case, a lack of sovereignty and, in the

when both its actions and rhetoric showed an increasing interest in foreign-educated persons. For instance, a considerable share of ministers in Bashar al-Assad's cabinets was foreign-educated,[9] a Ministry of Expatriate Affairs was founded in 2002, and Abdullah al-Dardari– who has an immense international working experience and degrees from UK and US universities (Zorob 2006) – was until 2011 influential deputy prime minister for economic affairs and *the* driving force behind the 10th Five Year Plan of 2005, which introduced Syria to market economy. President Bashar al-Assad and his wife Asma themselves are foreign-educated, though to a very dissimilar degree: While she grew up in London and pre-marriage worked as an investment banker, he spent just one and a half years in London before prematurely returning to Syria in 1994 after the accidental death of his older brother Basil. Despite the brief duration, his sojourn abroad earned him the reputation as a cosmopolitan 'moderniser'.

The recruitment and promotion of highly-skilled and often foreign-educated technocrats was obviously meant to give the impression that clientelist relations and party membership do not suffice for being promoted into high political ranks – though some say that the government was more interested in expatriates' investments than in their actual return.[10] Appointing foreign-educated persons – no matter how many were in fact regime cronies who got their position through *wasta* (mediation, connections) – provided an excellent opportunity to convey a modern image. This practice helped to convince international observers that Syrian politics had become more meritocratic, therefore contributing to regime legitimacy.

The meritocratic image campaign was, however, subject to the availability of knowledgeable and loyal persons. Western-educated persons with fluent English language and technical skills were most needed; regarding loyalty, former state-scholarship holders provided the obvious choice. However, because of its Cold War alliance with the USSR and in contrast to regimes which sided with the capitalist West or changed into the Western camp (e.g. Egypt), Syria does not have a large pool of Western-educated, state-sponsored returnees. Instead, it sent large student delegations to Eastern Bloc countries,[11] whose returnees were deemed less suitable

---

Jordanian case, the regime's problematic relations with the Palestinian majority of migrants preclude a more effective rallying of their diasporas.

9   This was especially significant in his early cabinets (see e.g. OBG 2005) but also almost half of the 2006-2011 cabinet members (15 of 31 persons) had studied abroad, mostly in Western countries (11) and for a PhD (13; see Syrian Arab News Agency's profiles of cabinet members, available at: www.sana.sy/ara/article/5-sec.htm [accessed 28 January 2010].

10   'I think expats' return is not wished for by the establishment because they would push for influence and change the political balance' (interview 12 May 2010).

11   Between 1975 and 1995 Syria sent ca. 3,600 university staff and 1,600 ministry employees for postgraduate studies abroad, mainly to Eastern Bloc countries (see SAR/MoHE: 70, 66). After the collapse of the Soviet Union few scholarships were given out in a period of reorientation. Only after 2000 numbers rose again and were redirected towards Western countries, especially France, Germany and Great Britain. But, until today, Eastern-

for undertaking reforms and image campaigns.[12] Therefore, during the 2000s, the Syrian government tried to reach out, e.g. through the Ministry of Expatriate Affairs, to those foreign-educated persons who had studied in the West on their own or foreign agencies' expenses. Since the authoritarian regime was less able to count on the gratitude and allegiance of individuals, who had not received a government scholarship, it was quick to exploit another source of loyal transnationality; many regime cronies had sent their children abroad, especially to Lebanon or the US. For wide parts of the political and economic elites this – like attending a private English- or French-speaking secondary school – had been the rule rather than the exception.[13] Furthermore, many well-situated returnees were happy to work with the regime as a transnational expert since this would brush up their families' reputation. For example, the same privileged group helped the regime to uphold a modern and secular image through a 'custom-made' (Kawakibi 2009: 241) civil society: Several foreign-educated businessmen engaged in philanthropic activities such as business-related ventures like the Syrian Young Entrepreneurs Association (interview 6 April 2010), and returnees were overrepresented in upper staff levels in the newly established developmental NGOs.[14]

Technocrats added considerable authority to some reforms, helping to push them through against hardliners in the ruling elite. A prime example is Abdullah al-Dardari's 10th Five Year Plan, for which he got full presidential support against less reform-minded cabinet members:

> The Minister of Finance: for the first two years of the plan, he was 100% opposing the plan [...] After two years, he understood that the president is accepting this plan and that he is supporting this person and his plan, so he had no other choice: either he resigns or he comes back to this person. (Interview 5 April 2010d)

Yet, returnees were granted decision-making powers only for already officially rubber-stamped reforms, keeping those reforms which were 'unwanted' by the

---

educated persons are still heavily overrepresented, especially at state-run universities (see Zintl 2009: 20).

12    Eastern-educated personnel's public standing and reputation is lower and the quality of their education was frequently called into question by Syrian entrepreneurs and even politicians (e.g. George 2003: 149, Selvik 2009, several interviews). Also, their international contacts helped little *vis-à-vis* the potential donor countries favoured during the 2000s.

13    E.g. interviews 18 March 2010, 27 March 2010, 1 April 2010a. It is thus interesting to note that beneficiaries of the socialist nationalist Baathist regime chose to send their children to schools and universities with 'Western' curricula: Business cronies must have realised quickly that an American MBA would be more fruitful for their family business than a Syrian degree.

14    Many of these NGOs, most notably the Syrian Development Trust running several projects, were established under the patronage of the Syrian First Lady and thus called GONGOs (government-organised NGOs).

authorities out of reach.[15] Furthermore, as many interviewees pointed out, giving foreign-educated returnees a political voice was not a planned strategy since the regime lacked the willingness to defend returnees against both old guard hardliners and non-elite critics: 'It is not clear, it's not organised. In one phase, this idea was in mind [...] they invited experts from outside as a part of [the] executive administration. Just some persons here or there, they were not organised in a kind of an institution or in a forum' (interview 23 March 2010b). Several influential figures were accused of insufficient re-adaptation to local circumstances and prematurely dismissed – well-known cases in point are for instance Minister of Industry Issam al-Zaim (2000-2003), Minister of Economics and Trade Ghassan al-Rifai (2001-2004), and Presidential Advisor Nibras al-Fadil (2004-2005). The 'double learning process' when going abroad and upon return is a challenge that can impede returnees' productivity and influence, and one which can be taken as a pretext for criticising their output.[16]

Even before the advent of the 'Arab Spring', the 'international contacts' element of transnationality was under especially close surveillance by the authoritarian regime: numerous interviewees described their transnational social capital as a blessing and a curse at the same time (e.g. interview 18 March 2010). It seemed that these contacts add to foreign-educated persons' clout only if officially 'accredited' through 'loyalist' local contacts or through employment with a well-known international organisation. 'International contacts are a harm if you are quite connected. Because you will face [...] accusations that you are recruited as a spy! [...] It is like a ready accusation, okay?' (interview 29 March 2010a). This accusation became official policy when, not even two weeks after the beginning of the uprising, Bashar al-Assad publicly blamed the unrest on a 'foreign conspiracy'.[17] Additional two weeks later, Syria's Ministry for Expatriate Affairs was merged with the Ministry of Foreign Affairs, thus losing its own clout (al-Baath 2011). Though the demonstrations had not been started by foreign-educated nationals – rather by disadvantaged unemployed youth who, at most, had been 'transnationalised' through the internet – returnees' international contacts were suddenly devaluated, as both interviews and cancelled interviews in spring 2011 demonstrated.

---

15 In particular, foreign-educated persons had little influence on policy areas related to national security or foreign policy (e.g. interviews 22 March 2010, 4 May 2010b).

16 One respondent illustrated this: 'If you are only foreign-educated and you don't know how the country operates you get surprised and you spend your tenure in government discovering how things are done. You need to know the system, the *gigantic* system that has been operational for 40 years. They brought in for example Ghassan al-Rifai from the World Bank: [He is a] brilliant guy but he spent his two years in government discovering how the ministry operates! Because it was too alien for him' (interview 4 April 2010b).

17 An English translation of al-Assad's speech in front of the parliament on 30 March 2011 is available at: http://www.joshualandis.com/blog/?p=8917 [accessed 2 May 2011].

Spurred by Russia's crucial support for weathering the uprising,[18] returnees educated in the former Eastern Bloc seemed to experience a sudden revival in the regime's staffing decisions: For instance, in summer 2012 Qadri Jamil, a Soviet-educated communist party leader, became both head of a newly-established Ministry of Internal Trade and Consumer Protection and Deputy Prime Minister of Economic Affairs, i.e. Dardari's old post. Even options for re-strengthening cooperation in higher education with 'Eastern' countries have already been explored.[19] These examples show that the 'symbolic capital' component of returnees' transnationality can, probably more than their cultural capital, provoke a change in how they are perceived and treated by other agents.

*Western Countries' Cooperation with Foreign-Educated Arabs*

From the perspective of international actors, foreign-educated locals are ideal cooperation partners. Fluent in at least one foreign language and familiar with the required state-of-the-art concepts and jargon, they can tune into a neoliberal and/ or democratising discourse most credibly. In a country like Syria, which had in the second half of the 2000s partly recovered from its international isolation and Axis of Evil-image,[20] they provided a first point of access for Western diplomatic and developmental agencies. Recruiting foreign experts with similar qualifications – obvious difficulties are fluent Arabic skills and local contacts – involves costly incentives for moving to the 'conflict-stricken Middle East'; moreover, foreigners tend to be internationally more mobile and difficult to win over for a long-term commitment. For example, one UK-graduated Syrian who worked as chief editor for a recently opened English-language publication complained that it was 'frustrating' to employ foreigners: while they had originally constituted almost half of the team, within only half a year they had left and had been replaced by foreign-trained returnees or locals (interview 4 May 2010). Furthermore, during the 2000s many foreign-educated Syrians were attracted to work for foreign institutions or newly-established Syrian institutions emulating the foreign 'model', not least because the salary paid is often considerably higher than in other Syrian

---

18    In addition to continued arms deliveries, Russia – along with China – repeatedly made use of its right to veto proposed UN Security Council resolutions condemning Syrian regime violence since 2011.

19    For example, a Ukrainian delegation visiting Damascus in March 2012 announced that Syrian (government-financed) students would be welcomed at Ukrainian universities (see Syrian Arab News Agency. *President Bashar al-Assad: Power of Every State Lies in Popular Support*, available at http://www.sana.sy/eng/21/2012/03/07/404504.htm, [Online, 7 March 2012], accessed: 9 March 2012).

20    Especially after the assassination of Lebanese prime minister Rafiq al-Hariri in early 2005 with alleged involvement by Syrian officials, Syria was ostricated. Only after Bashar al-Assad's invitation to the launch of the Union for the Mediterranean in summer 2008, had Syria regained some diplomatic foothold with the West.

organisations but also because the pressure tore-adaptat to local working culture is mitigated.

On a more critical note, foreign-educated Syrians are indeed so well-suited for cooperating with foreign institutions that there is the danger of them driving out other Syrians, who might be more representative or suitable to a job. Foreign-educated returnees thus belong to the 'cocktail civil society' as Salam Kawakibi calls the key contacts for foreign embassies:

> European embassies and the European Union delegation are content simply to associate with members of the 'cocktail civil society', an easily accessible category of people, listed in the directories of embassies as being 'Francophone or Anglophone', and thus facilitating the task of diplomats who are rarely familiar with the land and language. Such an attitude excludes those people who are truly representative of civil society. (Kawakibi 2009: 243-244)

This seemed to be the overwhelming pattern which, to some extent, was reinforced by the fact that some foreign donors for student grants favoured applicants from the entourage of international organisations.[21] There was less international cooperation with the mostly non-foreign-educated[22] activists of civil rights-oriented local NGOs, though this is above all due to the fact that too close cooperation with foreign organisations could undermine the respective NGO's security, ability to manoeuvre, and public legitimacy. Most such cooperation was indirect and low-key because formalised and open initiatives like the EU-funded European Centre for Human Rights – opened and closed in 2006 (Kawakibi 2009: 241) – were short-lived. The dilemma for international organisations was to cooperate with organisations 'on the ground', which were more representative for Syrian civil society, but not to endanger them by doing so. Since foreign developmental organisations sourght to build a positive track-record of successful projects, they preferred to cooperate with local partners with at least some domestic influence, often falling back on the above-mentioned 'cocktail civil society'.

Furthermore, though Sunni NGOs and charities constituted the majority of Syrian civil society international cooperation with them, and even scholarly research on them, was rather low.[23] Western institutions were reluctant to associate with Islamic organisations because they feared being accused of financing a

---

21    For instance, one interviewee recounts that her first application for a British grant was unsuccessful but she was advised to re-apply after having acquired work experience with a foreign institution in Syria (interview 24 March 2010).

22    See e.g. interview 23 March 2010. Some of them only later participated in brief capacity-building workshops abroad, by invitation of their international partners (interview 18 May 2010).

23    Donker urges the West to at least inform themselves about this religious stratum of NGOs, though he admits that cooperation is unlikely over the short run (Donker 2009: 11); maybe the 'Arab Spring' will provide a trigger to this effect.

terrorist organisation. Besides, cooperation with these organisations has always been more difficult because they lack 'obvious' key contacts who share Western partners' views and backgrounds – in short, they lack Western-educated persons.[24] Foreign-educated returnees, who frequently but not necessarily share Western experts' more secular worldview, were preferred cooperation partners.

Thereby, returnees' transnationality gave rise to a new form of the 'othering' discourse, as described in the Logics of Action framework. It created a positive stereotype of 'the modern, secular, and democratising foreign-educated Arab' which upset the 'normal' European-vs.-Arab dichotomy and Orientalist 'othering'. Because Western organisations and media tend to automatically add them into 'their camp', Western-trained individuals unconsciously helped nurture an Islamophobic and more complex 'othering' between modernity and secularism, on the one hand, and backwardness and religiosity, on the other. Individuals familiar with 'the West' were often perceived by Western partners as most credible, as diverse examples from the region show.[25] Consequently, authoritarian states' recruitment of foreign-educated nationals was interpreted in strictly positive terms,[26] expecting them to push through liberalising, or even democratising reforms. Though unintentionally, the West aided the secular Syrian regime's divide-and-rule approach which marginalised Sunni NGOs by stigmatising them as 'Islamist'.

With the 'Arab Spring' turmoil, Western governments found themselves accused of having pursued self-serving interests through close contacts with authoritarian regimes in the region. In 2011, due to the closure of international development agencies and embassies and spurred by the constantly widened economic sanctions against the Syrian regime – the pendulum swung back

---

24    Religious leaders, who frequently also gained a higher degree abroad – but in Islamic countries like Egypt, Sudan, or Indonesia – continued to be seen primarily as contacts for church representatives and Islamic studies scholars, i.e. confined to theological matters.

25    Three examples from 2011 can illustrate this point: First, the international attention and sympathy for 'a gay girl in Damascus' in spring 2011, a blog which later was revealed as an American man's fraudulent fabrication (e.g. Whitaker 2011), was a particularly sad example showing that Westerners are willing to believe the accounts of 'westernised' persons (the fictitious character held both American and Syrian citizenships). Second, Western expectations were particularly high that Mohammad el-Baradei, former head of the International Atomic Energy Agency, would become an 'agent of change' after his return to Egypt in 2009 and during the 'Arab Spring' in early 2011. Third, the West's 'shock' that Libya's Saif al-Islam al-Gaddafi, who helped his father in ruthlessly suppressing the popular uprising against his rule, had earned his doctorate from the prestigious London School of Economics turned into relief when rumors became louder that this degree had been plagiarised (e.g. Sellgren 2011).

26    One interviewee exemplified this point by complaining that Western media praised some foreign-educated reformers in the cabinet while deliberately ignoring other Western-educated ministers whose politics did not fit into the Western vision of successful neoliberal reforms (interview 4 November 2011a).

from the use of 'linkages' to 'leverage' – most of the cooperation with foreign-educated returnees was suddenly suspended. Instead, the West's attention shifted to an alternative group of transnational Syrians, i.e. those residing abroad, and forged a – though uneasy – cooperation with the newly-formed Syrian National Council (SNC), a hybrid expatriate opposition group[27] which, at least for some time, came to be regarded as a quasi-government-in-exile. Leading figures of the SNC like academics-turned-activist sociologist Burhan Ghalioun or researcher Basma Kodmani found themselves engaged in diplomatic and supportive talks but, at the same time, overburdened by Western expectations. Contrastingly, the considerable share of SNC-members affiliated to the Muslim Brotherhood or other Islamic groupings (e.g. Pierret 2011) was less courted – if not largely ignored – by Western politicians and media. Western linkages to the Syrian opposition on the ground remained rather timid as well, both to peaceful demonstrators sometimes organised in so-called Local Coordination Committees and to armed groupings like the Free Syrian Army. While this cannot be derived for sure from the available empirical data, it seems that the international community resorted during the uprising to another group of transnational Syrians and built new partnerships with Western-trained expatriates, i.e. the cosmopolitan wing of the SNC.

*Foreign-Educated Syrians' Perspective*

Foreign-educated persons have the above-mentioned considerable advantages of transnationality at their disposal. One should assume that they are able to secure influential and well-paid positions and have notable political and economic influence, especially in interregional relations. However, access to positions of influence is often twisted since taking advantage of transnational skills depends very much on both work-related and political contexts, i.e. on factors which returnees themselves cannot control. This is especially true for the 'Arab Spring' shaking Syria longer and more violently than, e.g., Tunisia or Egypt and raises the question whether, or not, foreign-trained returnees are better suited to weather historical changes than their non-transnationalised peers.

To begin with, whether and in what way foreign-educated Arabs make use of their transnationality depends on their respective positions towards their respective host country and their native country. While these relations are shaped by numerous factors, first of all their funding source for studying abroad, has some influence on where their loyalties lie since it was the reason why they could go abroad and build up their transnationality. All three groups of agents investigated here are potential sources for financing studies abroad: 'Southern' governments give out scholarships, mostly stipulating graduates' immediate return to their native country and employment in an agreed-on position in the public sector

---

27   For more information on the SNC see their webpage: www.syriancouncil.org [accessed 20 August 2012].

for several years; 'Northern' governments or institutions provide scholarships;[28] lastly, the foreign-educated persons themselves, or their families, bear the costs of studying abroad.

This influences the likelihood that they return to their native country after completion of their studies. Government-financed scholars were most inclined to return – because otherwise they paid considerable fines – but for all three groups returning to their respective native country is not self-evident. In addition to personal and cultural reasons for return, structural factors like labour markets or legal regulations on migration provide push and pull factors that influence the return decision. While the global financial crisis in the West in 2007-2008 *pushed* and Syria's conversion to a 'social market economy' in 2005 *pulled* numerous expatriates back home,[29] the starting conditions were not always favourable: Building a career, in particular establishing a successful business, continues to be a daunting experience in most Arab economies – the soaring unemployment rate, especially amongst young university graduates, was one of the underlying causes for the 'Arab Spring'. Successful resettlement is extremely difficult without local contacts and a comfortable financial allowance: 'It's hard to start something new here without proper contacts, connections and/or financing. So if you don't have [either of them], this is hard to work' (interview 4 April 2010a) and consequently the 'reverse culture shock' and re-adaptation difficulties will be higher. In contrast, children of the established business elite and regime cronies were more able to effectively capitalise on their transnational skills: by virtue of their local contacts and 'weight', they 'converted' their transnational skills into local currency (e.g. interviews 1 April 2010a, 4 May 2010).

Many – especially younger – respondents believed that meritocratic recruitment of 'transnationals' was on the rise: Education abroad, particularly in English-speaking Western countries, was associated with an extremely high social status, providing 'a winning card from the beginning' (interview 5 April 2010) because 'in the US you are a nobody, here you can do something [...] you are special' (interview 27 March 2010). However, by far not all foreign-educated returnees were successful or optimistic.[30] Many interviewees addressed the difficulties of re-adaptation: While most had been prepared for a culture shock when going abroad, many did not anticipate another, reverse culture shock when going back

---

28    Some well-known options are Chevening (UK), Fulbright (US), and DAAD (Germany), or grants by individual Western universities.

29    As late as 2010, a respondent enthused: '[More] people will come back. Because Syria is a land of opportunity now. And I tell you, many things conspired [means: coincided] to make this happen: the financial crisis, the world is in chaos and Syria was surviving. Some people want to come here ... not only because there are opportunities now available in this country but because there are no opportunities there' (interview 7 April 2010a, similarly 6 April 2010a and 27 March 2010).

30    For instance, stories about unsuccessful attempts with subsequent re-emigration as well as alcoholism and psychological problems circulated (e.g. interview 23 March 2010d).

home (e.g. interview 6 April 2010). They also struggled with transnational skills' and qualifications' limited applicability: 'They need a few years time to adapt, to study, to understand and *then* to apply. You cannot come with a model, it's not a push-button, you see?' (interview 1 April 2010a). On top of that, colleagues' envy and suspicion were much reported problems,[31] *vice versa* respondents criticised that many foreign-educated persons exhibited 'arrogant' behaviour towards their colleagues or society at large (e.g. interview 23 March 2010b), sometimes trying to exclude non-foreign-educated colleagues from discussions by using English or overly complex jargon (e.g. interview 11 April 2011).

Several foreign-educated Syrians, especially those not endowed with a privileged background, continued to see better career opportunities abroad and decided against returning. There are little statistics, both for expatriates[32] but especially so for return migrants who, from an official and legal point of view, are not different from their fellow countrymen and do not figure in any statistics. Expatriates' ties to their native country – if still existent – were often confined to the private sphere: During its short lifespan, the Ministry of Expatriate Affairs seemed most occupied with enabling short visits[33] as well as exchanges and other cultural networking events with Syrian associations abroad. Arab expatriates staying in Western countries also enjoy benefits through their transnationality but lack the distinct home field advantage. Because of their Arab roots they are deservedly seen as experts on this region and can take influence e.g. through academic work or business activities. Yet, at least pre-uprising, large parts of them 'stayed out of politics' and were more active in purely professional fields. For some expatriates, this changed with the onset of the 'Arab Spring' when more lobbying activities were triggered and bundled through associations like the above-mentioned SNC.

As was already mentioned, transnational social capital – one of the resources foreign-educated possess that should give them an advantage *vis-à-vis* their peers – was seen in a rather critical way. Some respondents did not see their international contacts as major added value, stressing that they were useful only in conjunction

---

31    For instance: 'They are locked in the mentality of positions: This is my position and I should protect my position. [… If anybody] has more degrees or more knowledge or even more international experience, simply they would not accept it, they would not accept [working with] him: They will look at you as a threat' (interview 1 June 2007).

32    There is no reliable figure of Syrian expatriates. While rumours claim that there were as many expatriates as resident population inside the country (ca. 22 million), actual numbers seemed to be much lower. The Syrian Ministry of Expatriates (2013) estimated 12 to 15 million 'Syrian expatriates or expatriates of Syrian descend', thereby including the descendents of numerous nineteenth- and early twentieth-century migrants to Latin America, who often neither hold a Syrian passport nor speak Arabic. This illustrates a problem encountered by all estimations on diasporas as up to which generation somebody will be considered an expatriate.

33    E.g. new regulations detailed circumstances under which expatriates, who had not completed Syrian military service, were allowed to temporarily return to Syria without being conscripted, for instance for family celebrations.

with other assets like local contacts, education, and financial resources and that these other assets would 'automatically' bring about international contacts (e.g. interview 5 May 2010). More alarmingly, several interviewees stressed that international contacts were more an 'impediment' than an asset (interview 4 April 2010b), alluding to the authoritarian regimes' fear of hardly controllable influence by foreign powers which, as described above, morphed into a 'foreign conspiracy' narrative during the uprising.

The uprising-turned-civil war came as a 'shock' not only for foreign-trained returnees but the Syrian population at large. Whether transnationalised persons, who already lived through two 'culture shocks' and re-adapted to changing circumstances, are better able to cope with quick changes like the uprising than their peers without this 'learning experience' is rather questionable. On the one hand, even the literature on re-entry and cultural learning disagrees over whether adaptation gets 'easier' with practice, i.e. whether adaptation is a learnable and transferable skill (e.g. Szkudlarek 2010: 5). On the other hand, adapting to new cultures is arguably very different from adapting to rapid and profound changes in one's home society – especially since, in the latter case, there is no way back to the original position while, in the first case, one can travel back to one's culture of origin.

To date, Syrian returnees seem to have either left the country, especially those who have double nationality or who own business ventures in the Gulf, the US, or elsewhere (e.g. interview 26 April 2011) but also those who have maintained close contacts abroad, which helped them to resettle and find employment (e.g. interview 4 May 2010a). Other foreign-educated returnees with successful careers or enterprises inside Syria were more reluctant to leave but in most cases also unwilling or afraid to openly join the revolution. They thus formed part of a 'Silent Bloc' (Mufleh 2012) of passive fence-sitters, which has been largest in affluent neighbourhoods of Syria's largest cities Damascus and Aleppo. In contrast, lower-skilled transnational citizens like migrant labourers and transient lorry drivers in the region of Dar'a, where the Syrian uprising started, were more outspoken in oppositional politics and even actively involved by smuggling communication equipment, weapons, medicines, or baby food (Leenders and Heydemann 2012: 147-148). By way of conclusion, my interviews showed that many highly-educated returnees had believed in the advantages of a slow and gradual reform process as well as in Bashar al-Assad as the suitable reformer. This constituted one of the reasons why they had returned and accommodated themselves to Syria's 'authoritarian upgrading' in the first place. For them, both the uprising and the regime's ruthless repression of it must have come as an unwelcome surprise – making them less inclined to adjust their logics of action to the new 'Arab Spring' situation.

### Conclusion: Transnational Returnees as Weak or Strong Actors?

As shown by this chapter, very diverse hopes, expectations, and fears are projected on foreign-educated returnees. On the one hand, most Western actors seem to see them as preferred cooperation partners; at least this is the image that Western governments and media so far upheld even if it got troubled by developments and dynamics of the 'Arab Spring'. On the other hand, and often ignored or played down by Western media and scholars, authoritarian states or states in transition have also been courting transnationalised persons and benefited from their multiple resources, if they managed to present them with sufficient incentives.

Foreign-educated Arabs themselves, despite their common 'transnational' logics of action, lead very different lives because they react to (dis-)incentives and interact with other people in very diverse ways. Politically, they continuously position and re-position themselves between different 'sides' or take no stance at all. 'Cosmopolitans' are however not privileged enough to pick and choose which side to represent because they need to be 'groomed' by the South or the North. The number and backgrounds of foreign-educated Syrians is broad enough so that their home and respective destination country can select which intermediaries to trust or whether to trust them at all. In fact, in the present violent conflict, Western-educated Syrian returnees seemed to be recruited by neither side: The international community shifted its attention to foreign-educated expatriates in the SNC and other exiled opposition groups and, to a lesser degree, to – mostly locally-educated – Free Syrian Army fighters or protesters on the ground. Meanwhile Bashar al-Assad's leadership began to fully rely on military and security personnel and, with the exception of a few official spokespersons and military advisors, has not anymore been particularly interested in westernised personnel. In the current struggle, the educational background of actors takes a backseat.

The Logics of Action framework helped to show that foreign-educated returnees' room for manoeuvre is 'negotiated' by different agents as well as shaped by numerous ideational and material structures. Returnees illustrate, probably more than any other group, that every actor has a distinct background and history that makes him or her behave in a particular way and, to a certain degree, resistant to quick changes. This personal 'path dependency' is challenged during revolutionary times like the 'Arab Spring', which necessitate persons to gradually adapt their logics of action to the new realities. To what extent foreign-trained returnees can draw on their previous experiences in (re-)adaptation, and thus retain a comparative advantage towards other actors will need to be substantiated in further research. While, on the one hand, foreign-trained returnees might be less versatile than other actors because they fear losing their privileges, on the other hand, those from wealthy backgrounds may be better able to absorb the shocks of societal upheaval. In a post-'Arab Spring' or civil-war-situation, their skills and experiences as professionals, academics, or entrepreneurs will be needed for rebuilding their country, to create economic stability and jobs for a mass of unemployed – and by then traumatized – youth. Yet, maybe as their biggest challenge, Western-educated technocrats might be perceived as 'too secular' and 'not pious enough' if an emerging new order takes the form of a more Islamic-oriented political system, like in post-revolution Tunisia and, at first, Egypt. Such an outcome would not only change the logics of action of foreign-educated Arabs but also those of the international community which, so it seems, would have preferred their better known foreign-educated partners.

## Bibliography

al-Baath newspaper. 2011. *Legislative decree 50* [in Arabic]. 15.4.2011.

Al-Mufleh, G. 2012. The 'silent bloc'. Acquiescing to tyranny willingly or out of fear. *Arab Reform Brief*, 55 (February). Available at: http://www.arab-reform. net/sites/default/files/Silent_Bloc_-_Syria.pdf [accessed: 8 February 2012].

Bourdieu, P. 1986. The Forms of Capital, in *Handbook of Theory of Research for the Sociology of Education*, edited by J.E. Richardson, New York: Greenwood Press, 241-258.

Brand, L. 2006. *Citizens Abroad. Emigration and the State in the Middle East and North Africa*. Cambridge: Cambridge University Press.

Donker, T. H. 2009. *Moth or Flame. The Sunni Sphere and Regime Durability in Syria*. Knowledge Programme Civil Society in West Asia, Working Paper 1, HIVOS/University of Amsterdam.

George, A. 2003. *Syria. Neither Bread nor Freedom*. London: Zed Books.

Heydemann, S. 2007. *Upgrading Authoritarianism in the Arab World*. Analysis paper no. 13, Saban Center for Middle East Policy, Washington D.C: The Brookings Institution.

Kawakibi, S. 2009. Syria's Mediterranean Policy, in *Mediterranean Politics from Above and Below*, edited by I. Schäfer and J.-R. Henry, Baden-Baden: Nomos, 237-250.

Leenders, R. and S. Heydemann. 2012. Popular Mobilization in Syria: Opportunity and Threat, and the Social Networks of the Early Risers. *Mediterranean Politics*, 17(2), 139-159.

Levitsky, S. and L. Way 2010. *Competitive Authoritarianism: Hybrid Regimes After the Cold War*. Cambridge: Cambridge University Press.

Levitsky, S. and L. Way 2006. Linkage and Leverage: How do International Factors Change Domestic Balances of Power?, in *Electoral Authoritarianism. The Dynamics of Unfree Competition*, edited by A. Schedler, Boulder and London: Lynne Rienner, 199-216.

Moon, B. 1985. Consensus or Compliance? Foreign-Policy Change and External Dependence. *International Organization*, 39(2), 297-329.

OBG (Oxford Business Group). 2005. *Emerging Syria 2005*, London: OBG.

Onley, J. 2004. Britain's Native Agents in Arabia and Persia in the Nineteenth Century. *Comparative Studies of South Asia, Africa and the Middle East*, 24(1), 129-137.

Pierret, T. 2011. Syrie: l'islam dans la révolution. *Politique étrangère*, 76(4), 879-891.

Robinson, R. 1986. The Eccentric Idea of Imperialism with or without Empire, in *Imperialism and After: Continuities and Discontinuities*, edited by

W.J. Mommsen and J. Osterhammel, London: Allen & Unwin for the German Historical Institute, 267-289.

Robinson, R. 1972. Non-European foundations of European imperialism: sketch for a theory of collaboration, in *Studies in the theory of imperialism*, edited by R. Owen and R.B. Sutcliffe, London: Longman, 117-142.

SAR/MoHE (Syrian Arabic Republic/Ministry of Higher Education) year unknown. *Achievements in Higher Education under the Glorious Correctionist Movement. 1970-1996.* Damascus.

Sellgren, K. 2011. LSE investigates Gaddafi's son plagiarism claims. *BBC* [Online, 1 March] Available at: www.bbc.co.uk/news/education-12608869 [accessed: 5 May 2011].

Selvik, K. 2009. It's the Mentality, Stupid: Syria's Turn to the Private Sector, in *Changing Regime Discourse and Reform in Syria*, by A. Sottimano and K. Selvik, St Andrews Papers on Contemporary Syria. Boulder: Lynne Rienner, 41-70.

Szkudlarek, B. 2010. Reentry – A review of the literature. *International Journal of Intercultural Relations*, 34, 1-21.

Syrian Ministry of Expatriates. 2013. Ministry of Foreign Affairs and Expatriates [online]. Available at: http://www.mofa.gov.sy/ [accessed: 10 February 2013].

Whitaker, B. 2011. Gay Girl in Damascus was an arrogant fantasy. *The Guardian* [Online, 13 June 2011] Available at: www.guardian.co.uk/commentisfree/2011/jun/13/gay-girl-in-damascus-hoax-blog?INTCMP=SRCH [accessed 19 June 2011].

Zintl, T. 2009. Modernisierungspolitik durch Kompetenztransfer? Syrische Remigranten mit deutschem Hochschulabschluss als Katalysatoren von Brain Gain in Syrien unter Bashar al-Assad. *Volkswirtschaftliche Diskussionspapiere Nr. 104*, edited by D. Weiss and S. Wippel, Berlin: Klaus Schwarz Verlag.

Zorob, A. 2006. Abdallah ad-Dardari, Stellvertretender Premierminister für wirtschaftliche Angelegenheiten in Syrien. *Orient*, 47(3), 323-333.

# Conclusion

Jakob Horst, Annette Jünemann, Delf Rothe

Two years after the self-immolation of Mohamed Bouazizi started the 'Arab Spring', the political reality in North Africa and the Middle East mirrors the multifaceted and contradictious nature of transformation processes. In these two years we have seen both peaceful protest and opposition as well as a vicious circle of state repression and a radicalisation of resistance leading into a situation of civil war. We observed how people could freely vote for their governments for the first time and how elected rulers have used their position to monopolise power and turn back the achievements of the revolutions. One could hear strong voices in Brussels proclaiming a fundamental shift in EU's Mediterranean policy and notice that since then very little has actually changed.

The contributions in this volume dealt with this dialectics of persistence and change. They investigated contradictions and fissures that mark the political transformation processes set in motion through the 'Arab Spring'. At the same time, they searched for explanations for persistence in times of change beyond simplified narratives of the backwardness of Muslim societies. The rationale of the Logics of Action (LoA) approach adopted by all the authors in this volume was to identify broader patterns of political action without reducing the complexity of inherent political rationales and practices. And although the contributions in this volume have dealt with quite different countries and policy fields, they nevertheless revealed several broader logics across the cases that could explain the tenacity of regimes and practices in the Euro-Mediterranean space. Let us summarise the most important of these overarching logics.

## Persistence through Cooptation

A first broader logic identified in several cases refers to practices of coopting actors or societal groups in order to stabilise a given political regime. A prominent example for this logic is given by Harders with regard to the Egyptian Mubarak regime and its strategies to coopt potential change agents. Challenged by Islamist movements in the 1980 and 1990s the Egyptian regime reacted by strategically taking up Islamist discourses. This led for example to censorship, scandals about 'blasphemic' literature, anti-Western campaigns or show trials against homosexuals. The same logic of cooptation can be identified in what Harders calls the 'authoritarian social contract', through which important subject positions such as capitalist elites, middle classes or the military have been granted economical privileges. It is a crucial explanation for the resilience in many of the authoritarian regimes in MENA-countries.

Horst confirms this assumption in his case study on Algeria where natural resource abundance and oil rents allow for cooptation practices that function as an instrument of power-preservation for the Algerian regime. Algeria's ability to coopt specific social or political groups in order to mitigate political or social protest became obvious during the first half of 2011, when the Algerian authorities appeased emerging protest-movements by salary increases for specific groupings and subsidies on important staple foods like oil and flour. Jünemann describes in her contribution on the promotion of gender democracy a similar practice through which many secular feminist actors have been coopted by authoritarian governments. Thereby, the regimes could not only display themselves as progressive and politically open actors but could also construct a strategic alliance against Islamist parties which for them clearly represented the most dangerous oppositional force.

However, the logic of cooptation does not always work the way it is meant to. According to Zintl's findings in her contribution on foreign-educated Syrians, neither the authoritarian Syrian regime nor the EU succeeded in ultimately coopting foreign educated Syrian citizens. These transnationals can therefore neither be labelled as stakeholders of the old regime nor as change agents of a democratisation or even Europeanisation. Each case seems to be very specific, according to the concrete personal context with its variety of additional parameters.

## Persistence through Pragmatism and De-Politicisation

Another logic of action that is particularly important when it comes to explaining persistence is the logic of pragmatism and de-politicisation, which is often interlinked with the aforementioned logic of cooptation. A logic of pragmatism refers, on the one hand, to political practices informed by strategic or practical rationales rather than ideology, beliefs or affects. On the other hand, it refers to those policies which are pragmatic or apolitical in outcome – i.e. through an economisation of public tasks or by substituting political contestation with technocratic governance. Ouaissa highlights the nexus between both logics when he describes the political effects on those Islamist parties in Algeria, which have been successfully coopted by the regime. Instead of ideology they are today far more driven by a neoliberal economic ratio and thus by an obvious shift towards pragmatism. The pragmatic arrangement with the authoritarian regime helped to end the civil war. At the same time, however, it stabilised the persistence of the authoritarian regime in Algeria. Fritzsche and Lübben observe similar political effects with regard to the cases of Morocco and Jordan. In Jordan the Muslim Brothers since decades honoured being coopted into the ministry of Religious endowments and education by the acceptance of the legitimacy of the throne even after the conclusion of the peace treaty with Israel. Here too pragmatism prevailed over ideology, although the liberation of Palestine is a core aspect of the Islamists ideological conviction. This said, one must be careful not to generalise the findings of single case studies. In the case of Jordan the trend towards pragmatism among some Islamist groupings is balanced by the strong impact of their national identity as Palestinians. For them solidarity with Palestine is a policy core belief not easy to be sidelined by pragmatic logics of action. Thus, they are more resilient against any attempt of cooptation through the regime.

Another case in point is the Egyptian Muslim Brotherhood. Their logic of action during the revolution when they remained in the background was equally informed by a logic of pragmatism as Morsi's first action as president aiming solely at the retention of political power. According to Harders, the logic of action of the Morsi government in this respect was absolutely coherent with that of the Mubarak regime. Going one step further, El Masry's contribution on Egypt sheds light on the nexus between the logics of cooptation and pragmatism. Her analysis predicts persistence also in Egypt's labour-capital relations, which underpin the economic privileges of the military that go back to Mubarak's times. Despite the fact that labour and union movements have been basic pillars of the 2011 overthrow, effective change within Egyptian labour-capital relations remains unlikely. From a short-term perspective this pragmatism might be mollifying European worries. One should bear in mind however that this pragmatism stabilises some of the traditional foundations of the Egyptian authoritarian state, among them the political leverage of the military. Such a policy is likely to inhibit necessary socio-economic reforms and thereby ignore the demand for 'bread and justice'.

The logic of pragmatism applies not only for the old and new MENA-regimes, but also for the EU. On the one hand, for the EU pragmatism refers to practices that seek to bypass political conflicts because of the potential stalemate they can induce on the regional level of cooperation in the Mediterranean. The institutional setting of the Union for the Mediterranean with its focus on merely technical cooperation in functional project reveals this logic. This can be well observed in the field of energy policy in which the EU concentrates on rather technical cooperation below the ministerial level or on the support of a few lighthouse projects. In his contribution Rothe exemplifies this tendency for the case of renewable energy. Similarly Horst's contribution, relating to the EU's trade policy in Algeria, shows that the EU continues to focus on its external 'core-business' of bilateral trade, even though there is evidence that the EU itself contributed to the socio-economic distress that partly explains the political upheavals in the MENA countries. In times of political flurries the EU pragmatically concentrates on the less politically sensitive field of economic cooperation.

On the other hand, pragmatism in the context of EU-Mediterranean policies refers to practices that seek to bypass self-imposed norms and values. In his contribution on EU-migration policies Seeberg reminds us that right from its beginnings in the 1990s European Mediterranean policies were guided by an overwhelming interest in security and stability. After 9/11 the security paradigm became so strong that virtually all other policy-goals were perceived predominantly through these lenses. Migration policies were securitised to an extent that the EU and its member states engaged in unreserved cooperation with authoritarian MENA regimes, thereby subordinating human rights to a norm-free pragmatism. Seeberg comes to the conclusion that the 'Arab Spring' did not fundamentally change this pragmatic approach of the EU or its member states concerning migration policies. Nevertheless it remains to be seen whether the changed political realities in the southern partner countries will challenge the long established patterns of cooperation between the EU member states and MENA countries such as Tunisia or Libya in the field of migration policies.

## Resilience through Adaptation Strategies

Some of the contributions do not focus so much on the question of persistence and change, but rather on the *quality* of change. Since the LoA approach integrates main assumptions from the concept of political learning, the contributions of Maggi and Harders draw on the belief system to qualify the degree of the political change observed. With regard to the case of Morocco Maggi shows very clearly how political elites strategically adapt to a novel situation such as the 'Arab Spring' without fundamentally changing their political stance. We call this pattern of behaviour logic of adaptation. A logic of adaptation refers to patterns of behaviour change in which actors adapt their secondary beliefs to novel contextual settings and situations, while fundamental deep-core and policy-core beliefs of these actors remain the same. In the Moroccan context this implied that the deep-core belief of the King as 'commander of the faithful' remained unquestioned when the government slightly adopted its economic and ecological reform patterns to prevent unrest and upheaval. The investment in water projects or the creation of government-funded jobs are cases in point. With regard to Egypt, Harders comes to similar yet differentiated conclusions: Whereas deep core and policy core beliefs of the former regime actors, the military and the security apparatus did not substantially change so that they merely adapted their strategies to the new political realities, the ongoing confrontations and the high degree of political mobilisation are an indicator that the deep core beliefs of some parts of the Egyptian public did indeed change. Most important in this context is their seemingly irreversible loss of fear requiring Egyptian military and security forces to adopt ever more violent measures to silence political contestation,

In contrast to increasing politicisation of the Egyptian public Ouaissa comes to different findings with regard to the economic middle classes in Algeria, which follow a rather persistent logic of rent-seeking. What is more, they used considerable material and ideal resources to adapt their rent-seeking strategy to the respective political context. This behavioural pattern of adaptation in the middle classes in Algeria helps a lot to explain the resilience of the current regime even in times of recent mass protests and political unrest. Lübben and Fritzsche identify a similar logic of action concerning the Islamist party IAFP in Jordan which adapted its behaviour to the new political circumstances and tried to take advantage of new opportunities for improving its political leverage within the Jordanian political system.

## Persistence Due to Discursive Path-Dependency

But it is not always the logic of a particular group of actors which decides over the question of persistence and change. Several contributions in this volume have shown that actor's behaviour is strongly influenced by their discursive context. And this is often characterised by such a strong path dependency that dominant narratives and storylines are not even changed through a critical juncture like the 'Arab Spring'. Jünemann's contribution for example showed that European Mediterranean politics is informed by narratives and binary identity constructions which are so strongly ingrained that they are hardly challenged by an event such as the 'Arab Spring'. The culturalism that undergirds EU action, for example, in the field of gender policy but also democratisation approaches in general hinders a more productive approach in these policy fields. In the case of gender policy the patriarchal character of MENA-societies is reduced to the seemingly backward ideology of political Islam. As a result other impact factors for gender injustice are blurred and potential partners for cooperation are overlooked.

Equally ingrained on the EU-side are discourses on economic modernisation or neoliberal economics. The persistence of an economic modernisation discourse is perfectly illustrated by Horst against the backdrop of the Algerian case. In line with neoliberal economic discourse and the conviction that 'the market would do better' the EU's bilateral cooperation with Algeria concentrated on market liberalisation and the abolishment of trade barriers. This liberalisation, according to the economic modernisation storyline, would spur liberalisation and development also in the social and political field. The EU held up this strategy even despite serious doubts about positive effects for the economic and social development in Algeria.

The contributions of Harders and Seeberg also proved a strong impact of the discursive context on EU's Mediterranean politics, here the dominant stability and security discourse. In the case of migration policy, described by Seeberg, it has been the fragmentation of EU member states as well as diverging threat constructions that up to now hindered the development of a coherent EU immigration policy and hence unwillingly provided persistence. This fragmentation became particularly apparent in the aftermath of the revolutions in Tunisia and Egypt when a perceived 'flood' of immigrants prompted quite different reactions by Mediterranean and other EU member states. Harders instead describes a rather coherent stability discourse that has informed European and US approaches towards the region in the past – and still does. The stability discourse informing the EU perfectly matches with a logic of action of MENA-governments to retain power and to suppress political opposition. In Egypt this symbiotic convergence of EU-MENA governmental rationales clashes with an ever more courageous civil society leading to a situation of continued violence and political instability.

Moreover there seems to be little change in the discourses informing energy or environmental policy. In the case of the European Union there are two interrelated meta-narratives informing the EU's approach to energy policy in the region, as Rothe shows in his contribution. This is on the one hand a discourse of energy security, which constructs a twofold threat of a climate and energy (supply) crisis. On the other hand an economic modernisation storyline undergirds energy policies in the region. This holds all the more true for the unstable situation during and after the 'Arab Spring'. Economic growth and related positive social feedbacks due to renewable energy projects, it is hoped, could help in producing political stability and foster socio-economic progress. As Maggi's contribution in this volume showed such discourses perfectly match with the logics of action of MENA countries' political elites who used solar energy or water generation projects in order to demonstrate their willingness to foster socio-economic or ecological progress. Such political 'marketing' projects to prove the willingness for political change are all the more important in a situation such as the 'Arab Spring' in which Moroccan elites feared that protests might spill over to their country. In this respect, progressive policies such as cooperation on renewable energy might paradoxically have the effect of stabilising a quasi-authoritarian regime such as the Moroccan one.

Yet also MENA countries are characterised by ingrained discourses or ideologies. This holds true for ingrained enemy constructions such as Israel or 'the Western world' which represent a strong motive for example of Islamist actors as the contribution of Fritzsche and Lübben demonstrates. The importance of the Middle East conflict and the handed-down enemy figure remain important motives for many MENA-actors before and after the 'Arab Spring'. Moreover, neoliberalism as political discourse not only informs European Mediterranean policies but also many MENA actors have internalised neoliberal rationales into their logics of action. Ingrid El Masry shows in her contribution that since the 1980s the Egyptian regime not only arranged with but also actively promoted neoliberal policies such as structural adjustment programmes. As other important socio-political actors, such as the military or Islamists, adopted this discourse there seems to be a strong persistence of neoliberal discourse amongst Egyptian elites after the Arab Spring.

**Prospects for Change?**

The framework applied by the authors in this volume demonstrated the tenacity that characterises many logics of action and underlying discourses in Euro-Mediterranean relations. Yet, this does not imply that there is no prospect for change. After all, the so-called 'Arab Spring' still represents a window of opportunity for substantial change within MENA-countries and with regard to Euro-Mediterranean cooperation. The 'Arabellions' have made visible the contradictions of past approaches of European Mediterranean politics such as the strategic cooperation with authoritarian regimes. As Jünemann in this volume showed this applied for example for the field of gender policy with the EU's focus on a state feminism in MENA countries that ultimately stabilised the position of authoritarian governments. It remains to be seen, whether or not the EU will alter this position and open its perspective for actors other than Westernised feminist groups that have been coopted by MENA regimes in the past. The same applies to security and immigration policy. On the one hand, the 'Arab Spring' has shed some light on the cooperation between the EU and authoritarian rulers, such as Muammar al-Gaddafi in Libya in the field of migration control. On the other hand, the 'Arab Spring' brought grist to the mills of security actors and national politicians articulating immigration from North Africa as a security threat. This situation opened a discursive struggle between rather liberal and more securitised discourses on migration within the EU which is nowhere near decided.

Within many MENA countries there is still a strong momentum of change – as many contributions in this volume have shown. Above all this holds true for the situation in Syria which is marked by an ongoing civil war. The contribution by Zintl showed that actors such as foreign-educated Syrians have to adapt to this unstable and quickly changing situation. As her contribution demonstrates this adaptation does not follow one coherent logic. Neither do the 'transnationals' function as change agents, i.e. do not play any leading role in the Syrian opposition movement – as a European perspective might hope; nor are they completely coopted by the Syrian regime or adopt any important position in the regime's struggle for survival. The continuing violence between Islamist supporters of the degraded President Morsi, the Tamarod protest movement, and state forces perfectly demonstrates the complex interplay of persistence and change. While the Egyptian public is increasingly politicised but split into two antagonistic camps – the military establishment is violently defending its established socio-economic place. Ongoing violence and protests show that the renegotiation of the Egyptian social contract will be a question of years rather than months. And the outcome of this process is more open than ever.

One of the most important issues with which the newly elected governments in the revolutionary countries are confronted, is the ongoing socio-economic crisis that on the one hand nurtured the dynamic of revolutionary movements but on the other hand was reinforced by the political instability that followed the regime overthrows. The possibility of effective change and sustainable political liberalisation in the MENA countries depends heavily on the ability of new political leaders to deal with this issue in order to fulfil the high expectations of populations in the post-revolutionary MENA countries.

The merit of the LoA approach applied by the authors in this volume is that it helps explain the versatile situation without falling back on simple narratives and patterns of thought. It helps overcome binary identity constructions that divide the Mediterranean in 'us-versus-them', North versus South or the West versus

Islam. The pragmatic logic of action characterising many Islamist actors, for example, challenges the predominant perception of these actors as being irrational, ideological and emotional. Also Zintl's study of the transnational subjectivities of foreign-educated Arabs helps in transcending binary identity constructions. Zintl convincingly shows that their action and social position is influenced by a complex interplay of context factors – amongst them material structures like political economy as well as discourses, for example on identity. Jünemann's analysis of gender relations provided a similar result and argued against European discourses that attribute gender injustices in MENA countries solely to political Islam. Jünemann's contribution is a perfect example how the LoA approach can help to deconstruct simplified narratives about the backwardness of the MENA region.

The LoA approach allows developing explanations of transformation or persistence of political processes in the Euro-Mediterranean that are more flexible and context-sensitive than a causal-law approach in political science. It paid particular attention to the particularities of the 'region' and the concrete context in each transformation process studied. All the contributions in this volume have made clear that *context matters* and that a detailed consideration of context parameters prevents simplified explanatory narratives or premature diagnoses. Due to the common LoA perspective it was then possible to crystallise some broader logics of political action that are able to explain the tenacity of many political processes in the Mediterranean. Starting from the co-determination of agents and structures the LoA framework allowed authors in this volume, on the one hand, to take the practices and logics of particular actors as a starting point and show how these influence broader political structures. A perfect example is Ouaissa's chapter in which he shows how the rent-seeking behaviour of middle classes reproduced and stabilised authoritarian government structures. Authors like Rothe or Jünemann, on the contrary, started from discursive structures – the securitisation of energy or gender discourse – and investigated how those discourses impact the behaviour of different political actors in the Euro-Mediterranean space. Lastly, the LoA perspective allowed for grasping the quality and not only the mere occurrence of change as especially the contributions of Harders and Maggi demonstrate. This volume offered a diversified multifaceted overview of processes of persistence and change during and in the aftermath of the 'Arab Spring'. As the contributions showed the events that many of the MENA states went through since the beginning of 2011 can certainly be labelled as a fundamental change in the sense that they effectively altered the political power structures in many MENA countries and partly revised discursive patterns within the Euro-Mediterranean political space. However, throughout the different chapters it became clear that it is meaningful and worthwhile to look at the specific logics of action of different actors in different policy fields in order to understand the concrete meanings and the quality of change as well as to identify logics of persistence. Equally it became clear that the process of change, which began with the 'revolutions' of the year 2011, is far from concluded. Euro-Mediterranean relations will continue, in the years to come, to be influenced by the repercussions of the 'Arab Spring'.

# Index